She was born *Stefani Joanne Angelina Germanotta* on *March 28, 1986* to parents *Cynthia Bissett* and *Joseph Germanotta*.

Music, obviously, was a huge part of her childhood. She learned piano at age four.

She even wrote her first ballad at 13 years old. How many of us can say that they accomplished something like that at age 13?

She attended a private Catholic school in Manhattan but has been very adamant that she wasn't wealthy as a child, instead talking of how her family worked for everything they wanted or needed.

She sang at open mike nights while still very young...

She was an actress in high school, and well known for her acting abilities. It is something we can definitely see today in the *Gaga* persona.

But high school wasn't all fun and games. She was different and people made her feel like a freak for who she was. At least, that's how she felt. Others might not agree with that history, but to *Gaga*, that's the truth.

Things changed from then on.

At 17, she was admitted to NYU and the Tisch School of the Arts, a feat that proves her dedication to her craft and her abilities.

She studied music and her songwriting became more advanced...

She worked hard, and felt like she was more creative than others, that she wanted it more. But school stopped appealing to her and she withdrew...

At 19 years old, she singed with *Def Jam Records* after being discovered and heard a few feet from the CEO's office.

It didn't last, and in 3 months she was dropped, but managed to get together with producer *RedOne*.

She produced her first song called *Boys Boys Boys* with *RedOne* and from there, her career was moving forward.

Soon, she became *Lady Gaga*. There are conflicting reports on how the name came to be, but one of the most prevalent, and interesting, is that she loved the song *Radio Ga Ga* by *Queen* and because of an autocorrect error on a text from her producer, she became *Lady Gaga*. And that was that. Such a better story than just some marketing meeting, right?

Before striking it big on the music scene, she performed in New York's club scene with Lady Starlight as performance art with the Lady Gaga and the Starlight Revue.

...And began to focus on her musical career. But she made a promise to her father.

She and *Starlight* played *Lollapalooza* in 2007 and the crowd went wild.

Fusari, her recording partner who helped her come up with the name *Lady Gaga*, sent the songs they worked on to another producer and record executive. From there...

...She was quickly signed to a record deal with *Streamline Records*, part of *Interscope*. This was it. Here she was. *Lady Gaga* had arrived.

She struck a deal writing songs for people like **Britney Spears**, **New Kids on the Block** and others. She was writing her own songs as well, and starting to make a name for herself. Pretty soon, everywhere you looked, **there** would be **Lady Gaga**.

She became one of the *go to* writers in pop music, working all over the industry and continuing on her own stuff as well.

Her own music became *The Fame*, released in 2008 to critical praise and acclaim from the public as well.

She swept the charts, taking the world by storm...

Her first single, *Just Dance*, became not only a chart-topper, but a hit music video and a phenomenon of its own.

And it was a huge song, up until her second single dropped...

...*Poker Face*. She was noticed almost immediately all over the world, and her album was playing everywhere she went.

The song would go on to win her Grammys for Song of the Year, Record of the Year, Best Electronic/Dance Album and just swept the world.

She was all over the place, and to most, seemed to have popped up over night. It was surprising, and her newfound *Fame*...

...Allowed her fashion sense to be noticed by people and not questioned. She was a pop superstar, winning *MTV Video Music Awards*, topping the charts all over the world, and finding her own niche...

...She could wear whatever she wanted and people would talk about it. It was part of her persona as *Lady Gaga* and we were all along for the ride

She dropped her album the *Fame Monster* and went on tour in its support, and even released another hit single, *Bad Romance*. She rocketed to the top...

...Even performing for the *Queen!*

Beyond the music, she is not just some flash-in-the-pan superstar. She has a message. She has appeared on the *Ellen Degeneres Show*, praising Ellen for being an inspiration to both women and the gay community. Gaga is very outspoken about her support of gay rights...

...And equality for everyone.

But it was her music and her fashion sense that first got her noticed, and gave her the ability to speak out and speak her mind.

And in her vocalizing about herself and her thoughts on the world, she's been open about her musical influences, from *Queen* down the line to *Britney Spears*. She's a superstar who is very open about who she is and where she's come from...

...And even enjoys when comparisons are made between her and other superstars like *Christina Aguilera*. She doesn't hide from them, she takes them head-on, just like the critics...

...And like the rumors or urban legends. When asked by *Barbara Walters* about her androgyny and the possibility of her being intersex, she took it head on, dismissing the claim and acknowledging that she revels in the androgyny on-stage and again, revels in the questions.

THE
100
MOST
INFLUENTIAL
PEOPLE
IN THE
WORLD

Like I said, she's all over the place, and this is just the tip of the iceberg.

She took the world by storm and she's now not only seen all over the news media and in magazines and newspaper articles, but on television too.

She's been on *Saturday Night Live* and there's even been an episode of *Glee* devoted to her music.

But no matter what she does, whether it be collaborations with *Beyonce* or her outlandish outfits or just going on television, we can't stop talking about her.

It's part of the *Fame Monster* she's talked about and sung about. We constantly want to know what she's doing...

As is the *Haus of Gaga*, not to be confused with the *House of Gaga*, her own music publishing company. *The Haus* is her collective of artists, performers and back-stage presence that help her become *Lady Gaga*.

They build the sets, do the make-up, make the films that play during the performances; they all play a role in the persona of *Gaga*. Made up of close friends and new friends, they have all contributed to who Stefani is today.

She's taken the world by storm. She's a superstar. And all we hear is *Lady Gaga*. In spite of that, in spite of her being everywhere, people just can't seem to get enough of her. And that will be her true claim to *fame*: her staying power.

THE END

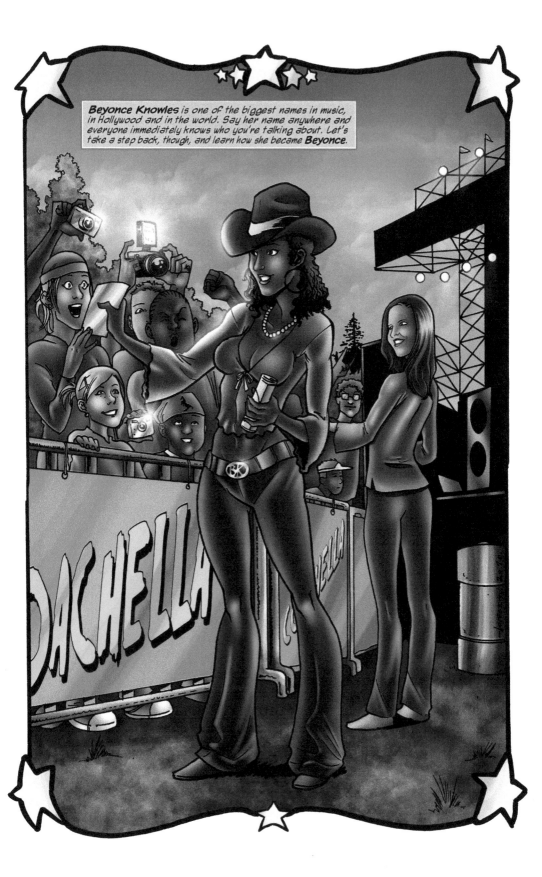

Beyonce Knowles is one of the biggest names in music, in Hollywood and in the world. Say her name anywhere and everyone immediately knows who you're talking about. Let's take a step back, though, and learn how she became Beyonce.

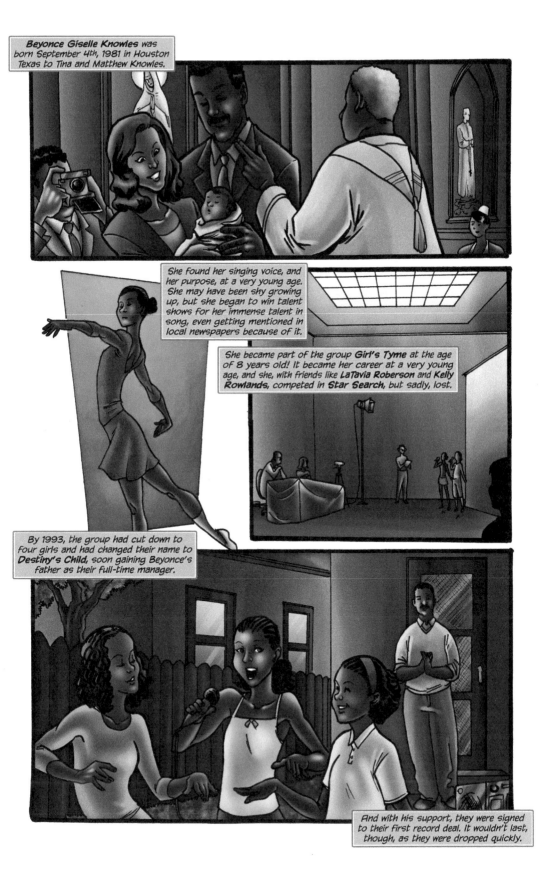

Beyonce Giselle Knowles was born September 4th, 1981 in Houston Texas to Tina and Matthew Knowles.

She found her singing voice, and her purpose, at a very young age. She may have been shy growing up, but she began to win talent shows for her immense talent in song, even getting mentioned in local newspapers because of it.

She became part of the group *Girl's Tyme* at the age of 8 years old! It became her career at a very young age, and she, with friends like *LaTavia Roberson* and *Kelly Rowlands*, competed in *Star Search*, but sadly, lost.

By 1993, the group had cut down to four girls and had changed their name to *Destiny's Child*, soon gaining Beyonce's father as their full-time manager.

And with his support, they were signed to their first record deal. It wouldn't last, though, as they were dropped quickly.

Beyonce and Destiny's Child spent the next four years performing at small venues and getting people talking about their stellar group. Their first major label debut would come in 1997...

...with the song *Killing Time* on the *Men in Black* soundtrack. The next year would be big for them too...

...Destiny's Child released their debut album and had their first major hit the same year. It lead to a number of awards and the beginning of their recognition, all before Beyonce was 18 years old.

The group's second album, *The Writing's on the Wall*, rocketed them into the music stratosphere. They won Grammy awards, had number one hits and were becoming household names.

It wasn't all glory, though. There were lawsuits against the group and Beyonce's father and group changes.

It didn't stop them, though. They continued to make music, some of which appeared on albums for the *Charlie's Angel* film, like *Independent Women Part 1*.

Their next release, 2001's *Survivor*, was the number one album on the Billboard charts.

It has sold over 10 million copies worldwide to date and had numerous number ones, such as *Survivor* and...

...*Bootylicious*. One of their biggest and best known hits. It was also one of the songs that brought Beyonce into the limelight, both for her skills and for her image.

After their Grammy Award wins for this album, the group recorded a holiday album and then went their separate ways for solo careers. Beyonce's career would now soar.

Beyonce would move on to not only a solo career, but would begin acting as well. She signed her first solo contract and acted in her first two films...

...Carmen: A Hip Hopera and Austin Powers in Goldmember. As Destiny's Child before her was starting to become a household name, Beyonce herself was as well.

She signed a contract with Pepsi, starring in a number of commercials for them, some of which included many other singers...

...Such as Pink, Britney Spears and others. She was taking off in the world...

She even was in the music video and song of then boyfriend Jay-Z's music video for O3 Bonnie and Clyde. She also signed on with L'Oreal and Tommy Hilfiger's True Star fragrance, garnering more and more commercial deals.

She released her first solo album in 2003, *Dangerously in Love*, after a number of collaborations had come out before that. It debuted at number one and went four times platinum.

She had two number one singles from the album and was a success both in the US and the UK with this album, proving her own mettle as a solo performer.

She won five Grammys in 2004 for the album and her efforts, putting her in an elite group of women.

That same year her and her mother founded the company *Beyond Productions* which did all the licensing for Beyonce's acts. It was a big step forward in her move toward not only being a solo act, but a businesswoman.

Also in 2004, **Destiny's Child** recorded and went on tour for their final album and toured for that same album. The album and tour, **Destiny Fulfilled...**

...And *Lovin' It*, scored them another three hits and was where they announced the disbanding of the group. It was the end of Destiny's Child, but another chapter in Beyonce's career.

In 2005, Beyonce and her mom introduced the *House of Dereon*, a new fashion line that was named after her own grandmother.

It was yet another step into her takeover of the fashion world, music world and film industry.

It was a clothing line that sells sportswear and other clothing for women that is both contemporary and fashionable. She made waves that same year...

...As Destiny's Child received a star on the Hollywood Walk of Fame, they released their greatest hits album and were seen as the best-selling female group of all time. A lot of accomplishments for Beyonce, before her 25th birthday.

#**1**s DESTINY'S CHILD

2006 was another big year for Beyonce. She starred opposite *Steve Martin* in the *Pink Panther* and had another hit song on its soundtrack.

2006 was the year she co-starred in *Dreamgirls* by Bill Condon.

Alongside **Jennifer Hudson, Jamie Foxx, Eddie Murphy** and many others, she wrote and performed in new songs for the film and received praise for her performance.

People began to see Beyonce not just as a musician, but also as a full-fledged crossover star.

DREAMGIRLS

DREAMGIRLS

She was nominated for two Golden Globes for the film.

Her second album on hold because of her movie work, she would find time to work on it between everything else she was doing at this time.

Besides her worldwide success in films and music, she has become a sex symbol as well, ending up on the **Sports Illustrated Swimsuit Issue** and in countless commercials and billboards around the world.

She was a seminal figure for womanhood and for strength, but her status would slightly change as a sex symbol...

...As she married **Jay-Z** in 2008, putting numerous rumors to bed about their pending nuptials or about their breaking up. They had been together since at least 2003 and were seen together often, but their marriage put all the rumors to bed. And their happiness was seen everywhere.

Later that year saw the release of her third solo album, *I Am... Sasha Fierce*. Probably her biggest album yet.

She stated that the name *Sasha Fierce* was her onstage persona; her performing name. The album actually saw the release of two singles before the official release of the album.

Both songs topped numerous charts all over the world, and *Single Ladies* became one of the biggest songs in both her career and in 2008. It was huge for her as a performer and as a singer but also...

...As a *married* woman. She revealed her marriage to Jay-Z at a listening party for her new album in a video for it. She was proud of her man, and he of her, and it was now common knowledge.

The release of this album seemed to be her biggest release yet.

Not only did it hit all the right notes for her creatively, but it took the world by storm.

She saw four singles released from the album, and her world tour became one of the highest grossing tours of 2009.

She was not only a household name, but a worldwide phenomenon.

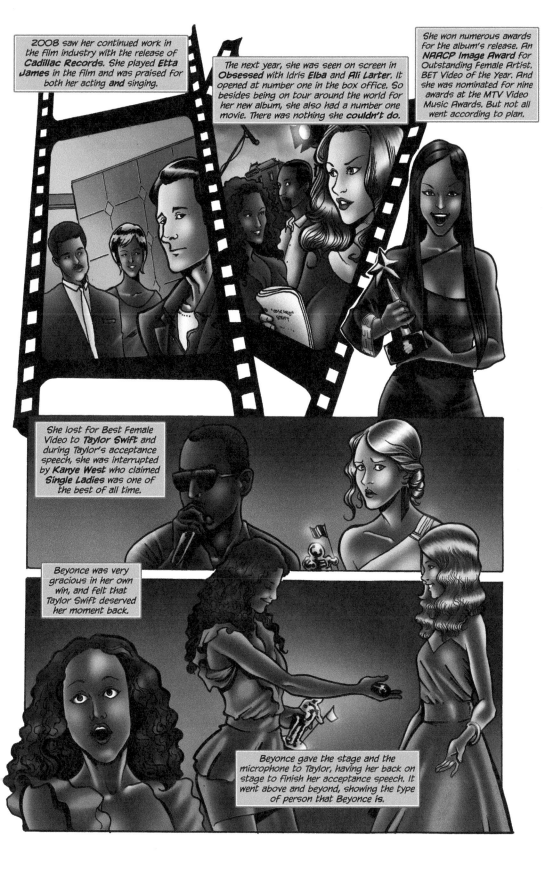

2008 saw her continued work in the film industry with the release of **Cadillac Records**. She played **Etta James** in the film and was praised for both her acting **and** singing.

The next year, she was seen on screen in **Obsessed** with Idris **Elba** and **Ali Larter**. It opened at number one in the box office. So besides being on tour around the world for her new album, she also had a number one movie. There was nothing she **couldn't do.**

She won numerous awards for the album's release. An **NAACP Image Award** for Outstanding Female Artist. BET Video of the Year. And she was nominated for nine awards at the MTV Video Music Awards. But not all went according to plan.

She lost for Best Female Video to **Taylor Swift** and during Taylor's acceptance speech, she was interrupted by **Kanye West** who claimed **Single Ladies** was one of the best of all time.

Beyonce was very gracious in her own win, and felt that Taylor Swift deserved her moment back.

Beyonce gave the stage and the microphone to Taylor, having her back on stage to finish her acceptance speech. It went above and beyond, showing the type of person that Beyonce is.

She has not only seen fame, but also parody. Her song, **Single Ladies**, has seen countless people performing the song in parody or in reverence.

It has seen countless interpretations, many of them very funny.

She's even played a role in them on shows like **Saturday Night Live**, being gracious and having fun with her own image.

She worked with *Lady Gaga* on the song *Telephone* and was featured on both the song and the video.

Beyond this, she took home six Grammys in 2010, setting the record as the most Grammys won by a woman ever.

She continues her charity work to this day, seemingly never taking a moment to stop working or working with others.

SURVIVOR FOUNDATIO

She even has her own fragrance now.

"WHERE THERE IS A
WILL WE WILL HELP
MAKE A WAY "

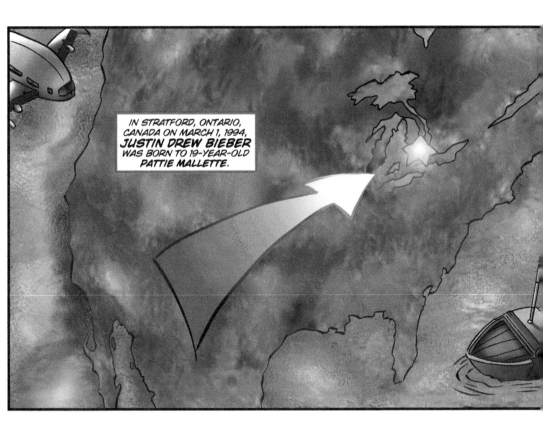

IN STRATFORD, ONTARIO, CANADA ON MARCH 1, 1994, **JUSTIN DREW BIEBER** WAS BORN TO 19-YEAR-OLD **PATTIE MALLETTE**.

AT AGE 2, JUSTIN BEGAN HIS CAREER IN MUSIC BY LEARNING TO PLAY THE DRUMS. HE THEN TURNED TO THE PIANO, AND EVENTUALLY GUITAR...

...WHICH HE PLAYED IN FRONT OF STRATFORD'S AVON THEATRE TO MAKE MONEY TO GO GOLFING WITH HIS BUDDIES.

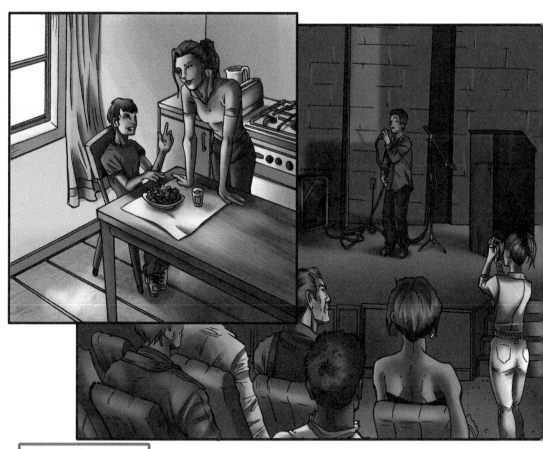

ACCORDING TO JUSTIN, "NOTHING EVER CAME OUT OF STRATFORD."

SO JUSTIN'S MOTHER DECIDED TO GO GLOBAL. SHE TOOK TO *YOU TUBE* WHERE SHE UPLOADED FOOTAGE OF HER SON PERFORMING AT A LOCAL SINGING COMPETITION. INITIALLY, THE FOOTAGE WAS MEANT FOR FAMILY...

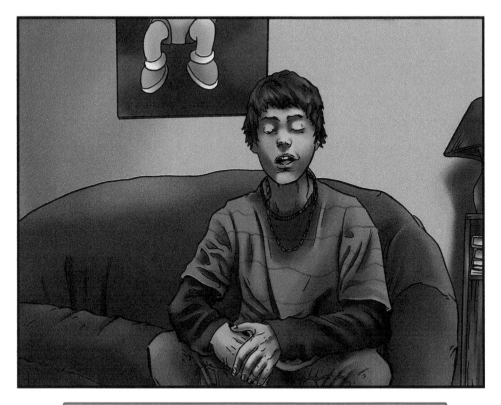

...BUT IT WASN'T LONG BEFORE THE WORLD TOOK NOTICE. IN 2007, JUSTIN BECAME A **YOU TUBE** SENSATION COVERING ARTISTS SUCH AS ALICIA KEYS, EDWIN McCAIN, USHER, NE-YO AND CHRIS BROWN AT REQUEST FOR HIS FANS. IT DIDN'T TAKE LONG BEFORE JUSTIN'S VIDEOS REACHED OVER **10 MILLION VIEWS.**

AFTER 7 MONTHS OF **ONLINE PERFORMANCES**, FORMER **SO-SO DEF** MARKETING EXECUTIVE SCOOTER BRAUN ACCIDENTALLY CLICKED ONE OF JUSTIN'S **YOU TUBE** VIDEOS AND WAS DETERMINED TO MEET THE YOUNG PERFORMER.

BRAUN CONVINCED JUSTIN'S VERY **PROTECTIVE** MOTHER TO FLY INTO ATLANTA, GEORGIA FOR A MEETING.

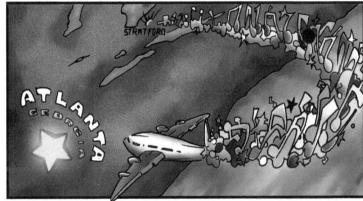

IT WAS HERE THAT A 13-YEAR-OLD JUSTIN MET **USHER** FOR THE FIRST TIME.

STRATFORD

ATLANTA
GEORGIA

HEY *USHER!* I LOVE YOUR SONGS. DO YOU WANT ME TO *SING* YOU ONE?

NO, LITTLE BUDDY, JUST COME INSIDE. IT'S *COLD* OUT.

BUT THE MUSIC CAREER HE WAS BORN TO DIDN'T TAKE OFF RIGHT AWAY. A WEEK LATER, JUSTIN AND HIS MOTHER FLEW TO ATLANTA FOR A SECOND MEETING WITH USHER.

THEY ALSO MADE A TRIP OUT WEST TO MEET WITH ANOTHER POP TITAN, JUSTIN TIMBERLAKE. BEFORE LONG, BIEBER FOUND HIMSELF IN THE MIDST OF A BIDDING WAR BETWEEN THE TWO LABELS.

MEANWHILE, HIS LIFE HAD TRANSFORMED FROM LAZY DAYS OF SKATEBOARDING WITH FRIENDS TO A STRICT SCHEDULE OF *VOICE LESSONS* AND PRIVATE *TUTORS.*

IN OCTOBER 2008, JUSTIN SIGNED WITH **ISLAND RECORDS**. BACKED BY **USHER**, HIS MANAGER SCOOTER BRAUN AND SONGWRITER AND RECORD PRODUCER, L.A. REID, HE **IMMEDIATELY** WENT INTO THE STUDIO WHERE HE RECORDED HIS FIRST SINGLE "**ONE TIME**."

NOT LONG AFTER, THE MUSIC VIDEO FOR THE SAME SINGLE MADE ITS DEBUT ON MTV.

DESPITE THE COOL **LOOK** IN HIS EYES, JUSTIN HAD A FIRE INSIDE OF HIM, AND ON NOVEMBER 17, 2009 HIS FIRST ALBUM, "**MY WORLD**," WENT **PLATINUM**.

THE RELEASE GAVE BIEBER SEVEN SONGS ON **BILLBOARD'S HOT 100 CHART**. THIS WAS A RECORD NUMBER OF CHARTED HITS FOR **A DEBUT ARTIST**.

BEFORE HIS FIRST ALBUM *DROPPED*, JUSTIN WENT ON *THE ELLEN DEGENERES SHOW* WHERE HE TALKED WITH ELLEN ABOUT HIS LOVE LIFE, PERFORMED AND MET WITH SOME OF HIS TEARY-EYED FANS.

YOU ARE VERY CONFIDENT. DID YOU ASK *RHIANNA* OUT? IS THAT *TRUE?*

IT *DID* HAPPEN. YES I ASKED HER OUT.

AND WHAT DID RHIANNA *SAY?*

UMM... I MEAN, I'M NOT *DATING* HER.

AFTER THE WILD SUCCESS OF **"MY WORLD,"** IN DECEMBER OF 2009, JUSTIN HAD THE OPPORTUNITY TO PERFORM STEVIE WONDER'S **"SOMEDAY AT CHRISTMAS"** FOR PRESIDENT OBAMA AND FIRST LADY AT THE WHITE HOUSE FOR CHRISTMAS IN WASHINGTON, DESPITE 'BREAKING A LEG' IN LONDON WHILE OPENING FOR **TAYLOR SWIFT.**

REGARDLESS OF THE FRACTURED FOOT, JUSTIN WENT TO NEW YORK TO RING IN A ROCKIN' NEW YEAR BY PERFORMING ON **DICK CLARK'S ROCKIN' NEW YEAR'S EVE** SPECIAL WITH RYAN SEACREST.

THE NEW YEAR WOULD PROVE TO BE A GOOD ONE FOR JUSTIN. IN JANUARY, HE RELEASED THE SINGLE *"BABY"* FEATURING *LUDACRIS.* THIS WOULD PROVE TO BE HIS BIGGEST HIT TO DATE EARNING THE FIFTH SLOT ON THE US TOP 100 CHART.

HE WOULD ALSO MAKE A SHOWING AT THE 52ND GRAMMY AWARDS AS A PRESENTER ALONGSIDE *KESHA.*

JUSTIN IS AS DEVOTED TO HIS FANS AS THEY ARE TO HIM. ONE WAY HE IS SURE TO KEEP HIS FANS UPDATED IS THROUGH HIS *TWITTER* UPDATES. KEEPING IN TOUCH WITH HIS FANS ALSO KEEPS HIM GROUNDED.

AND AT THE END OF THE DAY, JUSTIN IS YOUR AVERAGE TEEN WITH THE SAME DREAMS, FRIENDS, AND FAMILY WE ALL HAVE.

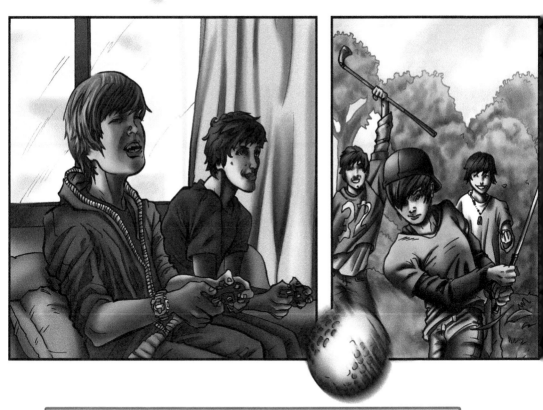

KEEPING IT HUMBLE IS SOMETHING JUSTIN STRIVES TO DO. HE KEEPS HIS FRIENDS CLOSE AND REGULARLY HEADS HOME TO STRATFORD TO SPEND TIME WITH THEM, ESPECIALLY HIS BEST BUD RYAN BUTLER. BIEBER IS ALSO A SELF-PROCLAIMED "MOMMA'S BOY," AND ON OCCASION, HE STILL GETS GROUNDED.

WHAT PART OF HOME BY 10 O'CLOCK DO YOU NOT **UNDERSTAND?**

NO PHONE FOR **FOUR DAYS.**

BUT **MOM...**

I LOVE YOU. NOW OFF TO BED.

ON MARCH 1ST, 2010, JUSTIN TURNED 16. HE CELEBRATED BY PARTYING IN LA WITH FRIENDS AND SEEING AN *L.A. LAKERS* GAME WHERE HE MET *KOBE BRYANT*. THEN IT WAS BACK TO TORONTO FOR A CELEBRATION WITH HIS FAMILY, A LITTLE CAKE, SOME BOWLING...

...AND A NEW *RANGE ROVER* WHICH HIS MENTOR, USHER, HELPED HIM BUY. BUT THE CELEBRATION *DIDN'T* STOP THERE. AFTER RIDING AROUND IN HIS NEW WHEELS...

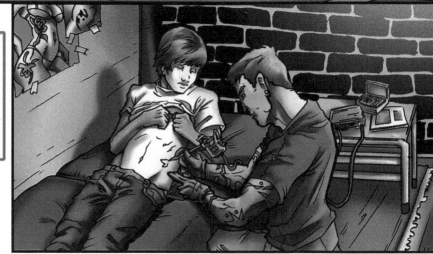

...HE GOT A TATTOO! JUSTIN RETURNED TO HIS HOMETOWN OF *STRATFORD*, WHERE A FRIEND OF JUSTIN'S FATHER GAVE HIM HIS FIRST *INK*. THE SEAGULL TATTOO ON HIS LEFT HIP IS RUMORED TO BE A FAMILY TRADITION.

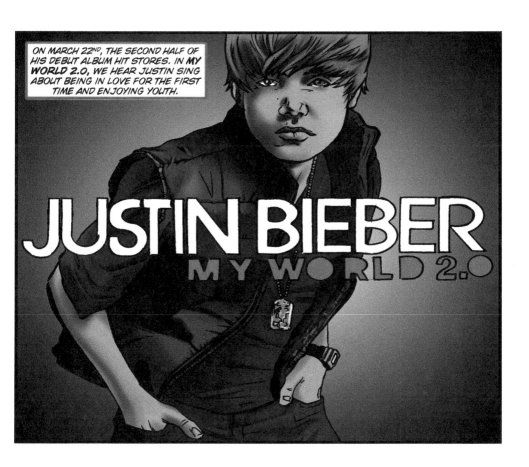

ON MARCH 22ND, THE SECOND HALF OF HIS DEBUT ALBUM HIT STORES. IN **MY WORLD 2.0**, WE HEAR JUSTIN SING ABOUT BEING IN LOVE FOR THE FIRST TIME AND ENJOYING YOUTH.

HE EVEN PENNED THE SONG **U SMILE** FOR HIS FANS. THE ALBUM IS FULL OF SURPRISE GUESTS: LUDACRIS RAPS WITH JUSTIN ABOUT HIS FIRST LOVE IN **BABY**, JESSICA JARRELL HELPS JUSTIN GO **OVERBOARD** AND THE DUET OF SEAN KINGSTON AND BIEBER TELL HER TO MAKE UP HER MIND IN THE REGGAE INSPIRED "**EENIE MEENIE.**"

ON APRIL 26, POLICE IN SYDNEY, AUSTRALIA, **CANCELED** ONE OF JUSTIN'S EVENTS DUE TO UNRULY FANS.

TWO DAYS LATER IN AUCKLAND, NEW ZEALAND, AN OVERZEALOUS GROUP OF FANS, OR "**BELIEBERS**" AS THEY ARE SOMETIMES KNOWN, WOULD RUSH JUSTIN AT THE AIRPORT KNOCKING DOWN HIS MOTHER AND STEALING HIS HAT IN THE PROCESS.

THESE INCIDENTS WOULDN'T BE THE FIRST CASES OF BIEBERMANIA'S CHAOS. IN NOVEMBER OF 2009, FANS AT A LONG ISLAND MALL IN NEW YORK GOT SO OUT OF HAND THAT AN ALBUM SIGNING WAS CALLED OFF.

AFTER THE AUCKLAND INCIDENT, JUSTIN TWEETED A GENTLE WARNING TO HIS FANS BY TELLING THEM THAT SAFETY SHOULD ALWAYS COME FIRST AT HIS EVENTS. HIS MOTHER HAD NOT BEEN HARMED AND BIEBER DIDN'T SEE A NEED TO FILE CHARGES FOR HIS STOLEN HAT SINCE IT DID GET RETURNED.

DESPITE THESE SETBACKS, JUSTIN MADE THE MOST OUT OF HIS TRIP BY VISITING A LOCAL NEWS STATION, PERFORMING A PRIVATE CONCERT AT A SCHOOL AND BUNGEE JUMPING OFF THE AUCKLAND HARBOUR BRIDGE, WHICH HE TWEETED ABOUT LATER THAT EVENING.

BUNGY! I **LOVE** NEW ZEALAND!

AT THE END OF APRIL, JUSTIN WAS NAMED TO PEOPLE MAGAZINE'S MOST BEAUTIFUL LIST FOR 2010 ALONGSIDE ROBERT PATTINSON AND JULIA ROBERTS.

BUT WHAT MAKES JUSTIN SO BEAUTIFUL? SOME ARGUE THAT IT HAS TO DO WITH THE FAMOUS "SWOOSH" OF HIS TRADEMARK HAIRSTYLE.

I SPEND FIVE MINUTES ON MY HAIR. I USE SHAMPOO, CONDITIONER --BASICALLY WHATEVER IS IN THE HOTEL-- AND BLOW-DRY. IT'S PART OF MY IMAGE. IT'S NOT WHO I AM.

BUT THERE IS CERTAINLY MORE TO THIS SIXTEEN YEAR OLD THAN GOOD HAIR AS HIS MAY 19TH *AMERICAN IDOL* PERFORMANCE CONFIRMED.

DESPITE HIS GOOD LOOKS AND HIS REPUTATION AS A PRANKSTER, JUSTIN TAKES HIS MUSICIANSHIP VERY SERIOUSLY.

TO PREPARE FOR HIS 2010 SUMMER TOUR, JUSTIN INSISTED THAT HE SIT IN ON THE AUDITIONS FOR HIS DANCERS AND TOURING BAND.

ONE MONTH BEFORE HEADING OUT ON TOUR, JUSTIN PRACTICES WITH HIS NEWLY AUDITIONED BAND, PERFECTS HIS DANCE MOVES AND WORKS ON HIS VOCALS.

BUT AS JUSTIN PREPARES FOR HIS UPCOMING TOUR, NO ONE KNOWS QUITE WHAT TO EXPECT. THERE IS THE PROMISE OF MEET AND GREETS BEFORE AND AFTER SHOWS, GREAT DANCING AND A FIERCE DRUMMER, SINCE JUSTIN LOVES THE DRUMS.

AND RUMORS ARE FLYING THAT HE MAY PULL A GIRL OUT OF THE AUDIENCE TO SERENADE. BUT FANS IN 31 STATES THROUGHOUT THE US AND IN CANADA WILL HAVE THE OPPORTUNITY TO SEE THE TOUR THAT PROMISES TO BE THE MUST-SEE EVENT OF THE SUMMER.

AT 16, JUSTIN BIEBER HAS SUNG TO SUPPORT THE VICTIMS OF THE HAITIAN EARTHQUAKE WITH "WE ARE THE WORLD - 25 FOR HAITI," AND HE HAS MINGLED WITH SUPERSTARS AND APPEARED ON COUNTLESS TELEVISION PROGRAMS IN ADDITION TO TOPPING MUSIC CHARTS WORLDWIDE, BUT WHAT'S NEXT FOR THE KID FROM CANADA WHO HAS WON OVER THE HEARTS OF TWEENS AND TEENS ACROSS THE GLOBE?

We dissect her clothing more than her music, and even argue about the outfits on television, determining if she's a fashion icon as well as a music icon.

It's all part of the *Lady Gaga* persona.

BRITNEY SPEARS

IN THE YEAR 2000, ANOTHER SMASH: "OOPS, I DID IT, AGAIN." WAS THIS THE VOICE OF THE NEW MILLENNIUM? FAME MOVES *FAST!!!*

ON THE SET OF "OOPS," A FALLING CAMERA ALMOST MAKES BRIT A ONE-HIT-WONDER!

WHAT IS *WRONG* WITH YOU PEOPLE? CAN WE TRY TO *NOT* KILL AMERICA'S SWEETHEART, TODAY? AM I BEING UNREASONABLE?

FOUR STITCHES LATER...

MOMMA, I'LL BE FINE. I'M A STAR, NOW! THIS IS BRITNEY, INC.! I'M GONNA BE ON THE SUPERBOWL! I GOTTA GET IT RIGHT!

STOP BEING SUCH A PERFECTIONIST. I WORRY ABOUT THESE FREAK ACCIDENTS THAT HAPPEN WHEN YOU WORK CRAZY HOURS, FLYING SO MUCH.

THE DAY'LL COME WHEN I WON'T EVEN *RECOGNIZE* YOU.

OH, MOMMA... THAT'LL *NEVER* HAPPEN. I'VE GOT JUSTIN TO KEEP MY FEET ON THE GROUND.

WOW! IT'S ALL OVER THE CHARTS. THEY SAY THIS NEW CD IS SO MATURE AND PERSONAL! NOTHIN' LIKE THE LAST TWO!

YEAH. I HATE IT!

WOW! HER FIRST MOVIE! HAD STUFF ABOUT BECOMING A WOMAN AND DEALING WITH EARLY PREGNANCY. IT WAS SO GROWN-UP.

YEAH. I HATE IT!

DAN AYKROYD, YOU'RE *THE* BLUES BROTHER. WHAT ARE YOU DOING PLAYIN' A POPPA IN A BRITNEY SPEARS MOVIE?

HEY, BRITNEY'S OKAY BY ME. SHE MAKES SOME ROCKIN', POPPIN' TUNES.

WELL, THAT'S *ONE* DAD WHO SUPPORTS ME. AT LEAST I HAVE JUSTIN.

NOT FOR LONG.

HE BROKE UP WITH ME, AND MADE A VIDEO SAYING I CHEATED ON HIM....

THIS CAN'T BE HAPPENING.

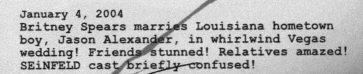

January 4, 2004
Britney Spears marries Louisiana hometown boy, Jason Alexander, in whirlwind Vegas wedding! Friends stunned! Relatives amazed! SEiNFELD cast briefly confused!

DID, UM, WE GET MARRIED A FEW HOURS AGO?

YUP.

CAN WE, LIKE, MAKE THAT, UM...NOT.

YUP.

IN TWELVE HOURS, IT WAS HISTORY... BUT NOT A BAD IDEA.

...MAYBE SOMEBODY WHO UNDERSTANDS THE MUSIC...LIKE A DANCER ... LIKE KEVIN FEDERLINE...

BUT KEVIN FEDERLINE'S ALREADY WITH SOMEONE! HE'S A FATHER WITH ANOTHER ONE ON THE WAY!

AND A NOBODY!! THINK OF YOUR CAREER!

MOMMA. THIS CAREER IS *NOT* A LIFE. I JUST WANT A LIFE. *A HOME?*

SOUND FAMILIAR? SINCE YOU AND DADDY UPPED AND DIVORCED, I DON'T HAVE ONE. NOT FOR REAL. SO I GOTTA MAKE MY OWN.

September 18, 2004
Britney Spears Stuns World! Another Wedding! Spears marries Kevin Federline in secret ceremony! But is it official?

...I'LL FINALLY HAVE IT ALL...

THE NEXT DAY...

I CAN'T ARGUE WITH THESE REVIEWS. AND THEY'RE *TERRIBLE!*

Brit's Crazy for It

WHAT WENT WRONG?

I WENT WRONG. I MADE A *FOOL* OUT OF MYSELF. I DIDN'T WORK NEARLY HARD ENOUGH.

SO YOU'RE QUITTING? WON'T YOU MISS IT?

NOT ALL OF IT, DADDY... I'LL JUST MISS THE DANCING AND SINGING.

YOU MEAN THE THINGS THAT MADE YOU FAMOUS? THE THINGS YOU LOVE? WHY NOT TRY THOSE AGAIN?

BUT REALLY WORK AT THEM. LIKE YOU USED TO. IF YOU FEEL LIKE A SUCCESS, IT WON'T MATTER WHAT *THEY* THINK.

I JUST NEED AN ESCAPE.

THEN YOU MIGHT AS WELL ESCAPE INTO THE *WORK YOU LOVE*, RIGHT?

Taylor Swift has become one of the hottest musicians in recent years, taking the world by storm. But how did she get here? What path did she take and where will that path lead her?

She was born on December 13, 1989 to parents Scott and Andrea. Her parents became immediate **fans**.

She was followed into this world by her younger brother **Austin**, and the family was complete.

Her first taste of success in **art** came in the 4th Grade...

...When she entered a national poetry contest with her poem "**Monster in my Closet**"...

...And **won** for the three page poem. It would place her in the public eye, albeit briefly, for the first time in her life.

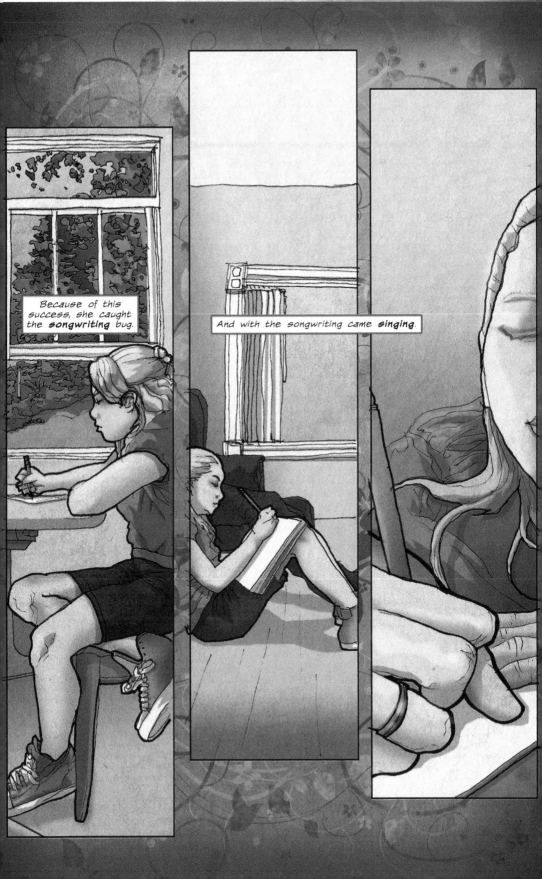

Because of this success, she caught the **songwriting** bug.

And with the songwriting came **singing**.

Like so many of us, she **loved** to sing from an early age on. She loved karaoke, and even spent time doing contests for best **singing** in karaoke.

She performed in front of small groups at fairs, festivals and other places around her home in Pennsylvania.

She became a member of a kid's comedy group where her comedy blossomed and shined through, something the world would get to see later on when she hosts Saturday Night Live. But even **better** for her was what these performances **did** for her...

Her time in *TheatreKids Live!* pushed her into a spotlight that would only intensify. She started on her path to *Country* singing and began to perform in front of groups at malls, more fairs, and open mic shows as well.

But the singing didn't come without its **problems** or its **perks**. She was picked on at school. She was **different** from other girls.

Songwriting became her way to escape this world, to escape the torment of the other girls.

It allowed her to think of the future, and plan for that to happen.

But it wasn't until she learned to play guitar, with the help of a local repairman, that she would then write her first song, in its entirety.

And this would be the last piece of the puzzle that she needed. She was on her way to making music.

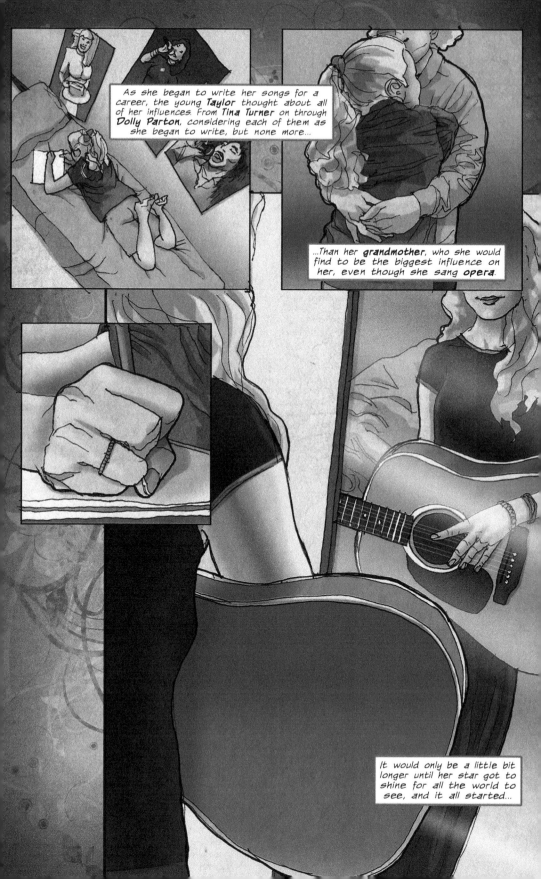

As she began to write her songs for a career, the young **Taylor** thought about all of her influences. From **Tina Turner** on through **Dolly Parton**, considering each of them as she began to write, but none more...

...Than her **grandmother**, who she would find to be the biggest influence on her, even though she sang **opera**.

It would only be a little bit longer until her star got to shine for all the world to see, and it all started...

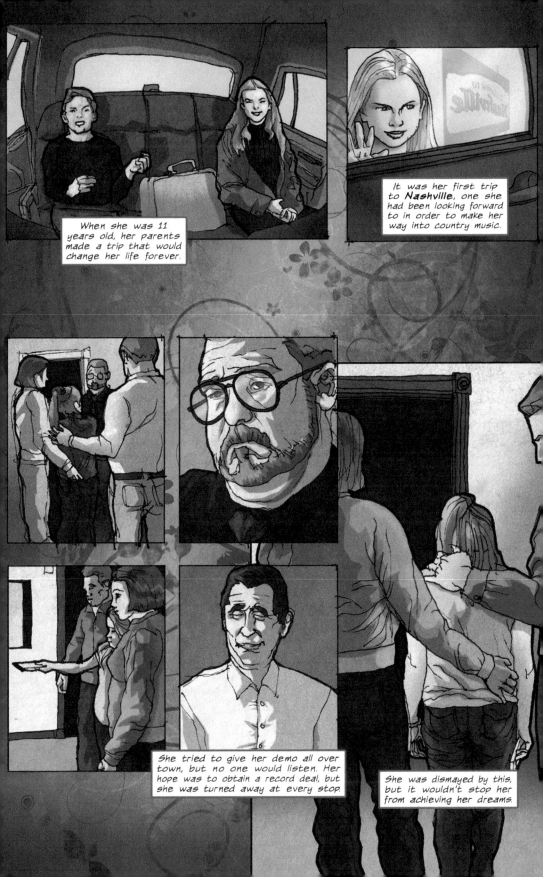

When she was 11 years old, her parents made a trip that would change her life forever.

It was her first trip to **Nashville**, one she had been looking forward to in order to make her way into country music.

She tried to give her demo all over town, but no one would listen. Her hope was to obtain a record deal, but she was turned away at every stop.

She was dismayed by this, but it wouldn't stop her from achieving her dreams.

It would be her first step in taking the world by storm.

Her dreams of singing were quickly met when she sang the National Anthem at the US Open tennis tournament. People took notice of her immediately...

It was because of this attention that her parents decided to take the family outside of Nashville to live, when she was 14 years old.

When her parents moved outside of **Nashville**, things began to take off.

Her parents rejected an offer from one record label in order to allow her the freedom to write and sing her own songs, and because of this, she was found by **another** producer who signed her to his **new** record label.

Taylor Swift

It was a whirlwind for her, leading her to her first release ever.

Her first single, **Tim McGraw**, hit #6 on the Billboard Hot Country Songs chart from her self-titled album.

TIM McGRAW
Taylor Swift

On the album, she wrote nearly all of the songs herself and it did **remarkably** well, especially being her first release and at such a young age.

Her album hit **#1** on the Billboard Top Country Albums and spent the next 8 weeks in that exact same spot. It managed to do well on the Billboard 200 as well.

1 TAYLOR SWIFT
Taylor Swift

Taylor Swift's Friend Space (Top 37)
Taylor Swift has 1767204 friends.

Because of her popularity, **MySpace** took notice of her very quickly, giving her one of the highest music streams in MySpace history and putting her in the Top Ten musicians in all music and first in Country Music. She was officially...

...A **star!**

Taylor's growing popularity took her all the way to the 2007 Academy of Country Music Awards, where country's biggest stars receive top honors.

She found herself side-by-side with some of her biggest influences in music.

She took the stage, the **lights** came up...

...And Taylor found herself **face to face** with the inspiration for her first hit song.

After that night, she **joined** Tim McGraw's tour as an opening act.

Taylor releases even more singles on her way to the top of the charts.

Taylor's single, **Teardrops on My Guitar**, climbed up to #2 on the Billboard charts in February 2007.

Later that year, Taylor warmed homes with her holiday album, **Sounds of the Season: The Taylor Swift Holiday Collection**.

The album contributed to Taylor's first Grammy nomination. It wouldn't be the last.

The success of her singles landed her on the prime-time stage again, this time at the 43rd Annual Country Music Awards.

Taylor finally had the chance to do the performance of her dreams for the world to see.

Taylor's popularity continued to rise.

She continued working hard, shooting a video for the first single from her 2nd album, "Should've Said No".

But she never forgot the people responsible for her success: her *fans*.

Taylor's star even shone on the **sports world**.

She sang the **Star-Spangled Banner** at the 2008 World Series to a packed stadium of fans.

From there, she traveled to New York City as the youngest country music guest ever on **Saturday Night Live**.

It would be her first time on the show but most certainly not her last.

Taylor sparked a romance with **Jonas Brother Joe Jonas** in 2008.

But the **fame** and touring took their toll on the young romance, ending almost as **quickly** as it began.

She explained on **Ellen's** show that one of the songs on her album, **Fearless,** is based on her experience with this heartbreak.

But Taylor remained strong, **touring** and **performing** more than ever.

Even at such a young age, Taylor has been recognized by her peers and fans as one of the most talented country acts around, resulting in numerous awards.

Taylor won **5** American Music Awards in 2009, and was nominated for **8** Grammys that same year.

Taylor was quickly becoming one of the fastest growing Pop/Country stars of 2009, and her **popularity** has shown no signs of stopping.

At the 2009 MTV Video Music Awards, Taylor was blindsided by **Kanye West** as she accepted the award for Best Female Video as he exclaimed that **Beyonce's** video for **All The Single Ladies** was "one of the best of all time".

Later in the show, Taylor appeared on stage with Beyonce. She was given the opportunity to finish her acceptance speech as Beyonce stepped aside for her moment.

Following the VMA's, Taylor appeared on **The View** to discuss the incident. Kanye later called and apologized.

In spite of the apology, it has been mocked by fellow country musicians as well as comedians the world over.

THE VIEW

In May 2009, Taylor hosted **Saturday Night Live**, allowing her to show the acting range she'd had since her time with the **TheatreKids Live!**

Saturday Night Live became her first major test as a budding actress, one which would be tested very soon.

In early 2010, Taylor's feature film debut arrived in the form of **Valentine's Day**, a romantic comedy featuring a talented ensemble cast such as Bradley Cooper, Julia Roberts, Jamie Foxx and one other actor she'd come to know...

Valentine's Day

...It was during the filming of **Valentine's Day** that she met and began dating Taylor Lautner. It would not last, however, but it wouldn't stop her in the slightest.

Taylor has successfully shown her range as a country singer, pop star and now is showing the world what she can do as an actress.

Despite all her success, Taylor has never forgotten her roots, and eagerly gives back to those around her.

No matter the cause, Taylor **repeatedly** finds ways to display her **generosity**.

Even on her own birthday in 2009, Taylor made it a point to share her good fortune with others when she donated $250,000 to schools across the country.

FORGIVENESS IN
A WOUNDED WORLD
Jonah's Dilemma

Janet Howe Gaines

Society of Biblical Literature
Atlanta

FORGIVENESS IN A WOUNDED WORLD
Jonah's Dilemma

Library of Congress Cataloging-in-Publication Data

Gaines, Janet Howe, 1950-
 Forgiveness in a wounded world : Jonah's dilemma / Janet Howe Gaines.
  p. cm. – (Studies in biblical literature)
 Includes bibliographical references and index.
 ISBN 1-58983-077-6 (pbk.)
 1. Bible. O.T. Jonah – Criticism, interpretation, etc. 2. Forgiveness – Biblical teaching. I. Title. II. Series: Studies in biblical literature (Society of Biblical Literature) ; 5.
 BS1605.52 .G35 2003
 224'.9206 – dc21   2003011519

09 08 07 06 05 04 03 — 5 4 3 2 1
Manufactured in the United States of America

To Gwendolyn and Jason
because when a child sings,
a mother dances.

Contents

Acknowledgments . . . .

Introduction . . . .

1. Approaching the Book of Jonah . . . .
   Genre
   Date
   Structure

2. Jonah's Disobedience . . . .
   Jonah and the Crew Spared

3. Jonah's Deliverance . . . .
   The Belly of the Fish
   The Psalm of Thanksgiving

4. Nineveh's Disobedience . . . .
   The Prophecy
   The Repentance

5. Jonah's Lessons . . . .

6. Jonah's Legacy . . . .
   The Inland Sunflower and the Island Prison
   Jonah and Jewish Liturgy
   Other Biblical Models of Forgiveness
   The Secular World: What Forgiveness Is and Is N

Works Cited . . . .

Index . . . .

Acknowledgments

Many people helped make this book possible. I would like to thank members of Congregation Albert in Albuquerque, New Mexico, including Rabbi Joe Black for providing me with opportunities to discuss forgiveness with congregants; Hedy Auerbach for allowing me to tell her Holocaust story in my introduction; and Rabbi Paul Citrin, my first Hebrew teacher, for patiently enduring my earliest slow and painful attempts to translate the book of Jonah and for helping me learn to chant excerpts for Yom Kippur afternoon. I am also indebted to scholars who reviewed a draft of my manuscript and made valuable comments, and to Professor Dennis Olson of the Princeton Theological Seminary and Rex Matthews at the Society for Biblical Literature for their faith in my ability to produce this book. I appreciate the many frank and honest conversations I had with South African friends, especially Laura and Thandile Ndukwana, for introducing me to their family and friends in the townships; Herbert and Shirley Hirsch for giving me the perspective of South African whites who grew up with and happily discarded apartheid; Miriam and Gunther Kleineibst, who fled Nazi Germany as children and led exemplary adult lives in South Africa; and Carole and Michael Rustin, transplanted Londoners who gladly watched the dismantling of the British Empire in South Africa. Most importantly, I want to extend sincere gratitude to my husband, Dr. Barry Gaines, who voluntarily functioned as my research assistant and was the most dedicated helper anyone could have. Without his hard work and unwavering support, this book could never have been completed.

Introduction

"Hedy will ask the first question," I said to my husband as we drove to synagogue. "It will be about forgiving those who killed her family during the Holocaust." To usher in the last High Holy Day season of the twentieth century, he and I would be doing our customary job of teaching. For the midnight religious service known as Selihot, a week before the Jewish New Year, our rabbi asked us to show a provocative film entitled *The Quarrel,* based on a play by Jewish theologian Joseph Telushkin. After the movie, we led the congregation's discussion of this probing look at two men, friends and study partners before the Holocaust, who accidentally meet after the war and resume their long debate on Jewish law and life. As I expected, Hedy was the first to rise and inquire, "How can I forgive when I can't forget?" My heart sank to my stomach. I had been preparing to answer that question for over a year. Researching the book of Jonah had given me many insights into the process of forgiveness, many stories I wanted to tell, many reassurances that forgiving and forgetting are not the same thing. But when the time came, I did not have the temerity to lecture Hedy. How could I give advice when she has suffered so much that I, born in America to affluent Lutheran parents well after World War II, have not experienced and could never truly understand? I ducked the question.

Several weeks before Selihot, I had made my first trip to South Africa, drawn there by some atavistic force. Growing up in a small North Carolina town during the long, hot summers of the 1960s Civil Rights movement, I had troubling memories of racism and therefore felt an old and profound connection to the victims of apartheid. I found South Africa to be a country of stark contrasts. Though some surprisingly upscale housing is found in Soweto and other townships, millions of black people still occupy acres of windowless, corrugated tin sheds, each one separated by only a few inches from the next. Not very far away from these shacks with no electricity or plumbing, wealthy white neighborhoods sprout mansions surrounded by tall stone walls topped with electrified wire and with armed guards standing at the gates. Yet all over the country — even in the tiny, poverty-stricken

Kalahari Desert town of Riemvasmaak — I found pamphlets entitled *Truth: The Road to Reconciliation*. The brochures outlined a national policy of forgiveness, designed to free victims and perpetrators of the burdens of the recently dismantled apartheid system of racial segregation. Though South Africa's young democracy faces enormous challenges resulting from the inexperience of politicians, AIDS, crime, poverty, illiteracy, and unemployment, I was inspired by the way the citizens of an entire country had avoided bloody revolution and instead reached out to forgive each other for wrongs committed in such a dark period of their history. Looking back to the Bible, I recalled how Jonah, his people so historically mistreated by the Ninevites, balked at forgiving them. How was the Bible story different from the present-day situation in South Africa? In the last chapter of this book I shall return to Holocaust and apartheid examples to demonstrate how they relate to Jonah's dilemma.

Months before my first trip to South Africa, Americans were besieged with seemingly endless television, newspaper, and magazine accounts of President William Jefferson Clinton's escapades with Monica Lewinsky. On August 17, 1998, the president gave videotaped testimony to a grand jury investigating his imbroglio with the young woman. Afterward, he appeared on national television and confessed to the American public his improper relationship with Lewinsky, a former White House intern. The tone of his speech, still defiant to the ears of many listeners, did not satisfy. Pundits, preachers, lawmakers, and ordinary citizens demanded a more sincere apology from the president. It took several days before Clinton actually uttered the word "sorry" and began to appear more repentant and contrite. On September 11 (a date that we did not know would come to have such significance to the issue of forgiveness in our national psyche), at a White House prayer breakfast, President Clinton finally said, "I don't think there is a fancy way to say that I have sinned" (Fineman 27). It was a commendable though perhaps tardy admission of the sort never made by the prophet Jonah. At the breakfast, Clinton also mentioned that a friend had given him a copy of the Jewish High Holy Day prayer book, *Gates of Repentance*. From the text he read, "Turn us around, O Lord, and bring us back toward You." The Jewish High Holy Days, with their emphasis on the book of Jonah and the forgiveness God extends to the erring prophet and the repentant Ninevites, contain appropriate liturgy for the president and anyone else seeking to understand the difficult dilemma of asking for and granting forgiveness. Nearly a year later, on September 29, 1999, the president publicly thanked his family and the nation for "unmerited forgiveness" extended to him after the sex-and-lies scandal with Monica Lewinsky (Hunt A1). Did the prophet Jonah and the Ninevites, I wondered, also receive "unmerited forgiveness" from God? Do we have to deserve forgiveness to obtain it? These and other questions troubled me. In the final chapter of this book I shall look at how Jewish liturgy helps people think about forgiveness.

As a person who is frequently in need of forgiveness, I am naturally drawn to the subject. My daughter, Gwendolyn, suggested I tackle the topic in a new book after she saw me struggling with the issue. For everyone — from those like Hedy who witnessed firsthand some of the darkest moments of the twentieth century, to those in South Africa who were persecuted by another (though noticeably less severe) incarnation of a white supremacy movement, to those like the former president whose positions of power put them under great public scrutiny and pressure to admit wrongdoing, to ordinary folks like me who have to grapple with the lacerations of everyday life — the topic of forgiveness looms large. How can we emulate God and forgive our fellow human beings when we are so much less than divine? How can we solve the dilemma of pardoning those who cannot or will not ask for forgiveness? How can we be true to ourselves while absolving those who are unaware of our misery and do not care about our largesse? The book of Jonah offers many suggestions. It has helped me know how to begin to comprehend the nature of divine forgiveness so that I can try to extend its power to myself and others.

Despite its diminutive size, the book of Jonah tackles several mammoth issues, forgiveness being just one of them. It is reductive to the book to suggest that it has a single idea, for it presents many themes. There are messages on the necessity of repentance, the brevity and frailty of life, and the nature of relationships between humans and God. The book of Jonah also discusses topics such as universalism versus particularism, false versus true prophecy, tolerance versus prejudice, fate versus free will, and clemency versus punishment. Furthermore, the book favors implicit over explicit theological, ethical, or psychological insights. The result is that a single, central theme that stitches together all the narrative's colorful threads into one pattern is elusive. Ambiguity remains a hallmark of the book of Jonah, and today no solid consensus exists on what constitutes its overriding idea. My intention, nevertheless, is to focus on forgiveness and leave direct discussion of other issues for another time. By honing in on one aspect of the book of Jonah, I try to explore it fully, not discounting and even sometimes amplifying the credibility and importance of other themes as they dovetail with pardon. The biblical story suggests forgiveness without using the vocabulary of forgiveness, and none of the characters, including God, is ever directly said to pardon anyone. Therefore, the story contains a treasure trove of hermeneutics, a sometimes weird and always wonderful collection of moral wealth, and implicit forgiveness is a glittering jewel.

Before plunging into a detailed analysis of biblical theme, chapter 1 of this book briefly relates the story's plot and then explores three literary issues that have a serious impact on how ancient and modern audiences could view forgiveness. The chapter assesses the influence of several possibilities concerning genre, date of composition, and structure on the way forgiveness messages are perceived and interpreted. Chapters 2 through 5 analyze the theme of forgiveness as it appears in each of the book of Jonah's four sections. Chapter 2 shows how the prophet's disobedience to divine calling reveals a very human protagonist in need of pardon. Jonah is contrasted to pagan sailors who, ironically, are more amenable to acknowledging God's power than Jonah. Chapter 3 discusses Jonah's deliverance in the belly of the great fish, a sign of God's protection and a recognition that salvation comes, perhaps when we least expect or deserve it, freely as a gift from God. Chapter 4 focuses on Nineveh and its turn from evil, noticed by a forgiving deity who renounces the plan to destroy the city and demonstrates a love of all humankind. Chapter 5 returns to a discussion of the prophet and his reaction to Nineveh's salvation, his physical and emotional discomfort, and his dilemma over how to forgive others. In Jonah's dialogue with God, the deity has the last word, and at its conclusion the text remains unclear as to whether Jonah ever understands the nature of divine forgiveness. Chapter 6 explores two twentieth-century echoes of Jonah's predicament as they relate to forgiving others — the Holocaust of World War II and the post-war apartheid regime of South Africa. Providing opposite conclusions to the open ending of the book of Jonah, these two separate and distinct historical events show how individuals who were directly affected can feel either prevented from or compelled to grant forgiveness to those who committed some of the most egregious wrongdoings of the century. More biblical models are also explored, as are contemporary views on what forgiveness is and what it is not. In this way the Bible's lessons on the dilemma of how to forgive are applied to our world.

One final note is needed concerning my outlook and tone. This examination of the book of Jonah is viewed from the perspective of a believer who accepts the notion of a Higher Power and desires to question and explore the nature of divine authority as well as human action. Nonbelievers might not look first to the Bible as a behavioral guide, but I find that the biblical text provides timeless and enduring advice on the process of forgiveness.

Perhaps secular readers may relate to the writings of psychologists, sociologists, and other academic scholars whose ideas are discussed alongside those of theologians in this work. My own experiences, based on biblical models as well as nonreligious critical analyses, tell me that forgiveness assists in exorcising my demons and bringing me closer to God. It is a healing process for a wounded world.

CHAPTER 1

Approaching the Book of Jonah

To err is human, to forgive divine.
— Alexander Pope,
"An Essay on Criticism"

It was not an auspicious beginning. God commanded, "Go!" but Jonah's actions screamed, "No!" The original audience of Israelites must have sat spellbound as they heard an intriguing story about one of their prophets. Jonah refused to obey God's directive to visit faraway Nineveh, capital city of enemy Assyria, and deliver a message of doom to its citizens. Awestruck Israelites would hear how a giant fish then swallowed Jonah, only to spew him out onto dry land again so he could start the journey to the distant city. Some listeners would be sympathetic and others perplexed when the Ninevites repented and Jonah became angry about God's decision to forgive Israel's powerful foe. The oral storyteller related a captivating incident concerning Jonah's startling encounters with a group of sailors, a huge fish, an infamous archenemy, and the Lord. It would be a tale for the ages.

If history had taught the people anything, it was that Yahweh, their single and incorporeal deity from days of old, expected compliance to divine decrees. Enthralled, the listeners would immediately realize that this tale of Jonah was no ordinary homily. The successful prophet and the redoubtable God of Israel were locked in a battle of wills. How could both emerge victorious? Surely one side would lose, and the likelihood was small that Jonah could escape God's will and justice. From the beginning, the Israelites would suspect that forgiveness would have to be an integral component of the narrative concerning such an insubordinate servant of God.

The book of Jonah has always seemed bigger than its diminutive size indicates. It takes up scarcely three pages in many Bibles, a mere four chapters comprising forty-eight verses, but it is the mighty mite of the Hebrew Scriptures (also called the TANAKH or the Old Testament). The Bible has other small books — Nahum, Haggai, Zephaniah — but who knows them well today? Few prophets have a name more widely recognized by ordinary people than Jonah's, and the short work is sacred text for three major religions — Judaism, Christianity, and Islam. The book of Jonah is placed roughly in the middle of the Jewish TANAKH, clumped with other prophets at the end of the Christian Old Testament, and spaced out in various surahs (or chapters) in the Islamic Koran. Prophetic books usually contain oracles of doom, warnings, and curses, but the book of Jonah also carries the compelling force of a sustained narrative. Jonah's is the story we have always known, the tale so ingrained in our culture that it is part of our collective memory, inseparable from our very selves (Hampl 291). The story of Jonah is simple enough to delight a child and complex enough to confound a scholar. It invites reflection and contemplation on a number of important levels and themes. The book of Jonah is a high point in the Hebrew Scriptures, a pinnacle in divine revelation on the dilemma of how to forgive.

As the tale opens, the Lord orders Jonah to leave his homeland, go north into the enemy territory of Nineveh, and tell the people that their days are numbered. Immediately it is clear that the way Jonah handles his existential conflict will have far-reaching effects. Refusing to obey, Jonah plays the truant and flees instead in the opposite direction, toward Tarshish. There he boards a ship and quickly goes below deck to sleep. Just after it embarks, God assails the vessel with a great storm. The sailors, men who are probably experienced navigators, are frightened of the squall's intensity and pray to their various gods. The captain awakens Jonah and pleads with him also to call upon his deity. In an effort to determine who is causing the storm, the sailors draw lots. When the lot falls on Jonah, he tells them to throw him overboard so the ocean will cease raging. After trying other means to save the ship and those aboard, the mariners comply with Jonah's suggestion and toss him into the sea. The storm abates, and instead of drowning, the prophet is rescued by a giant fish that swallows him whole. Inside the fish for three days and nights, Jonah prays and apparently receives divine forgiveness for his disobedience, for he is delivered safely back onto dry land. Then the word of God comes again to Jonah, commissioning him to go to Nineveh and preach a divine message, the nature of which is not yet revealed to the prophet. This time Jonah submits, journeys to Nineveh, and delivers his brief warning that soon the city will be overthrown. The people believe and repent, thereby hoping to change God's mind. To Jonah's alarm and chagrin, the Lord relents and forgives the Ninevites. A pouting prophet begs God to let him die rather than witness what is to come. Jonah leaves the city and watches at a distance, under a cooling bush, to see what will happen next. When God commands a worm to attack Jonah's leafy ramada, the cranky prophet seems to care more for the bush than for the city's inhabitants.

God speaks to Jonah in the end, but whether Jonah ever understands and/or accepts the nature of God's universal love and forgiveness is unclear.

What amazement the original audience must have felt at encountering such a strange story of human disobedience and divine kindness. Perhaps some shocked listeners would view Jonah dispassionately (Payne 6), but others would identify strongly with the prophet. The Hebrew Scriptures, which establish Jonah's credentials as a prophet in earlier books, never mention Jonah again, although the New Testament gospels refer to the three-day fish interlude as the "sign of Jonah" that foreshadows Christ's experience in the tomb. The Bible does not trace the impact of the incidents in the big fish and the big city upon the rest of Jonah's life or career, but we nonetheless recognize that his story addresses modern as well as ancient concerns about how to forgive wrongdoers and accept outsiders. We see the prophet Jonah's wariness of foreigners as opposite to the message in the book of Ruth, which presents positive Israelite reaction to the main character, a woman born and raised among Israel's enemy Moabites. The book of Ruth demonstrates acceptance of outsiders who come to worship Yahweh, and the foreign heroine becomes the mother of a line of kings extending from David to Jesus. Jonah's negativity is thus unusual and disturbing when contrasted to the text of Ruth and high-minded Torah passages such as Lev 19:33–34: "When a stranger resides with you in your land, you shall not wrong him. The stranger who resides with you shall be to you as one of your citizens; your shall love him as yourself, for you were strangers in the land of Egypt. . . . " (All references to the Hebrew Scriptures, unless otherwise indicated, are taken from the 1985 Jewish Publication Society [JPS] version of the Bible entitled, *TANAKH: The Holy Scriptures, The New JPS Translation According to the Traditional Hebrew Text*. The translation is based on the ancient Masoretic text). The Ninevites whom Jonah seems to detest do not, of course, reside in Israelite land, and he fails to extend tolerance to them.

The reason Jonah's story resonates through time is that something of this prophet resides within us all. Though his travails are different from those of the hero preparing for death and judgment in the medieval morality play *Everyman*, Jonah in a sense becomes Everyone. He endures what feels to him like an unbearable burden; he faces an unassailable task that assaults his sensibilities and negates his personal wishes. He is a profoundly *human* being, an antihero who may fear he cannot live up to the onerous job God sets before him. Jonah's follies are ours. His uncompleted assignments remind us of our own. Because we associate with his struggles, we feel comfortable with his story. When we look in our mirror, we may see the reflection of Jonah. He is not an invincible hero in the classical sense, slaying ferocious monsters and saving fair damsels. We intuitively recognize his lack of heroism as inherent in our own personalities. He does not have superhuman strength or courage. Jonah in Nineveh is not Indiana Jones in the desert, bravely facing danger and outwitting villains who would steal the Ark of the Covenant. Nor is he Batman in Gotham City, crushing corrupt scoundrels who would infect the world with their poison. He is ordinary and, like us, he seeks to escape responsibility and has difficulty forgiving his enemies. He is, in effect, our second self or alter ego. Ironically, Jonah need not perform a superhuman deed — find the Golden Fleece or "leap tall buildings in a single bound" — to lead a fully realized, authentic life.

Jonah's enemy lies within. He knows what God wants him to do; he just does not want to do it. When we see Jonah leave his work undone, we bond and identify with him and his plight. Observing his unresolved conflicts, "we *become* Jonah. His unfitness in life painfully reminds us of our own daily struggle with meaning" (Lacocque and Lacocque, *Psycho* 50). As Jonah evades his vocation, he may actually motivate us to fulfill our obligations more readily. Jonah's dilemma, to accept all human beings as equal in the sight of God, represents a deeply rooted obstacle to our own emotional growth and maturation. As Everyone, Jonah shoulders the burden of our unresolved conflicts about accepting those around us who look different, hold different values, and follow different belief systems. Jonah is not alone in the ship on the tempest-tossed sea of life. His story reminds us that we follow him into those troubled waters. All humankind is in the same boat, threatened by the same dangers. Deep within our psyches, we understand that Jonah's problems are universal and that we ourselves cannot claim immunity to his reluctance to accept divine instructions on how to live, how to forgive. When the sailors' lot indicates Jonah's culpability for the storm, he expresses no shock. He has always seen responsibility heading his way. To be heroic he needs only to be obedient to his own conscience and impulse to do the good, which will automatically mean obedience to the divine plan, yet the biblical text offers no hard evidence that Jonah will ever live up to a conscience's demands.

Victory comes not only when the internal adversary is defeated, but earlier, when the process of confronting the foe begins. Whether Jonah's journey of introspection is motivated by his faith that the Lord will not destroy the Ninevites who were not raised to know God, his indifference to outsiders, his reluctance to minister to hostile heathens, or his belief that God belongs to the Israelites alone, his first impulse is to flee. As Jonah plunges into the sea, he dives into his own depth. Introspection is a life-renewing but grueling experience. When Jonah passes through the jaws of the mammoth fish and undergoes a psychological metamorphosis, he becomes one who knows that God commands the universe (P. Lacocque 222), but there is no such thing as a one-time, permanent defeat of the inner enemy's reign of error. Annihilation of the inner self and its conflicts may be impossible (and undesirable). When Jonah is reborn on dry land, he is still a mortal, not a god. Jonah after the fish and the subsequent journey to Nineveh is fundamentally the same as the earlier Jonah; he possesses the same character strengths and weaknesses after his sojourn as prior to it. The struggle to accept responsibility, grow emotionally, and extend forgiveness to others is ongoing, lifelong. To become fully human we must undergo the same journey as Jonah, a journey inside our own turbulent waters.

The book of Jonah is an excellent illustration of journey literature. Other examples abound outside and inside the Bible. In Mark Twain's *The Adventures of Huckleberry Finn,* Huck boards a raft and floats down the Mississippi River, maturing along the way and realizing the evils of slavery and the hypocrisy of society. In *Heart of Darkness* Joseph Conrad's characters are adrift on a serpentine African river that carries them deep into the recesses of the human soul. In Scripture, Joseph is forced to travel down to Egypt, where he will eventually become the savior of his people. Moses and the children of Israel wander in the desert for forty years. Their journey is designed to give them time to grow and change into a people worthy of the promised land. Likewise, Jonah sets off on a strange and wondrous adventure. It will not be a pleasure trip as he heads for sea and later for Nineveh. Characters ranging from Huck Finn and Charlie Marlow to the prophet Jonah explore their own psyches and embark upon perilous excursions. In the parching desert or murky depths of our hearts lurk impediments and monsters of all kinds. What is to be gained by confronting them? Benefits for those undertaking the journey include physical prizes such as the Golden Fleece and the Holy Grail. Spiritual rewards, such as the opportunity to exhibit bravery, overcome obstacles, learn cosmic truths, and discover one's identity, are even more valuable. In Jonah's case the prophet is presented with the challenge to learn obedience and forgiveness, to earn a second chance to do the right thing, to increase knowledge and tolerance, and to realize freedom from ignorance and bigotry. Meeting these challenges will be the struggle of his life.

Ironically, while Jonah attempts to flee from God and refuses to bend to divine will, the prophet is not free. "Only when one assumes responsibility for the commandment is one free, for the simple reason that it enunciates for the first time the *project* of a person, one's *raison d'être,* one's ultimate

meaning" (Lacocque and Lacocque, *Psycho* 71). The great Jewish philosopher Moses Maimonides (1135–1204) maintains that people are not created
free; we receive the commandment to become free (409). Our own volition
is necessary in order for us to transcend temporal concerns and choose freedom. Jonah acts alone when he seeks to rebuff God's expectations, but to
the prophet's credit, he does not battle with his fish. Rather, when he realizes the futility of hiding from God, Jonah submits to an examination of his
subconscious. Here he is not pusillanimous. Jonah risks being alone with
his inner self, heeds the messages of his unconscious, and tries to reform.
The Koran twice refers to Jonah as one to whom Allah gives inspiration and
favor, along with Noah, Abraham, Ishmael, Isaac, Jacob, Solomon, Job, and
Jesus (Surah 4:163; Surah 6:86). Jonah uses this inspiration to propel him
through a symbolic death inside the fish and resurrection on dry land before
he can attempt to overcome human limitations and start to be free.

The popularity of the book of Jonah should come as no surprise. The
tiny text with the big message excites our imaginations and calls us home.
Centuries before the birth of Christ, the book of Jonah was seen as an
archetypal story of tribulation and deliverance. Jonah is not a flat, unidimensional character. He is complicated enough to engage the reader and
encounter God. The book of Jonah is a gateway to solving the perplexing
dilemma of how to forgive our enemies. The narrative gestalt points to the
complexity of Jonah's relationship to the Lord.

Emphasizing any single element of the book of Jonah "can result in
quite different readings. That . . . ambiguity exists and that no single reading
is the 'true' one, is no more, and no less, a problem than the attempt to
recognize and understand the word of God" (Magonet 112). Though the
book's strategically mystical and ambiguous treatment of forgiveness is the
dominant issue here, at least three literary elements relate to that theme.
Genre, date, and structure all contribute to an understanding of forgiveness
messages. Analysis of the book's genre has an impact on one's understanding
of content. For example, if it fit well in the category of prophecy, one would
note where the book appears among prophetic oracles and how the Lord's
insistence that Jonah warn the Ninevites about impending destruction is
reconciled with God's later decision to renege on the punishment. If the
genre of satire dominated, the book would to the end remain highly critical
of Jonah's unforgiving behavior. Theories about genre therefore need to be
explored to see how they develop theme. The date of composition could also
have an impact on meaning. If the work were dated after the Babylonian
captivity, the original audience might be more perplexed by the dilemma of
pardoning their former Assyrian enemies than they would have been before

the exile. Structure also plays a key role in developing theme. Are the four chapters arbitrary, or does each play a role in fleshing out the forgiveness theme? Perhaps other ways of looking at the book's composition would make forgiveness issues clearer to readers. Opinions on these workhorses of literature — genre, date, and structure — vary and merit explanation.

Genre

While the story of Jonah is clearly unique in the Hebrew Scriptures, how the deceptively unassuming text should be labeled is not clear. Its four short chapters are just as sophisticated as much longer biblical books and more resistant to genre classification. The category issue has bearing on the theme of Jonah's dilemma — to forgive or not to forgive — though several literary genres are capable of communicating messages on the forgiveness of wrongdoing. Jonah is a moral narrative that has been labeled novella, poetry, prophecy, history, biography, midrash, wisdom literature, folk tale, fairy tale, myth, legend, allegory, parable, comedy, burlesque, parody, satire, tragedy, and tragicomedy. In truth, while the categories themselves may be antithetical, employing any of them to the Jonah story is possible to some extent. All of the genres potentially provide tools for those seeking to understand the nature of divine and human forgiveness; characteristics of all of them are at least partially applicable to the book of Jonah. Each literary type accounts for certain aspects of the text but fails to explain others. The original biblical author and audience were not concerned with labeling the tale's genre. Ancient Jewish tradition would find no need to distinguish among genres, for none would be seen as independent. All would combine to make a causal link between human actions and divine responses (Elata-Alster and Salmon 41). Our classification conundrum was not theirs.

By enjoying Bible stories as stories, we can learn much about God and ourselves. The book of Jonah contains no evidence that the prophet himself wrote it. The book simply tells a story about the prophet, as the two books of Kings relate narratives about Elijah. The work is certainly a moral narrative (Tigay 73) designed to disorient and then reorient our imaginations (Lacocque and Lacocque, *Psycho* 26) on major themes such as forgiveness. We are disoriented when our assumptions about life are challenged, then reoriented as we realize that we have misinterpreted a significant aspect of life, such as the necessity of forgiving enemies. We hear the message and have a breakthrough experience, realizing the need to think in a different way or go in a new direction. The book of Jonah resembles the moral narrative episodes introduced early in Genesis, including the expulsion from

Eden, the murder of Abel, the Tower of Babel, the flood of Noah, the covenant of Abraham and God, the destruction of Sodom and Gomorrah. Later
narratives, such as Job, are also similar. Indeed, what tale in the Bible is
not a moral narrative? The protagonists have specific names and locales,
but they represent the totality of humankind, our mistakes, and the results
of our errors. Alone among these stories, the book of Jonah gives special
emphasis to the efficacy of confession and the surety of divine forgiveness.
No prophet comes to warn the residents of Babel or Sodom so they can
repent and avert the crisis. Noah's generation is not given an opportunity
to change its behavior. The trajectory of Jonah's tale is different. It is more
optimistic and suggests that while God is free to execute sovereign will, the
Ninevites will not be punished for sin when they turn from evil ways. Good
vanquishes evil in the penitent heart.

Bibles nestle the book of Jonah in among the minor prophets, but one
could easily understand why the tale might be placed within the כתובים,
the Writings of the TANAKH, morality narratives such as the ones about
Ruth or Job. One could even place the book of Jonah alongside some of the
Apocrypha's fantastical tales, especially the book of Tobit, which contains
an episode reminiscent of Jonah's predicament in the city of Nineveh and the
belly of the fish. Tobit is a religious man who suffers blindness and poverty
in Nineveh as a direct result of performing the good deed of burying a fellow
Jew. His son, Tobias, journeys to Media and reclaims a sum of money that
Tobit has stashed there. Tobias's guide turns out to be an angel empowered
to extract magic spells from the organs of fish:

> Then the young man [Tobias] went down to wash his feet in the
> Tigris river. Suddenly a large fish leaped up from the water and
> tried to swallow the young man's foot, and he cried out. But the
> angel said to the young man, "Catch hold of the fish and hang on
> to it!" So the young man grasped the fish and drew it up on the
> land. (Tob 6:3–4)

They kill the fish and remove its innards, which are kept for medicine to help
Tobit regain his sight (11:8). The story is a strong moral tale echoing Jonah's
encounter with the great fish, though the book of Tobit is not prophetic or
insistent on the notion of forgiving the Ninevites. Alone among Bible and
Apocrypha narratives, the book of Jonah presents a uniquely imaginative
lesson on repentance and forgiveness (Roffey 10).

Like other moral narratives, the book of Jonah has a straightforward
(though fantastical) plot with tension, conflict, and some degree of resolution. Though poetry dominates chapter 2, the book is predominately a prose

piece. Built around a historical person, it is fiction designed to teach didactic lessons. The fact that there was an actual prophet named Jonah, first described in 2 Kings, gives way to the concept of Jonah representing a universal human predicament. The author uses imaginative details to spin the yarn, and the almost always present narrator can view Jonah up close or remain aloof and detached. The purpose of the moral narrative is to persuade the readers to accept certain theological principles — to admonish us against humankind's darker side and encourage us toward the light of forgiveness.

Despite the book's moral narrative qualities, from the beginning biblical scholars classified the work as prophecy. On the grounds of its placement among the נביאים (the Prophets) in the Jewish canon, prophecy is its proper genre. Jonah is one of the prophets who advises his monarch. In 2 Kings, located in the Hebrew Scriptures well before the book of Jonah, a prophet named Jonah, son of Amittai, is first mentioned as a contemporary of wicked King Jeroboam II, son of Joash from Judah. In a few verses Jonah proclaims important matters:

> [Jeroboam II] did what was displeasing to the LORD; he did not depart from all the sins that Jeroboam son of Nebat had caused Israel to commit. It was he who restored the territory of Israel from Lebo-hamath to the sea of the Arabah, in accordance with the promise that the LORD, the God of Israel, had made through His servant, the prophet Jonah son of Amittai from Gath-hepher. (2 Kgs 14:24–25)

The reference to Gath-hepher indicates that Jonah is a northerner, though in the book of Jonah he heads to Joppa, the port city for Jerusalem in the south. He successfully predicts the extent to which Jeroboam II will reinstate the boundaries of the northern kingdom of Israel many years before the Assyrians swoop down and destroy the country. Because of his accurate counsel, Jonah would have enjoyed a good reputation as a prophet in his native land.

Flavius Josephus, who lived between approximately 37 and 100 C.E., corroborates the biblical rendition of prophecy in *The Antiquities of the Jews.* Josephus writes in book 9, chapter 10:

> This king [Jeroboam, the son of Joash] was guilty of contumely against God and became very wicked in worshiping of idols, and in many undertakings that were absurd and foreign. He was also the cause of ten thousand misfortunes to the people of Israel. Now one Jonah, a prophet, foretold to him that he should make war with the Syrians, and conquer their army, and enlarge the bounds

of his kingdom on the northern parts, to the city Hamath, and on the southern to the lake Asphaltitis. (259)

The king successfully follows Jonah's advice. Thus, in biblical and extra-biblical accounts, an accurate but nonetheless ancillary prophet named Jonah is briefly mentioned as he helps the king reclaim Israel's land and reputation as a military force in the region. Based on these passages, the book of Jonah can be categorized as prophetic literature, the experiences of a veteran seer who might expect to have his prophecies come true and resent God's mercy to Israel's enemies.

Ancient fragments from Mirkhond, a Mohammedan writer, also pro-claim that Jonah becomes a prophet by virtue of the company he keeps. Mirkhond writes that Jonah's mother is the faithful woman of Zarephath who provides hospitality to Elijah in 1 Kgs 17 (Simpson 85). In the Bible story, the widow has a son who Elijah raised from the dead. The boy is never named, but Mirkhond calls him Jonah. In this tradition, Jonah is of the tribe of Asher or Zebulun and receives his commission as a prophet from Elijah's successor, Elisha. The theory is that Jonah is the prophet Elisha's unnamed disciple who anoints King Jehu in 2 Kgs 9:1–6 (Hirsch 226). This family history might also establish Jonah as a character who expects his word to be heeded.

Partly because Jonah is a known prophet, his short book has always existed alongside those of other great prophets — Isaiah, Jeremiah, and Ezekiel — but it is relegated to minor-league status. From the first sayings of Hosea to the final utterances of Malachi, the twelve Minor Prophets present a three-hundred-year compendium of prophetic insights. Several immutable concepts permeate these books, especially the notion that disobedience to God will bring destruction — to Israel as well as its neighbors (Gabel et al. 129). The book of Jonah contains several small similarities to other pro-phetic works. The phrase that opens the Jonah story parallels the beginning lines of Jeremiah, Hosea, Joel, Micah, Zephaniah, Zechariah, and Malachi. Furthermore, Jonah is hardly the first recalcitrant prophet in the Bible. Other representatives of God are eventually empowered after initial reluctance to obey the deity's call.

The Masoretic text, a medieval version of the Hebrew Bible from which translations are made and which dates from the ninth and tenth centuries, contains a remarkably well-preserved version of the Jonah story. Along with the Masoretic version, the partially complete Hebrew scroll of the book of Jonah discovered at Wadi Murabba'at near the Dead Sea in 1955 (and pub-lished in 1961) also places Jonah fifth among the twelve Minor Prophets.

The arrangement of the twelve is not accidental, but the book of Jonah is minor in length rather than in theological significance. By the second century B.C.E., the book of Jonah was canonized as part of classical prophetic literature. The prophetic works are grouped in rough chronological order, though issues such as size also factor into their placement within the TANAKH. After Obadiah comes the book of Jonah, a more sympathetic continuation on the theme of how foreigners, Edomites in Obadiah's case and Ninevites in Jonah's, should be treated. Micah's prophecy follows Jonah's in the sequence because Micah explores how Assyria, the nation that repents and is forgiven in Jonah's narrative, could destroy Israel (Dyck 72). Nahum is next after Micah, the link being that Nahum begins by delivering "a pronouncement on Nineveh" (1:1). In this context, ancient Israelites logically labeled Jonah's tale a book of prophecy. Not until modern times was any suggestion made that it should be classified in any other manner.

The book of Jonah is also prophecy because it contains familiar prophetic themes. God sees an evil king and people but determines to save rather than destroy them. In 2 Kings, the prophet Jonah speaks words that lead to Israel's salvation. God, demonstrating divine characteristics also found again in the book of Jonah, wishes to restore the world to order and to see the people repent rather than be blotted out. Jonah's commendable reputation as an Israelite prophet who is successful in Kings makes him an intriguing choice for the main character in this later story of a prophet's displeasure with his success in Nineveh. In 2 Kings he had proclaimed that in spite of King Jeroboam's wickedness, Israel's ancient frontiers would be restored through victory in war. Other than this single incident in 2 Kings, however, nothing more is revealed about Jonah until he reappears as the protagonist in his own book of the Bible.

One of the enduring reasons why the book of Jonah fits alongside other prophetic books is that many of them (notably Joel and Amos) are concerned with the destiny of "the nations." A prophet like Jonah, who predicts welcome news concerning the defeat of Damascus and the rise of Israel (2 Kgs 14:28), would enjoy royal favor at home and probably be treated as a palace fixture, an official staff member kept close to court and encouraged to foretell matters of national importance. When this same Jonah is found in a separate story about an encounter with a notable foreign city, he may be ideally situated in the minds of the Israelites to cry doom, not forgiveness, to the wayward foreigners. It is ironic that the author of the book of Jonah, probably desiring to criticize Israel's overly nationalistic policy run amuck and unforgiving attitude toward foreigners, would find fertile ground by exploring the character of royalist prophet Jonah. So the book of Jonah fits the prophecy category because it deals with Israel's relationship with foreign peoples, though the outcome is clearly different from other prophetic compositions. Nineveh will be destroyed in the future, but in the book of Jonah the people repent and are temporarily forgiven and saved. Surely the book also contains a message for the necessity of Israel's reformation.

The book of Jonah departs from other prophetic treatises in other ways too. For example, Jonah offers minimal proclamations, and though he is referred to as "the prophet" (הנביא) in 2 Kgs 14:25, the title is presupposed rather than stated directly in the book of Jonah. In fact, Jonah utters only a few words that predict the future. The rest of the book is preoccupied with the ordeals of the reluctant antihero. Generally, prophetic books extol the seer as a servant of God who often risks personal safety for the sake of revealing divine majesty and redemptive power, but Jonah is sometimes shown in a very poor light as he hesitates to forgive. Also, the content of Jonah's story varies greatly from all other prophetic books, and the predominance of narrative over oracle militates against prophecy as an adequate description of the book's genre. Jonah's predictions are subordinated to other elements of plot. Unlike other prophetic works, the book of Jonah contains a story about a prophet, not a series of predictions that he proclaims through divine revelation to sinful people. Fiery oracles, transmitted directly from the mind of God to the mouth of the prophet, are the mainstays of prophetic discourse, but Jonah is a noticeably laconic man. Other prophetic books are remembered for their sizzling oratory that demonstrates the blending of poet and prophet, but the book of Jonah is known instead for its recalcitrant prophet's obstreperous deeds rather than his onslaught of oft-repeated, blistering warnings to Israel and the nations.

Instead of being lauded only as prophecy, the book of Jonah is also considered as history. Since Jonah, son of Amittai, is a historical personage mentioned elsewhere in Scripture, a case is sometimes made that the tale, including details of his being saved by a great fish, is factual. Viewing the book as history would add the weight of fact to an otherwise fanciful tale of forgiveness and salvation. The history of the piece has always had its defenders, and two pillars near Alexandretta, Turkey, mark the place where the fish supposedly vomited Jonah onto dry land (Simpson 8). Today at a mosque near the oil fields of Mosul in northern Iraq, pilgrims can still view what is advertised to be the physical remains of Jonah's whale (Bickerman 4). The scholar Abravanel (1437–1509), displaying more faith than knowledge of gestation, posits that Jonah could have easily survived in the fish's belly for three days and nights because "after all, fetuses live nine months without access to fresh air" (Ginsberg 114). In the eighteenth century, German theology professors were forbidden to teach the book as anything but history. In the nineteenth century, numerous commentaries upheld the facts of the case (Salters 41–42). At Dayton, Tennessee's, famous 1925 Scopes "Monkey" Trial, leading anti-Darwinian William Jennings Bryan declared in response to Clarence Darrow's inquiry concerning the literal accuracy of the Bible: "I believe everything in the Bible should be accepted as it is given there.... I believe in a God who can make a whale and can make a man, and can make both do what He pleases" (Bryan). A 1956 Catholic encyclopedia and a 1962 Protestant biblical dictionary declare the story to be factual. As recently as 1995, Michael Corey has argued that

> it is a zoological fact that humans can survive quite nicely for brief periods within the large air-filled cavities of giant whales (which were called "fish" in Old Testament days). Indeed, there have been a number of reports over the years of people being consumed by whales and surviving. One man off the coast of Hawaii...is said to have been swallowed alive by a whale while swimming in the Pacific Ocean. He was able to survive for some 48 hours inside of the whale before he was expelled again in one piece into the sea. (5)

Corey further claims that the herbivorous whale, while skimming the surface of the water for plankton, could accidentally ingest a man and hold him in an air-filled cavity of the mouth without actually digesting him and then spit the man out again. In ancient times, religious rites were sometimes performed as dramatic pieces, recited by expressive narrators and actors. Over time, the story was accepted, and "in some instances these legends or myths were recorded as actual history" (Simpson 26). For the pious who insist on interpreting the work literally and historically, nothing is impossible for God, no matter how far-fetched the situation may be. Daring to question the power of the Almighty to perform miraculous deeds is blasphemous and unthinkable to some groups of Bible readers. "History" would reveal that if God can sustain Jonah in the fish, surely the Lord would have no trouble forgiving sinners.

Today some religious groups uphold the historicity of the piece so strongly that their belief in its message seems to depend upon its literal accuracy (Allen 178–79). Yet even one so devout as Martin Luther (1483–1546), German founder of the Reformation, questioned who would believe the story if it were not found in the Bible (Salters 40). Many critics and theologians through the ages reject the supernatural monster fish idea as they would the existence of jinns, vampires, and dragons. They scoff at the historical possibility of the story and prefer instead to think of Jonah as myth, folk tale, vision, or legend. Authoritative Jewish Bible scholar from Spain, Rabbi Ibn Ezra (1092–1167), attempts to explain away any literal interpretation of Jonah's story by asserting that the "experiences of all the prophets but Moses were visions, not actualities" (Ginsberg 114).

Prolonged debate over the story's historical and literal truth can obscure the great spiritual truths that it teaches, yet learned people write seriously and solemnly on the subject of a literal interpretation of Jonah's story. Looking at the text of the Jonah story is rather like looking into a fun-house mirror that distorts and renders strange reflections of our own selves. Biblical legend is a window into the human soul. The book of Jonah's miracle sequences, from the calming of the sea to the salvation of Nineveh, can be true even if they are not historical actualities. Biblical stories point to a deeper truth that transcends literal fact. Jonah's story achieves verisimilitude in the way of all great literature — by being true to the human heart, to our need to understand the universe and our place in it, and to our desire to be close to the divine. In this respect, historical facts are irrelevant to themes such as forgiveness and add nothing to the tale's profound meanings. The book of Jonah lacks conventional signposts of historical writing, and the author is noticeably unconcerned with physical fact and reality.

Little evidence exists to support the book of Jonah as history. The Nineveh that is described in the narrative is unrecognizable as a real city. The abundance of literary devices — such as hyperbole, repetition, allusion, and flashback — increase the likelihood that the story is more than an objective recitation of historical fact. Whether it is fact or fiction, the book contains awesome messages about forgiveness. The ancient Israelites probably made little distinction between history and narrative and had little need to differentiate between the two.

Some critics argue that the genre of Jonah is neither prophecy nor history, but rather midrash, a Hebrew term meaning "investigation." A midrash is a typically rabbinic form of instruction that employs Holy Scripture as a peg upon which to hang additional observations or fanciful discussions. Midrash, written after the original authors completed the Bible's final version, expands upon sacred text and seeks to derive further lessons from it. From this perspective, the book of Jonah is considered a commentary on Exod 34:6 (giving God's characteristics) and 2 Kgs 14:25 (mentioning Jonah as Jeroboam's prophet). The theory is that the story of Jonah, because of its independent value as midrash, was removed from its original location in 2 Kings, where it fit beside miracle stories of Elijah and Elisha, and placed as a book among the twelve prophets. One can easily understand that a midrash would be added to the biblical canon to explain the conundrum of why forgiveness is extended to a foreign, heathen people (Budde 229).

Another genre that is part of the Hebrew Scriptures, often aiming to instruct on such issues as forgiveness, is wisdom literature. The books of wisdom include Job, Ecclesiastes, and Proverbs, but some characteristics of the book of Jonah also fit the classification, especially if the label is modified slightly to "wisdom didactic." Jonah shares with wisdom literature concerns about human existence. The mysteries of the human condition — especially as we encounter divine judgment, punishment, love, mercy, and forgiveness — are typical topics in the wisdom books. Furthermore, wisdom literature questions God's design and its fairness to sentient mortals. Jonah's complaints to the Lord are consistent with this genre and its reflections on God's changing volition. In the book of Jonah, God recants the divine edict that Nineveh will be destroyed and forgives the people. The often-stern God of the Hebrew Scriptures is gentle to the Ninevites and offers only the mildest of rebukes to the wayward Jonah.

Other genres frequently associated with the story of Jonah are allegory and parable, two similar but not quite identical categories. Both are "figure-stories" (Cohen, *Twelve* 137), but an allegory is an extended metaphor in which characters, actions, and places symbolize general abstractions outside the story. If the book of Jonah is an allegory, the prophet represents Israel. His banishment from earth into the body of a fish symbolizes Israel's exile into Babylon. Allegorically, the sailors and the Ninevites represent the pagan world and Israel's enemies throughout time, yet they behave well. According to this interpretation, the prophet in the story is not Jonah but the author, who points out his people's shortcomings and affirms God's universal forgiveness. At the end of chapter 4, Israel (allegorically represented by Jonah) seems bereft of compassion and hope, yet "it can readily be deduced from the allegory that if the surrounding pagan world can earn Divine forgiveness and full remission of punishment, then so much more so is the door opened for God's treasured people" (Ephros 149–50). Allegorical approaches are not as popular as they used to be (Allen 181), primarily because allegory cannot directly explain all elements in the tale.

The Bible also abounds in parables, though the genre is more common to the New Testament than to the Hebrew Scriptures. A parable, such as Luke's Good Samaritan tale, is a kind of illustrative story that answers a question or points to a moral. The book of Jonah raises many queries about who should receive and give forgiveness. Parables often tell a story about what something is like, heaven for instance. Jonah's narrative could be described as a parable depicting what divine forgiveness is like. Parables are also generally shorter and less complex than the book of Jonah, which must be thought of as an extended parable if the genre is to apply. The Zohar — the Hebrew name for a fundamental work of Jewish mysticism also called the Kabbalah, first published in Spain between 1250 and 1305 — interprets the Bible in mystical and allegorical terms. Authors of the Zohar understand the book of Jonah to be "a parable of the totality of a person's career in this world" (Wineman 57). According to explication, Jonah represents the soul, the tempest is God's demand for judgment, and the great fish becomes analogous to the spiritual grave that holds the body until it is ready to reawaken to the kindness of a forgiving heart.

Most exegeses of the book of Jonah, whether they are prophetic or historical or allegorical, are deadly serious. The Bible is short on comedy, though humor can sometimes be an effective teaching device and is not equivalent to irreverent tomfoolery. The author of the Jonah narrative definitely has a roguish sense of humor that often masks didacticism, as when the great fish vomits after Jonah's pious peroration in chapter 2 or when the absurdity of animals fasting is shown in chapter 3. One rarely laughs when reading the Bible; even a knowing smile or a slight chuckle of derision is uncommon. Yet the healing power of comedy in the book of Jonah should not be denied (Canham 15), even when the topic is as crucial as the human dilemma and the divine proclivity for forgiveness. Two sub-genres of comedy may be considered part of Jonah's tale: parody and satire. The difference between the two lies in intensity. Parody educates; satire annihilates. Both rely on exaggeration of human foibles for comedic effect. The incongruity between what is and what ought to be is at the heart of parody. Satire is more heavy handed, more scathing, more overt in its exposure and ridicule of human folly than the milder irony found in parody (West 236).

The book of Jonah was perhaps originally intended as a parody dating from several centuries B.C.E., but in succeeding eras, the parodic signals were lost on more pious readers. When the book was being considered for canonization, strong theological need to overlook the parody could have caused a general shift in the way the work was viewed (Band 193–94). Parody assumes preexisting works that it imitates and distorts. Jonah's refusal to go to Nineveh is possibly a parody of obedient prophets whose stories are related in other books of the Bible. Readers may also find it humorous that Jonah thinks he can escape from God's directive to go to Nineveh. Additionally, the king of Nineveh's instant repentance is a parody of biblical rulers, Israelite and foreign, who disdain prophetic warnings and delay reform. Pharaoh despises Moses; Ahab fights Elijah; Zedekiah reviles Jeremiah. In a parody of this time-honored tendency to rebuff prophets, Jonah is the only successful seer whose prediction a king quickly heeds (Band 187). The immediately offered-up prayers of the heathen sailors and Ninevites are also a parody of Jonah's delay in petitioning the Lord. The prophet's religious conviction is thus called into question when pagans behave more piously than a supposed man of God. Jonah prays, but not as readily as those who are notorious nonbelievers.

Other scholars find the level of criticism in the book of Jonah to be more biting and serious than parody suggests. Satire is in evidence, for instance, when Jonah prays in the belly of the fish. The animal becomes so sick to its stomach over Jonah's newfound piety that it throws up. Jonah's antiheroic behavior makes him a target for the harsh ridicule of satire (Marcus 95; Crenshaw 380). He gives narrow-minded, nationalistic messages that are undermined by the overpowering, universal love and forgiveness of God. Clearly, the prophet who cares more for the life of a plant than for the continued existence of an entire group of people (Jonah 4:7–11) is a prime candidate for the full force of satire.

Serious difficulties arise, however, when discussing humor in the book of Jonah. While individual verses may be comical and the stubborn prophet may occasionally be mocked, surely the sublime theme of forgiveness is inappropriate subject matter for either parody or satire. The themes of the book are far too serious to evoke sustained laughter. In fact, the classical definition of comedy, wherein the plot machinations all turn out well in the end, does not necessarily apply to the character of Jonah. Chapter 4's final conversation between God and the prophet does not provide a tidy resolution to the conflict on the dilemma of divine versus human forgiveness. The mocking disdain found in satire and the lampooning irony found in parody ultimately disappear as an understanding narrator and a sympathetic deity deal gently with human weakness. Perhaps both satire and parody are terms too strong to apply to the book because the narrative observes the prophet's pain and gently exposes his failings, "but it is also forgiving. It sets the hero in his proper place without humiliating him" (Simon xxii). God's final scolding is soft rather than stinging (4:10–11). One must conclude that humorous elements are only on the surface of serious content (Lacocque and Lacocque, *Complex* 25).

Jonah's tale is not meant merely to amuse. In fact, the story has some tragic moments. The tragedy of a potentially uncomprehending Israelite prophet is set against the uplifted, foreign society that benefits from divine, merciful intervention. The book of Jonah appears to contain some of the characteristics associated with the genre of tragedy: a hero's tragic flaw, catastrophe, pain, wrong choices, and death (Woodard 5). Pride and stubbornness, common flaws found in a tragic hero, are evident in the personality of the prophet. His problems are primarily of his own making. Though Jonah does not die at the end of the piece, as is required in classical tragedy, he asks for death and, in fact, lives a kind of life-in-death because of his negativity toward the Ninevites. His personal life reveals the kind of downward spiral seen among tragic characters. The concept of a tragic hero brought low by his own imperfections is not unprecedented in the Hebrew Scriptures. A beguiling woman brings down Samson, but he is also a victim of his own weakness for beautiful temptresses. King Saul is undone as much by his own errors in judgment as by divine displeasure with his reign. In a similar manner, Jonah's successful career is threatened because of his reluctance to perform the will of God and to forgive his enemies. Perhaps the most conspicuous part of the tragedy is that Jonah's story ends without a clear resolution of his dispute with the Lord (Woodard 13–15). Recognition and reversal, elements of the classical Greek concept of tragedy, do not appear in this work, as Jonah never clearly states that he understands and accepts God's forgiveness of the Ninevites. Thus the book of Jonah fulfills some but not all the requirements of tragedy.

In the book of Jonah, comedy and tragedy are both present, as are parable and allegory, midrash and legend, wisdom literature and prophecy. It is a moral narrative containing elements of several literary types, and the book with its theme of forgiveness need not be restricted to any specific genre. Thinking about different genres may provide clues to meaning, but it is not critical that we decide upon one classification of the piece in order to appreciate its weighty content on forgiveness. The book's ambiguity is well served by uncertainty about its genre.

Date

Genre is not the only literary uncertainty that relates to theme in the book of Jonah. Though it is generally considered to be one of the oldest parts of the Hebrew Scriptures, debate persists as to exactly when the work was composed. The piece itself contains no clear reference to time; we are not told who was on the throne of Israel, what high priest Jonah may have known, or how many years it had been before or after the great earthquake mentioned by Amos and Zechariah. The anonymous author leaves no hint as to the date of the book, contributing to its timelessness. All we know for certain is that the collected work of the twelve prophets was codified and referred to in the oldest book of the Apocrypha — Ecclesiasticus, or the Wisdom of Jesus

Son of Sirach (49:10) — whose author probably lived about the third century B.C.E. Although the Bible's 2 Kings reference to Jonah dates from King Jeroboam II's reign in the eighth century B.C.E., this reference does not guarantee that the story of the prophet and the great fish was written at the same time. Nonetheless, the notion of Jonah's composition being contemporary to Jeroboam II (782–753 B.C.E.) has its supporters (Lawrence 121; Limburg 39).

The fantastical descriptions of Nineveh — the improbable three days required to traverse it, the silly fasting of the inhabitants' animals, and the implausible title of "king" assigned to the town's leader — also hint that when the book of Jonah was written, the real Nineveh had long since disappeared into legend (Budde 228). If someone could walk fifteen miles in a day, a three-day walk would be forty-five miles, and no ancient city could have had such colossal dimensions. Furthermore, prayer always accompanies fasting. People fast and pray to invoke God's favor, but it is unlikely that animals would also be required to participate in such a religious ritual. Calling someone the king of Nineveh is as absurd as referring to Elizabeth II as the queen of London. In 612 B.C.E., the Babylonians and Medes destroyed Assyria's capital city of Nineveh, which was never rebuilt. A commonsense analysis of the exaggerated description of Nineveh and its inhabitants suggests that the book of Jonah's composition considerably postdates the razing of the city. Probably, Nineveh had long since assumed mythical proportions when the book of Jonah was composed.

Convincing internal evidence demonstrates that the book of Jonah is postexilic, that is, dating after the Babylonian captivity. The exile refers to a period of seventy years. It began in 586 B.C.E. when King Nebuchadnezzar of Babylon besieged Jerusalem, destroyed the temple, and carted off the Jews to a foreign land to be made slaves for a second time in their history. A few Psalms, such as 137, indicate the anguish of the people who lived in captivity and could not forget their beloved homeland. The slavery continued until the 539 B.C.E. defeat of the Babylonians by King Cyrus of Persia. Soon thereafter Cyrus, called God's "anointed one" in Isa 45:1, freed the Jews and allowed them to return home and rebuild their temple (Ezra 1:1–2). Many scholars argue that the book of Jonah dates from sometime between the sixth and fourth centuries (Cohen, *Twelve* 137; Craigie 211). Diction, for example, shows an Aramaic influence to which the ancient Hebrew language was exposed in the years following the conclusion of the exile (Ginsberg 14). The book of Jonah reflects Persian practices, such as edicts emanating from the king and nobles (Jonah 3:7). Greek historian Herodotus (c. 485–425 B.C.E.) mentions the inclusion of domestic animals in mourning rites (3:8), an absurd idea in most cultures, as another Persian custom (Allen 186).

These factors suggest a postexilic date when the author is influenced by Persian rather than Assyrian rule.

The question of date is germane to the issue of forgiveness. If Jonah were composed in postexilic days when newly repatriated Jews were again establishing themselves in their homeland, concerned once more about instituting secure borders, and anxious to reestablish Yahweh as their exclusive God, then naturally the people's thoughts would turn to forgiving their former captors. In the early period following the end of the second slavery, the idea of rejecting heathens and their myriad gods would have much popular appeal. As the Israelites looked around at Jerusalem's battered city gates and the beloved but destroyed temple, bitterness would fill many hearts. A fragile Jewish community, dominated by a Persian Empire, would mistrust foreigners and feel surrounded and threatened. When Jerusalem was rebuilt, another destruction would not be inconceivable for those who remembered the terrors of the past. Survival would be paramount. Far in the future the broader concerns of a generous, loving God might be considered, but immediately after the return from Babylon, many Jews would feel the way Jonah does during his stay in Nineveh (Holmgren 130). Forgiveness would be a difficult topic among the Israelites immediately after they experience the horrors of war against the Babylonians. While dating the book definitively to either pre- or postexilic times is impossible, a strong case can be made for the major theme of forgiveness to be uppermost in the minds of the people after their return to Jerusalem. At this point a story about a long-dead prophet and a vanished foreign city would again become poignant, reaffirming for the people that forgiveness is a treacherous but necessary enterprise.

Structure

Although the date of the book's composition is in doubt, there can be no doubt about the long oral tradition of Jonah's tale. Yet through the centuries, this Jewish story was also written down, canonized, translated, and updated with the punctuation and organization conventions of more modern times. In the Middle Ages, the book was first divided into the four chapters that are accepted as standard today (Craig 35). This four-part structure shows the development of the narrator's theme of forgiveness. The brief tale presents a huge hermeneutics dilemma concerning who, when, and how to forgive. Each chapter presents a discrete episode, but all four work together to produce the overall message of divine mercy. Chapters 1, 2, and 3 develop a clear crisis → prayer → deliverance structure (Craig 100). The fourth chapter's open ending makes it more complex, but the book's overall architecture of division into four chapters is generally thought to enhance the literary quality of the whole.

At least one critic (Zimmerman 584) questions the accepted organization of the four chapters with chapter 3's scene in Nineveh and chapter 4's debate with God placed after the opening scene in Tarshish. According to this philosophy, the biblical compiler mistakenly located the Nineveh and its aftermath chapters toward the end of the book when they should have come first. Chapters 3 and 4 represent the deeds of a younger Jonah than the one we see in flight to Tarshish. The immature, selfish prophet should appear at the beginning of the story. If this were the case, God's message of forgiveness would not have to go unanswered by Jonah, the tale would not end so abruptly, and the book's arrangement would seem more reasonable. The older prophet — less physically adroit, fearing the long journey to Nineveh, and dreading his role of bringing a message of hopelessness to an alien people — should be presented as fleeing to Tarshish at the end of the tale. Such a rearrangement of events would, however, reduce the impact of God's final words to Jonah and ruin the power of the tale's open-ended conclusion. Zimmerman's notion is therefore the least tenable solution to the question of structure.

Given that the biblical author did not use chapter divisions, strict adherence to them may be superfluous or even obfuscate the original artistic design. Aside from a simple analysis of chapter organization, there are other ways of thinking about the structure of Jonah's story. One particularly useful technique is to examine the book's parallel composition: A-B-C-A′-B′-C′-D. The extra, unmatched dimension D contains the prime lesson on forgiveness and is the climax of the work:

A. Jonah commissioned to go to Nineveh: **his disobedience** (1:1–3)

    B. Jonah and the pagan sailors: the sailors cry out to Yahweh for mercy; **they are spared**; Jonah is swallowed by fish (1:4–16)

    C. **Jonah's response:** he is thankful to God for sparing him (1:17–2:10)

A′. Jonah recommissioned to go to Nineveh; **his disobedience** (3:1–4)

    B′. Jonah and the pagans of Nineveh: the Ninevites cry out to Yahweh for mercy; **they are spared** (3:5–10)

    C′. **Jonah's response:** he is angry at God for sparing Nineveh (4:1–3)

    D. The Lord's lesson for Jonah (4:4–11). (Dorsey 25)

Dorsey's analysis is consistent with a second view of the book as having two cycles and an epilogue rather than four chapters (Kahn 88). The first cycle consists of Jonah's flight from God, followed by the ordeal and prayer in the fish. The audience expects the story's complicating factor, Jonah's unexpected nonsubmission to God, to be resolved before the tale ends (Crouch 104). A critical transition scene occurs when Jonah is vomited onto dry land. After Jonah is deposited back on shore, the story seems to start up again (Wendland, 192). The second cycle then commences with Jonah's prophecy to Nineveh, the heathen people's repentance, and the concluding conversation between God and Jonah, wherein the deity tries to help the prophet comprehend divine forgiveness. God responds to Jonah's complaint and has the last word.

A slightly different method of understanding the structure of Jonah is to analyze it as a book in two parts, two existing chapters combining to compose each part. The beginning of each unit introduces a new incident. In part one a Hebrew sinner is saved. He is disobedient and punished for his transgression, but God creates a fish to preserve Jonah's life and then unceremoniously dumps him back onto shore. Jonah's sinfulness, surprising in a prophet, introduces a primary conflict of the narrative. The rest of the book will endeavor to resolve this tension. Also in part one, Jonah recognizes his good fortune in being spared from death at sea and praises God from the belly of the fish. Upon reaching dry land in part two, Jonah goes to Nineveh. The heathen sinners are saved. Jonah complains bitterly to the Lord over the Ninevites' salvation, though the prophet has a reasonable explanation for his distress. God then delivers a brief sermon to the recalcitrant prophet, a lesson in forgiveness that he may not fully grasp.

Both sections contain separate scenes with a beginning and ending, but they also double over on themselves (Lillegard 21). The anguished sailors in part one and the distraught citizens of Nineveh in part two are similar. Pagans all, the two groups of foreigners are isolated from one another, yet they turn to Yahweh for deliverance. There is a tripartite structure to the activity in each section: (1) impending disaster that (2) leads to repentance that (3) leads to deliverance and forgiveness (Craig 64). Furthermore, in the conclusion Jonah recalls how he fled to Tarshish, an obvious linking of the ending of the story to its beginning. Parts one and two both contain Jonah's journeys — a descent into the bowels of the ship and the depths of the ocean, followed by a descent into the depths of enemy territory. Part two begins in the same manner as part one: the word of God is sent to the prophet. The two sections of the narrative are thus symmetrically structured. Cycles one (chapters 1 and 2) and two (chapters 3 and 4) commence with God's directive to Jonah and his response to it. Each time the prophet is brought into contact with a group of pagans who cry to Jonah's God and receive help (Collins 32).

Jonah's utterance of thanksgiving to God in the fish (part one) and his plaint against God (part two) are also connected by Jonah's prayers. The prophet and the Almighty relate to one another as individuals. Both sections reveal much about the prophet's character and relationship to his deity. Jonah's extended lyrical prayer, offered while he is imprisoned in the fish, is a proper form of praise from one who has slumbered in an attempt to avoid the sea catastrophe that threatens his life. The prayer is also nicely contrasted to the final prose poem, God's message of kindness and forgiveness to all humanity. The dialogue provides God's answer to Jonah's petition to die and his distress over the sparing of Nineveh. The last event in part two is especially important because, while linked to earlier material, it represents a unique theological commentary of forgiveness, far more serious than the issues of the other scenes.

Yet another method of understanding the text is to view it as properly containing not four chapters or two parts but five scenes (Wolff 10). First (of the five), God directs Jonah toward Nineveh, but he flees and disembarks from Tarshish (1:1–3); second, the storm at sea rages, and the sailors cast Jonah into the sea and make vows to God (1:4–16); third, Jonah is swallowed by a great fish, prays while inside its belly, is vomited onto land, and continues to Nineveh (2:1–3:3a); fourth, Jonah quickly delivers his message in Nineveh and then disappears from the plot, the people and king repent, and God forgives them (3:3b–10); and fifth, Jonah becomes angry, begs to die, and receives direct revelation from God concerning the nature of forgiveness (4:1–11). For many audience members, the narrative would have reached a natural conclusion at the end of scene four when the Ninevites are forgiven. Jonah all but vanishes from the narrative. The conflict appears resolved when the Ninevites turn from their evil ways and are pardoned by God. But the narrator has other ideas, and the story swiftly continues with a fifth scene that draws attention back to Jonah and his attitudes. Although the external conflict of the pagans' behavior is resolved, Jonah's internal conflict about forgiveness is not. In other words, the story's main complication — Jonah's state of mind — has yet to be settled. The fifth and final scene suggests that the clashes with the sailors and Ninevites have only been secondary struggles to the conflict within Jonah and between God and Jonah over the issue of forgiveness.

Regardless of which plausible view one takes on structure, the crux of the matter is finally revealed. Three voices are heard in the book of Jonah: that of the prophet, the Lord, and the narrator, but the narrator has successfully concealed the most critical issue and built suspense by saving God's commentary on one of the book's most glorious themes for last. The most significant meaning is not to be found in the plot about sailors or Ninevites; rather, the heart of the story is contained in the book's final verses. The unidimensional foreigners appear in the story only long enough to help reveal Jonah's character traits, but the Lord and Jonah are more fully developed. A crucial theme lies in the difference between Jonah's and God's opposing views on how sinful humanity should be treated. At last the story apparently has not simply been about Jonah's adversity and anguish. God's pain over humanity's shortcomings is also at issue. The Bible purposefully leaves the discussion of forgiveness unresolved, a sophisticated narrative strategy that opens up space to bring in readers, to challenge them to enter the text's dilemma. Reopened is the problem that the audience thought had been settled when the Ninevites were spared God's wrath. Ought they to be forgiven? After intense dialogue between the two principal characters, God poses the question and Jonah does not respond.

Only the audience, who must fill in the story's gaps and supply an ending beyond the ending, can provide closure. What happens in Israel when Jonah is a missing person? Do people notice his absence and search for him? Is he one who finally agrees to go north because he loves to watch disasters such as tornadoes or the spontaneous combustion of civilizations? Do calamities put him in a party mood? As he sits in the booth of chapter 4, his compassion wilts on the vine and hangs lifeless. There in the cool shade, does he nurse some long-held vindictiveness that flourishes beneath his religious fervor like a subterranean fungus? Jonah holds back the core of himself from the sailors and the Ninevites. Is he a man known for his insularity? In the last verses of the Bible story, does he finally "get it," this message of compassion and forgiveness? Tectonic shifts cannot be seen because they move so slowly as to be imperceptible. Will Jonah begin to shift his position after the story ends?

What happens to Jonah after his last, crucial conversation with God remains a deliberate mystery that effectively engages the reader. There is no preaching here, no predictable oracular prophecy. Whether Jonah accepts God's forgiveness of foreigners or never learns the lesson of divine universal mercy is debatable, yet a skillful narrator and a watchful God attempt to guide the prophet and the audience to a right conclusion. At the beginning of the story, the Lord tries to command Jonah to do something; now God endeavors to persuade Jonah to comprehend something (Mather 282). Readers are compelled to provide for themselves an answer to God's final query about forgiveness, which will perhaps be the last and most important question we deal with on earth.

CHAPTER 2

Jonah's Disobedience

Will a man like me take flight?
—Neh 6:11

There is a simple principle in the Bible: God prefers obedience to disobedience. When we stray, we disappoint and anger the Lord, who then finds it necessary to punish us, as a loving parent would correct the behavior of erring children in order to teach them valuable lessons. We want to believe that if we repent of our wrongdoing and accept our punishment, God forgives us. The purpose of divine punishment is usually redemptive, not vindictive. God loves us and wants to bring us back into the fold as soon as we are ready to come. The prophet Jonah, like many of us, finds that it is often difficult to do what is right. We will go to great lengths to avoid our own consciences and God's will, capitulating instead to the emotional enslavement that disregard for right behavior brings. Virtually all the literary elements in chapter 1 unite to show a disobedient Jonah and to illustrate his need for divine pardon.

In contrast to Jonah, many prophets eagerly accept divine commissions. Nehemiah, governor of Judah around the year 445 B.C.E., is called upon to rebuild the walls of Jerusalem following the return of Jews from the Babylonian captivity. His job is dangerous; enemies want to kill him. When urged to hide in the temple, Nehemiah stands his ground and refuses to run away. In another episode when the Lord asks who should be drafted into service as a prophet, Isaiah initially protests his uncleanness but answers, "Here I am; send me" (Isa 6:8). How unlike Jonah, who flees the moment God commands him to go to Nineveh.

When given an opportunity to obey God freely, many of us behave not like Nehemiah and Isaiah but like Pharaoh's Hebrew slaves. Soon after liberation, they long to return to the security and familiarity of Egypt (Exod 16:3). The Israelites are out of Egypt, but Egypt is not out of the Israelites. The prophet Jonah is reminiscent of those disobedient former slaves who dread pursuing their destiny and turn away from God out of fear of what may lie ahead.

Jonah is one of the privileged few who hears the word of God without going through an intermediary. Noticing which biblical characters are in straightforward contact with God and which are not is always interesting. For example, after King Saul's disobedience, the Lord cuts off communication with the ruler. So distraught is Saul over God's silence that the monarch makes the heretical decision to consult a medium, the witch of Endor, in order to reestablish communication with God's prophet, Samuel, and foretell the outcome of an upcoming battle with the Philistines (1 Sam 28). Unlike Saul, those who enjoy God's favor have visions or dreams, or they receive Yahweh's direct command, thus establishing their credibility and showing that their authority originates with the divine source. At the beginning of chapter 1 of the book of Jonah, God speaks and emphatically dictates what the prophet should do. The story commences with, "The word of the LORD came to Jonah son of Amittai" (Jonah 1:1). This message emanating from God and going directly to the prophet is an orthodox beginning, the way several prophetic oracles start. Throughout this book, however, only Jonah speaks with the Lord. Messages come to the prophet and no one else, and none of the foreigners ever witness God and Jonah addressing one another. The sea captain, the sailors, the king, and the people of Nineveh speculate upon what God might do, but only Jonah hears directly from the deity. That God speaks first and last in the book of Jonah, thus causing an intriguing paradox, is also significant. Concluding with the Lord's comment would imply closure, yet the tale of Jonah's disobedience is by no means resolved.

The Lord's command is clear: "Go at once to Nineveh, that great city, and proclaim judgment upon it; for their wickedness has come before Me" (1:2). Yahweh summons Jonah to a very special mission, but God does not actually reveal to Jonah exactly what will happen to the Ninevites. The Talmud (an ancient compendium of Jewish law, tradition, and biblical scholarship) confirms this notion and states that "Jonah himself was not informed! — Jonah was originally told that Nineveh would be turned, but he did not know whether for good or for evil" (Sanhedrin 89b). What the prophet does realize is that he receives an unambiguous, clarion call to go to Nineveh, a summons designed to shake him out of his status quo and into a new and challenging undertaking. If God's statement were merely a prediction of Nineveh's fall, Jonah could have declared it from within the safe borders of Israel. Other prophets (notably Amos 1:3–2:3) give voice to oracles against the nations, but they do so from inside Jewish territory. Jonah is threatened by this calling that singles him out. Ezekiel willingly preaches to his fellow exiles far outside the promised land in Babylonia, but he is already a prisoner and his situation is very different from Jonah's call to enter enemy Nineveh. It would take a perceptive reader to comprehend at this point in the plot that Jonah's directive to travel to Nineveh as herald of divine wrath implies that God wants to give the Ninevites an opportunity to repent and be forgiven.

The exact nature of the Ninevites' wickedness (רעתם, sometimes translated as "evil" and implying immorality or calamity) is superfluous and therefore not specified. Nevertheless, we do know that the Ninevites deserve their reputation for brutality in foreign war and excessiveness in domestic matters. For example, if an Assyrian man's wife were found guilty of adultery, he could demand that her nose and the testicles of her lover be cut off (Klein 233). God's proclamation that the Ninevites' depravity has "come before" the deity (1:2) does not imply that God has heretofore been inattentive and failed to notice the people's corruption. Instead, the statement more likely suggests that the situation has recently deteriorated, causing divine patience at last to run out (Walton 14). The time has come for the Lord's disfavor to be revealed to those in the foreign city.

Swiss psychiatrist Carl Jung (1875–1961) has insights into pathological wickedness that can be applied to the Jonah story, but such interpretations are included here with the caveat that they represent a modern psychological imposition on the text and offer speculation on motive that lies outside the text itself. God's command to confront the evil can be compared to our own instincts, the urgings of our inner selves to do what is right. Yet Jonah resists that divine calling. Jung postulates that "the Shadow" is the portion of the personality we reject (Jung 419). The prophet's disobedience to God and desire not to confront the wickedness of Nineveh could thus be interpreted as his need to suppress and banish to the unconscious those aspects of his own character that he wants to deny. His reluctance to forgive the Ninevites after God has done so may even point to Jonah's wish for his own punishment. God's threat against the city's sinfulness is "directly symbolic of the profound self-destruction that will eventually take place in an individual's life if the ego doesn't come to terms with its Shadow" (Corey 11).

Jonah's flight to Tarshish at 1:3 can be understood to present not only a conflict between God and Jonah but also a conflict within the prophet. The "self is perpetually trying to persuade the ego into acquiring a state of psychospiritual wholeness" (Corey 7). Thus, the self is continuously pushing the ego to accept unwanted elements of the unconscious mind. The spirit of God, in the guise of the ego, disrupts human lives and causes great turmoil. God works for the good of the individual, to reconcile the Shadow's repressed elements of the personality with the ego so that the individual can become whole again and worthy of divine favor (Corey 9). Part of Jonah knows that God's love and pardon extend to all people, but another part may have trepidation about aiding a perennial enemy. The text makes no specific reference to the cause of the prophet's loathing, but if Jonah must reconcile his inner conflict, God can be thought of as working to bring the two factions of the prophet's mind together again. The major area of internal warring for the prophet is his reluctance to complete his mission of caring for all of God's wayward children, especially if they are not born Israelites. Jonah's Shadow is his inability to forgive the Ninevites.

Not only does Jonah's Shadow cause disobedience and tear his psyche asunder; it also cuts him off from communion with whole segments of the human population. We are created to associate with one another, to help one another, to support one another in times of trouble. When we are in union with others, we are not alienated, separated, or divided from them. Through communion with others, we find a port in the storm, life's tempest, which literally howls around Jonah as he is tossed upon the sea. Yet Jonah, like so many people, avoids what his soul needs: "It seems as if we keep running away from the communion we most desire. Maybe we are afraid that if we really stop running, there will be a horrible silence or an accusing voice" (Nouwen 11). After being coughed up by the great fish at the end of chapter 2, Jonah will finally abandon the Shadow's flight, and the word of God will come to the prophet again with clarity and force.

The actual physical distance between the prophet and the city of Nineveh symbolizes the gigantic psychological chasm between the conscious and the unconscious mind. Modern psychological probing into the meaning of the book's opening may produce lukewarm responses from traditional Bible readers. To take a religious manifesto and transform it into a psychological treatise on the human condition is foreign to some devotees of the Bible. But to treat the book of Jonah as a psychological tableau as well as a religious work is valuable, though not the only option.

No single notion of why Jonah flees to Tarshish answers all possibilities that the text raises. From a purely practical narrative perspective, transgression must precede forgiveness, so Jonah's disobedience is an essential ingredient because one theme of the story is to demonstrate divine love. The reader, faced with the tale's ambiguity about the prophet's motives, may alternatively reject and sympathize with Jonah's behavior. Thus the author indirectly presents a lesson about tolerance and accepting another's point of view. We may change our minds about Jonah's character as often as he flip-flops on accepting his duty. Several motifs of chapter 1 combine to establish

Jonah's insubordination: the role of the narrator, Jonah's symbolic name, the prophet's solitariness as he flees, the raging sea, and the unexpected humanity of the sailors. Each helps to develop the audience's awareness of Jonah's disobedience and his need for forgiveness.

Apparent to virtually all Bible readers is that the narrator provides scant exposition in the book's first chapter concerning major characters, locations, and conflicts. Besides being the son of Amittai, who is Jonah? From where does he come? What are his qualifications? When does the story take place? Who are Jonah's friends and family? What is his occupation before being called to Nineveh? How can God still accept Jonah despite all his flaws? How can Jonah know God and remain defiant? These and other mysteries remain, and except for the skimpy background information given in 2 Kings, we know nothing about the prophet. The book of Jonah foregoes the niceties of exposition and plunges forward with the principal matter at hand, the prophet's noncompliance.

The narrator is the one who provides a dominant voice in the text, the one who guides us through Jonah's world. Ostensibly the author, the narrator recounts the story. In the book of Jonah, the narrator tells the tale from an omniscient point of view, not only relaying reliable information about the plot but also freely commenting upon it whenever he chooses. (The original storyteller was almost certainly a man.) His function is to introduce characters, probe their inner thoughts, and interrupt their actions. An omniscient narrator has privileged information not readily at the disposal of other characters or readers. He knows details and secrets, and he apprehends the true nature of situations that readers might not discern from observing action. An omniscient storyteller is always capable of providing a periscope on plot and meaning, but our narrator sometimes withholds clues to personalities and themes. He, in typical biblical style, avoids lengthy immersions into the hearts and minds of the characters. He never uses the term "forgiveness," never directly applies it to any characters in the piece, and never has them speak the word. The narrator could inform us at any time what motivates Jonah, what the complications and consequences of the plot will be, what lies behind the marvels. Often, however, he does not share such insights with us, though the result is more significant than building suspense for its own sake. This book is not like a modern pulp thriller or mystery novel that introduces a problem but deliberately keeps readers in the dark until the final scene just so we feel compelled to read through to the end. Jonah's narrator develops the riddle of the prophet's disobedience and forgiveness, tightens the knot of intrigue, heightens audience emotion, and encourages us to solve the moral puzzle ourselves. The storyteller will occasionally suspend narrative summary and allow characters to develop by speaking for themselves. Sometimes the narrator is neutral, and sometimes he leads the way to theological exegesis. Always he postpones the moment when outcome and meaning will become clear to us. Obviously, at the beginning of the piece, we are not ready for the forgiveness dénouement; some of us even have trouble understanding it at the end.

In the beginning, the narrator shapes the story and thus the audience's reaction to it. The prose is terse. No strong warning is sounded of what lies ahead for a prophet of God in Nineveh, but the original audiences would already know enough about the city to realize that going there is no ordinary journey, no cause for celebration. To be sent to Nineveh is pulling tough duty. Jonah balks. The audience is drawn into the narrator's story and would speculate that the central conflict is the ideological and religious differences between the chosen people of Israel (represented by Jonah) and wayward nonbelievers (represented by the people of Nineveh).

Perhaps Jonah's very name is a clue to his personality and mission. At least one critic (Lewis 163) maintains that "Jonah" stems from the Hebrew word for "oppress." The prophet's dangerous mission to distant Nineveh thus makes him an oppressed person. More typically, his name is translated as "dove." In the Hebrew Scriptures approximately forty different animals are associated with human beings through nicknames and comparisons. Many of them are uncomplimentary links to pests such as fleas, moles, or pigs (Wolff 98). In several passages, the dove also receives less than flattering descriptions. Isaiah 38:14 compares King Hezekiah's lament to a dove's soft but complaining noise in "I moaned like a dove." In Hos 7:11, Israel (poetically called Ephraim) is compared to a dove, but it is representative of an undiscerning person, a birdbrain: "Ephraim has acted / Like a silly dove with no mind." In this instance, the dove is a fickle creature, incapable of sustained devotion. In the book of Hosea, the Lord is loyal to the people, despite their faithlessness to the deity.

In the story of Noah, of course, the dove is a positive symbol of reconciliation after the deluge of God's justice (Gen 8:11). The dove is also one of the birds used by ancient sailors to guide them to dry land (Hamel 344), a practice that has implications in the book of Jonah when, after meeting the prophet, the mariners pray to the Lord. Elsewhere in the Torah (the first five books of the Bible, also called the Pentateuch) a dove is even used as an acceptable means to restore "unclean" persons to the community. For example, a woman who seeks purification after giving birth could, if financially strapped, substitute two doves for a sheep in her sacrifice at the Tent of Meeting (Lev 12:8). Throughout the Song of Songs, "dove" is a term of endearment used by lovers, and in Ps 74:19 the "lowly ones" who should not be ignored in a community are compared to doves. Associating Jonah with a dove therefore has both negative and positive connotations in the context of other Bible passages — connections echoed in more modern symbolic and psychological interpretations of Jonah's story and reflecting his disobedience and ambivalence to the divine call.

Jonah is also the son of Amittai (אמתי), a word that derives from the Hebrew root אמת, truth. So Jonah's name may be broadly interpreted as either "Peaceful bird, son of human truthfulness" or "Birdbrain, son of God's enduring truth in the face of human capriciousness." Ambiguous interpretations of the prophet's name imply a major problem of the book: how to view Jonah's character. If Jonah is a dove, his actions are sometimes far removed from the dove of hope in Noah's story. The peaceful dove symbol may seem appropriate for Jonah at the beginning of the tale, but by the end it appears to be the opposite of his true nature (Hauser 22). If he is a son of truth, he is not particularly faithful to his prophetic calling or keen to fulfill it. Jonah and Yahweh are the only characters in the book who have names; everyone else — the mariners, the captain, the king of Nineveh, the nobles — remain anonymous. Yet even Jonah's name reveals the potential for dispute over what his character entails.

Jonah's first dilemma is how to react to God's commission, and the third verse of chapter 1 reports Jonah's disobedience. Here he begins to look like an alienated, wounded outsider. Instead of heading toward Nineveh, he "started out to flee to Tarshish from the LORD's service. He went down to Joppa and found a ship going to Tarshish. He paid the fare and went aboard to sail with the others to Tarshish, away from the service of the LORD" (Jonah 1:3). This verse's verb "to flee" (ברח) is used another forty-six times in the Bible and is always an overland flight, usually by camel or donkey (Zimmermann 581). Jonah's route is by sea, but his departure begins on land, for he "went down" to Joppa. Thus begins his descent into the world of noncompliance to divine decree, action that will require him to seek forgiveness. At present Jonah desires the anonymity found in a lower realm of existence.

Jonah is unnerved by God's command and craves release from the yoke of duty. The Talmud (Sanhedrin 89a) lists several different kinds of prophets and cites Jonah as "he who suppresses his prophecy." Jonah's flight could be an impulsive act of desperation. When he buys passage in advance, he shows extreme eagerness to escape divine injunction, for the custom in ancient days was to pay the fare at the conclusion of a voyage. One tradition even relates that Jonah, in his joy to find a ship to take him far away, gladly pays the full value of the vessel — four thousand gold denarii (Hirsch 226). In the Talmud, Rabbi Yohanan alleges that all prophets are rich, the proof being Jonah's ability to purchase the whole ship bound from Joppa (Bialik and Ravnitzky 472–73). Another interpretation of the Bible's statement that Jonah paid for passage indicates that the sailors realize his overzealous need to leave town quickly and therefore overcharge him (Cohen, *Twelve* 139).

Jonah's flurry of activity in 1:3 has a comedic effect. He becomes the caricature of a typical Hebrew prophet who intercedes on behalf of sinful people and becomes a shepherd to lost sheep. A false prophet might panic and behave as Jonah does, but Jonah is portrayed as a true prophet. Surely he knows that he cannot evade God. Soon Jonah will become passive while everyone around him bursts into action, but in the beginning of the story, he vigorously seeks to thwart divine will. We smile at his immaturity. Like a two-year-old child, Jonah throws a temper tantrum and defies authority. Readers know that Jonah can run, but he cannot hide. Adam and Eve discover this basic truth in the Garden of Eden (Gen 3:8–10), and Cain learns the same lesson soon after (Gen 4:14–16). Ultimately, the flight of the truant prophet will fail, for the Lord's omniscience is inescapable, and Jonah will eventually have to seek forgiveness for his disobedience. The story admonishes us concerning our lack of commitment to good causes, for God sees our every action and inaction.

In ancient times, Jonah's flight may have been couched in terms of a deserting servant. The Israelites would have known the Torah's stories about runaways. Since the days of Hagar fleeing her abusive mistress, Sarah (Gen 16:9), the divine command is to return and submit to the legitimate authority placed over us. Legal documents of the day indicate that in countries all around Israel, a fundamental principle applies in the Near East: fugitives would have to go back to their masters (Ratner 287). Yet the Torah contains one sentence that is contradictory: "You shall not turn over to his master a slave who seeks refuge with you from his master" (Deut 23:16). Slave (עבד) also can be translated as "servant," depending on context. Jonah is a servant of God, not a slave, so the Deuteronomy injunction does not apply to him so well. Instead, Israelite custom would dictate that Jonah return to God and obey.

In modern times, the prophet's flight has been termed "the Jonah complex," which is defined as "not so much a fear of one's own immanent potentialities as it is a fear of actualizing one's vocation, i.e., to serve God"; it is "repression of the Sublime" (Lacocque and Lacocque, *Revisited* 15). The Jonah complex is connected, but with a religious twist, to the theories of Abraham Maslow (1908–1970), cofounder of the humanistic psychology movement. Maslow describes a "hierarchy of prepotency" in human motivation, a predictable order to the succession of desires that drive human beings. Maslow observes that when one need is fulfilled, another takes its place. In a few individuals, all low-level needs are satisfied and a new motive occurs — the drive for self-actualization, or the impulse to become everything they are capable of being. Self-actualized people are unusually healthy psychologically, but people at the opposite end of the spectrum are paralyzed by fear (Maslow, *Toward* 45). Frightened Jonah is the opposite of a self-actualized person. According to this notion, Jonah "exemplifies our call to our task. He is also a paradigm of our resistance to election by God, for nothing is more repulsive to us than to be designated (elected, chosen) by the Outer Voice for a self-transcending task, when we would rather follow our inner voice and our biological dictates ('what feels good') for our self-satisfaction and our self-aggrandizement" (Lacocque and Lacocque, *Revisited* 21).

Jonah's flight begins in Joppa, the port of embarkation most easily accessible from Jerusalem, capital of the southern kingdom. From there Jonah leaves for Tarshish, which was probably Tartessus, an ancient, remote Semitic colony located on the southwestern coast of Spain (Cohen, *Twelve* 138; Limburg 43). Since the days of King Solomon, a Tarshish fleet had brought precious cargo to Jerusalem once every three years (1 Kgs 10:22), and the Bible often refers to the ships of Tarshish (e.g., Ps 48:8). Departing for Tarshish means going in the opposite direction of Nineveh. Tarshish, a seacoast city familiar to the original audience, was literally the end of the earth, as the earth was known in Jonah's time. The city represents the farthest distance imaginable, the length to which Jonah is willing to go to avoid accepting God's commission, the polar opposite of engagement and duty. In English the equivalent cliché would be that Jonah heads for the hills or goes to Timbuktu. He seeks anonymity among the pagans in the Diaspora.

In 1851 Herman Melville published *Moby Dick*, a profoundly symbolic whale tale about good and evil. Father Mapple's sermon discusses Jonah onboard the ship:

> See ye not then, shipmates, that Jonah sought to flee worldwide from God? Oh! Most contemptible and worthy of all scorn; with slouched hat and guilty eye, skulking from his God.... How plainly he's a fugitive! No baggage, not a hat-box, valise, or carpet-bag, — no friends accompany him to the wharf with their adieux. (47)

Melville has an important point. Jonah is totally alone among strangers when he seeks refuge on ship.

More recently, Sigmund Freud and others have pointed out that people's actions are based on the pleasure principle, or the avoidance of pain, and Jonah's inner battle goes deeply to the issue of eluding distress. Clearly, Jonah's adventure represents an individual in conflict, struggling alone against God's will. Resolution can only come from Jonah's successful evasion of God, from God's rescinding of the order, or from Jonah's reconciliation to it.

Jonah is hardly the first reluctant prophet in the Bible. God has to ask Moses five times (Exod 3:11–4:20) before he accepts the mammoth job of leading the Israelites out of Egypt. Moses feels unworthy to accept such a huge responsibility, believes he does not speak well, thinks Pharaoh will pay no heed, and desires assistance. In his infancy, Moses is placed in a basket and set adrift among the Nile's bulrushes, a dangerous but nonetheless life-saving situation that invites comparisons to Jonah's salvation within the watertight enclosure of the great fish's belly. A second reluctant hero is Gideon, who to his credit refuses to become sovereign when the people encourage him to form a monarchy in Israel (Judg 6:22). A third example is the otherwise unflappable Elijah, who flees to Mount Horeb and despairs after Jezebel threatens his life (1 Kgs 19). In fact, many of the supernatural elements of Elijah's flight (the ravens, the cave, the number of days involved in the journey, the dialogue with God) suggest that the book of Jonah's author is already familiar with the Elijah cycle's theme of repentance (Wolff 77). The influential Isaiah is the fourth biblical great to protest that he cannot be a prophet because of his "unclean lips" (Isa 6:5), and Jeremiah is the fifth. Jeremiah objects because, like Moses, he does not speak well and is a mere boy (Jer 1:6). The original audience of the Jonah story would have more than a nodding acquaintance with these and other narratives and would have quickly detected their similarities.

Yes, other biblical heroes feel alone, shrink from duty, and express anguish over the burden of God's demands, but Jonah is unique. Elijah and Jeremiah flee from evil monarchs, but only Jonah flees from the Almighty. Moses and other prophets plead to be released from their missions, but with divine assistance they swiftly overcome their limitations. The gaps in their confidence quickly close. Abraham objects and argues vigorously when God proclaims the imminent destruction of Sodom and Gomorrah (Gen 18:22–32), but the patriarch does not protest the binding of Isaac (Gen 22:1–3). In both situations Abraham is expressing his faith that God will do what is right. Jonah's opposition is quite different. Early in chapter 1, idiosyncratic Jonah gives no hint that he will ever comply and, unlike Moses and others, does not even bother to offer up a verbal argument before running away.

In effect, Jonah's nonverbal protest is a denial of who he is and what he must do with his life. If God's summons to Nineveh were hollow or insignificant, Jonah might get away with rejecting his true vocation, stay forever unconcerned about the Ninevites, and remain untouched by God's call. At this point in the plot, the prophet indicates no reason for his blatant refusal to cooperate, takes extreme action to shirk his assignment, and later rails against God and humanity. Perhaps Jonah is merely afraid of his mission or his Lord, as a parallel story of Jonah in *The Antiquities of the Jews* asserts: "But [Jonah] went not, out of fear" (Josephus 259). In the Bible, Jonah seems more like a misfit than a man of God. The narrator does not tell us Jonah's motives, and we must try to fill in narrative gaps. Why does Jonah flee? By the end of the story, the reader will discover possible answers to this question, but not until considerably more plot and character development takes place.

Without the hero's hesitation to obey the instructions of his father's ghost, *Hamlet* would be a one-act play that teaches very little about human nature. Without Jonah's hesitation to obey God's command, this story would offer the audience no opportunity to learn important lessons about love and forgiveness. From this point of view, Jonah's resistance could be viewed as a necessary part of the literary as well as the divine plan. It certainly reinforces the way we identify with Jonah. Who among us feels truly qualified to do God's work? Who has not been disobedient at some time?

Jonah goes מלפני יהוה, "away from the service of the LORD" (Jonah 1:3), translated as "from the presence of the LORD" in the JPS's 1917 version of *The Holy Scriptures*. In an earlier story from Gen 41:46, Joseph does just the opposite. He leaves Pharaoh's presence in order to *fulfill* his mission of gathering food during the seven years of plenty, not to avoid his appointed role. It has been argued (Walton 14) that if Jonah actually believed time and space could put him forever out of God's reach, the flight would be expressed in more emphatic Hebrew language. Instead, Jonah merely hopes that stubbornness will cause God to look for someone else to do the job. Another venerable interpretation is that Jonah believes the presence of the Lord is localized in only three places: inside the land of the chosen people, in heaven, and in Sheol (the underworld of the ancient Jews). Psalm 139:7 asks rhetorically, "Where can I flee from Your presence?" At the time of Jonah's flight in chapter 1, he would have said to himself, "I will go outside the Land, to a place where the Presence neither dwells nor reveals itself" (Bialik and Ravnitzky 363). In the ancient Near East, the idea was commonly held that a god's presence could only be found in the territory of the worshipers

(*Interpreter's Bible* 6:879). No wonder Jonah is reluctant to minister in Nineveh.

Jonah is certainly seeking to be relieved of his commission and possibly hopes that God will transfer the duty to someone else or find work for Jonah to do closer to home. If Jonah is motivated by nationalistic desires not to leave Israel, his patriotism is not necessarily an indication of hostility to the Ninevites. He may simply feel that he has enough to do without traveling abroad.

Some things that God would have us do are difficult or unpalatable for a host of reasons; perhaps this is why God so frequently commands instead of endeavoring to persuade us to obey. Yet a credible interpretation, given little attention, is that Jonah flees because God's command to condemn the Ninevites is unethical. They are foreigners, unschooled in Torah and unacquainted with prophets of the Lord. To "proclaim judgment" (Jonah 1:2) upon a city of innocents who have never before heard the word of God is unfair and unkind. At this point in the story God does not reveal to Jonah that the prescribed punishment is conditional or that divine forgiveness of the Ninevites is imminent, though he later claims to have had faith in God's forgiving tendencies (4:2). In chapter 1 Jonah would be right to want no part in such a mission, and perhaps that is why he deserts his post. Skeptical readers may wonder if God is embroiled in an act that, for Jonah to comply, would require the prophet to forgive the deity. If so, the books of Jonah and Job begin to share a common theme: God's actions appear questionable, and it becomes humanity's task to point out ethical lapses and to evade compliance with harsh divine judgment.

Jonah's flight can also been seen as an unconventional version of the Oedipus story. Partly because people cannot escape their fate or outwit the gods, all the elaborate precautions undertaken to prevent Oedipus from killing his father and marrying his mother actually contribute to his fulfilling the oracle's prophecy. By the same token, all the activity that Jonah performs to avoid going to Nineveh is exactly what results in his going there, although the Israelite story conveys positive messages about forgiveness, and the Oedipus tale is a classical tragedy of doom and death (Goodhart 45). In Greek mythology, fate is inevitable and inexorable. In Hebrew theology people have free will, but fate cannot be avoided when equated with the will of God.

Josephus, whose text says that it relies upon "the Hebrew books" (259), simplifies Jonah's famous flight in *The Antiquities of the Jews*. Josephus's narrative follows only chapters 1 and 2 of the Bible's account and omits the rest of the story that takes place in Nineveh. In *Antiquities* Jonah goes to Tarsus in Cilicia, is thrown overboard by sailors, is swallowed by a whale, and asks God for forgiveness. Josephus's version ends when the prophet "obtained pardon for his sins" (260). He then departs for Nineveh, and Josephus does not mention the prophet again.

In the TANAKH the turmoil inside Jonah is more complicated. It is reflected by the hullabaloo that swirls around him: "But the LORD cast a mighty wind upon the sea, and such a great tempest came upon the sea that the ship was in danger of breaking up" (Jonah 1:4). "The History of Jonah," a Day of Atonement homily contained in chapter 10 of *Pirkê de Rabbi Eliezer* (a midrash of the ninth century), suggests that only Jonah's ship is adversely affected by blustery wind and waves; other vessels are seen sailing on smooth zephyrs (67). In the book of Jonah, however, the sea and ship are personified; one rages and the other is in danger of destruction. The narrator makes it clear that God is in full charge of natural forces, ויהוה הטיל. So desperate is Jonah to avoid his office as a prophet that he is willing to face the ocean, the great watery abyss of Gen 1:2. In ancient Israel, other nations blocked access to the Mediterranean Sea. Some people in landlocked Israel would have been frightened of the water, having had little or no exposure to it in their lifetimes. Rather than representing an act of cowardice, a sympathetic interpretation of Jonah's flight by sea could indicate his bravery, his willingness to face unknown, watery peril and to perish for his convictions. He puts his life on the line rather than undertake an unwanted prophecy job. From this perspective, the flight is not really a blot on the prophet's reputation and perhaps explains why God is not overly angry with Jonah. If the Ninevites are to be killed by God, then perhaps Jonah wishes not to be an accomplice in their murder. The possibility presents itself that, although at this point in the story Jonah offers no verbal corroboration of his motive, the prophet pities the Ninevites and cannot agree with what he assumes is Yahweh's intent to slaughter them.

The sea, unlike Jonah, has no independent volition and plays a terrifying role in fulfilling divine will. Bible critics nevertheless excuse the sea from culpability in causing alarm in the hearts of people onboard the ship. After all, the sea is merely doing God's bidding, just obeying orders. Alone among dissenters is Elie Wiesel. As a concentration camp survivor and winner of the Nobel Peace Prize, Wiesel is uniquely situated as a moral authority who can suggest that by being an accomplice, the sea endangers the lives of innocent sailors. Wiesel proposes that the ocean should protest when God orders a tempest to engulf Jonah's ship:

> If God wishes to punish or test Jonah, the sea has no reason to offer
> its services. . . . Could it not argue with God: "Listen, Almighty God,
> I understand that I must help You test Jonah, but he is not alone
> aboard that ship! There are other people on it! . . . You want me to
> help You punish or at least worry Jonah — so be it! But do not
> expect me to deliberately frighten innocent bystanders!" (141–42)

Yet even Wiesel finally concludes that the sea is not malicious or guilty. It is
God's instrument, knows its place in the divine order of the universe, rebels
at Jonah's presence, and refuses to bear the burden of the prophet's wicked
disobedience. The sea (as well as the wind and all other forces of nature
at God's command) cannot disobey. All do what they are created to do.
They do not have Jonah's free will. In nature, gale force winds can appear
at any time atmospheric conditions are conducive. The fact that they occur
at precisely the right moment to debunk Jonah's attempted escape points to
the literary artistry of the story.

In Gen 1:1, God sweeps over the water and creation begins. Yet in most
parts of the Bible the sea is more hostile. It represents chaos and contains
monsters like Leviathan (Isa 27:1; Ps 74:13–14). Noah's world is re-created
through the flood. The water represents disorder and confusion, but God
makes order of it in a manifestation of divine might. In the Elijah story,
the prophet is associated with God's control over drought, the opposite of
rainstorm at sea. Plunged into a deluge, Jonah becomes a kind of anti-Elijah.
At the conclusion of his wondrous career on earth, Elijah is swept up to
heaven in a whirlwind (סערה), whereas Jonah at the beginning of his trip is
cast into a tempest (סער).

From a psychological point of view the storm is caused by Jonah himself
and is symbolic of the ruckus we raise when we try to avoid our true selves.
The ship, as well as Jonah's life, is in danger of breaking up. The imagery is
strong and vivid. Like the raging heath on which King Lear falters, the sea
storm is a mirror of Jonah's soul; his environment is an echo of his interior
self. The sea — dark, violent, potentially deadly — also provides a display
of divine power. Jeremiah 30:23 reminds us that "the storm of the LORD
goes forth in fury, / A raging tempest; / It shall whirl down upon the head
of the wicked." Sails are of no use now; they would be quickly lowered as
the men on Jonah's ship begin to battle the wild waters.

The sea is also symbolic of water inside the womb, the amniotic fluid
that is both a sign of human immaturity and the potential for growth. In
watery liquid, life begins. So when Jonah embarks for Tarshish and gives

himself up to the forces of the deep, he is in a sense returning to his primor-
dial origin. God, who creates and manipulates life's mysteries, controls this
watery source of our existence. Though it is a sign of life, water may also
rage out of control and cause death, and the tale shows the close connection
between the two. People who, like Jonah, disobey the callings of conscience
risk self-destruction. When Jonah is tossed into the water, he simultaneously
loses his life and has the opportunity to regain it through divine forgiveness.
He may start out with limited ability to comprehend the concept of forgiveness, but his experience in the watery incubator/grave also teaches him to
understand divine deliverance better. The sea represents the demands of the
unconscious, and in this case its turbulence is associated with the agitation
caused when ego forces the unconscious into repressing part of its fuller self.
The stormy ocean is the consequence of Jonah's disobedience.

At this point in the story, we are introduced for the first time to Jonah's
polytheistic companions onboard ship, the sailors, המלחים. They are rough-
and–tumble men, but the Hebrew word for sailors sounds like the word for
"angels" (also translated as "messengers," המלאכים). This is not an example
of textual error; in Hebrew "sailor" and "messenger" would not be likely
to fool the eye of a diligent scribe, but in the oral presentation, the audience
might well be aware of both possibilities (Hoffer and Wright 147). Nowhere
in the Jonah text is the word "angel" found, so whether the author intended
and the audience caught any clever wordplay is speculative. Yet the sailors
function somewhat like angels, which in the Hebrew Scriptures are only
vaguely supernatural beings who bring news; they have not yet evolved into
the winged and haloed beings of the New Testament. Two angels, המלאכים,
tell Lot to leave Sodom (Gen 19:1), and the creatures appear bearing important tidings in many other TANAKH stories, so the original audience for the
book of Jonah could have been familiar with the idea of messenger-angels
and might have smiled at the wordplay in the Jonah story.

Surely these sailors have seen wild storms before, but despite their experience on the open sea, they are afraid of the severity of this particular
tempest. Assembling in Tarshish, they would be a motley crew, representative of humanity's diversity from all the nations of the earth, as the narrator
knew it. They are a microcosm of humanity, but mainly they are non-Jews —
the rest of the world, the opposite of Jonah's people. Phoenicians dominated
the seas in biblical times, and perhaps many of the mariners were Phoenician
worshipers of Baal and his consort Astarte. Assyrian sailors bowed down
before Ishtar, Shamash, and others; Babylonians praised Marduk. The biblical text hints that many nationalities of sailors are shipboard and that they
worship myriad deities (Walton 17). The sailors would be unacquainted with

the forgiving nature of Jonah's God and not know what to expect from the divinely caused tempest.

In spite of the swarm of gods worshiped among the crew, the portrait of the sailors is not uncomplimentary. Folk wisdom ascribes to sailors a terrible reputation. Greek historian Herodotus (c. 480–425 B.C.E.) tells of sailors stealing innocent passengers' possessions and money, or forcing travelers to turn over their worldly goods or be thrown overboard by a rowdy crew (Hamel 346). Lower-class people though they are in Jonah's story, they do comprehend the need to take positive action in this dangerous situation. In fact, they seem to be very decent human beings. True, they are afraid, but that is wise given their predicament. The sailors act quickly and religiously in their response to the squall. They cry out "each to his own god" (Jonah 1:5), something that the prophet Jonah fails to do. Could it be that these foreign mariners are more righteous than Jonah himself, more predisposed to call upon a deity in times of trouble, more trusting in divine rescue? Sailors, then as well as now, are stereotypically regarded as being superstitious if not downright nonreligious (Cohen, *Twelve* 139), but in the book of Jonah, they immediately offer up a prayer for deliverance. Ironically, by praying they provide a foil to the silent prophet. They have their own kind of honor, their own standard of religious piety. The Talmud even comments that while most "ass-drivers are wicked, ... most sailors are worthy men" (Kiddushin 82a), and many modern critics are only too happy to roast Jonah and toast the sailors in this episode.

In addition to praying, the men also "flung the ship's cargo overboard to make it lighter for them" (1:5). Their cargo — probably including precious metals, livestock, and ivory — is valuable to the ship's owner if not to the individual sailors, but the men are hired to deliver it safely to its destination. By performing this logical act of casting material goods overboard, the sailors raise the boat in the water and reduce the danger of sinking and shipwreck. Here they demonstrate an ethic that esteems human life (their own) over economic profit (their bosses'). Thus they involve themselves in spiritual and physical actions designed to take control of their desperate situation. By virtue of their behavior, the pagan sailors appear not only innocuous but also admirable.

As the men around him spring into action, Jonah becomes passive. He descends into the bowels of the ship and continues to sleep while the storm grows ever more intense: "Jonah, meanwhile, had gone down into the hold of the vessel where he lay down and fell asleep" (1:5). While Elie Wiesel argues (148) that a sensitive Jonah must cut himself off from humanity because he cannot bear to watch their suffering, most critics take the opposite view.

An emergency is afoot, a crisis of the worst magnitude, and Jonah does not lift a finger to help the panicked crew. The Septuagint — the oldest Greek translation of the Hebrew Scriptures, dating from the reign of Ptolemy II in the third century B.C.E. — ridicules the prophet's behavior by saying that not only does he sleep; he even snores (1094), signaling very deep slumber. Jonah's response to the problem presented by the tempest is to tune out, yet the actions of the mariners and the Almighty suggest that they forgive the prophet's avoidance behavior.

Jonah's sleep could also be a metaphor for symbolic death. Jeremiah (51:39) discusses repaying Babylon for the wrong it has done to Zion. The enemy will "sleep an endless sleep, / Never to awake." Jonah's sleep, deep within the womb of the boat, represents his further attempt to escape the reality of his prophetic calling. That Jonah is able to snooze right through a ferocious storm, just as the selfish ego obstinately denies the call to duty, is amazing.

Rabbi Abba is one of the first to interpret the importance of Jonah's subterranean slumber when he writes in the Zohar: "Jonah descending into the ship is symbolic of man's soul that descends into this world to enter into the body.... Man, then, is in this world as in a ship that is traversing the great ocean and is like to be broken" (4:173). While the Gentiles work feverishly to save themselves and the ship, Jonah escapes into the enjoyable release and quietude of slumber, all worry driven from his consciousness. He seeks to become as inconspicuous as possible, hoping anonymity will protect him. But Jonah's selective inattention to the crisis at hand is tantamount to deserting ship. For the moment he is oblivious to his fate. He descends אֶל־יַרְכְּתֵי, "into the hold" of the ship in the 1985 JPS translation and "into the innermost parts" in the 1917 JPS version of the Bible. Isaiah 14:15 uses the same word, יַרְכְּתֵי, to indicate Babylon being brought down to Sheol. Jonah's going down into the hold symbolizes disobedience and moral descent, yet it is also compared to the Lord's method of protecting Moses by concealing him in a cleft of the rock (Exod 33:22) while the divine goodness passes by (Havazelet 30).

Modern critics are likely to see Jonah's descent into the bowels of the ship as a withdrawal comparable to clinical depression (Lacocque and Lacocque, *Complex* 48), representing Jonah's wish to return to an embryo-like state of nonbeing and nonaccountability. He seeks the protection of isolation and noncommunication. Jonah's desire to run away from responsibility is labeled a pathology by Carl Jung, who names it the "Jonah-and-the-Whale complex" (419). Though Jonah's sleep is often cited as evidence of his single-minded pursuit of self-preservation, perhaps it is not. A truly self-centered person would go to any lengths to save himself during such a crisis (A. D. Cohen 170). At this point, Jonah seems to have given up on life willingly (Telushkin 99).

Abraham Maslow has defined the "Jonah Syndrome" as "partly a justified fear of being torn apart, as losing control, of being shattered and disintegrated, even of being killed by the experience" ("Neurosis" 165). Maslow believes that our greatest fear is knowing ourselves because such self-knowledge might force us to make fundamental, unwanted changes in the way we view our lives. Who could blame Jonah for avoiding life's obstacles? While developing his prophetic talents would be exciting, it would also be dangerous. It would disrupt Jonah's comfortable, safe life as a successful prophet in his own land and mark him as one destined for unforeseen, perhaps impossible tasks in the future.

The captain of the vessel, the foreigner in charge who will later be compared to the king of Nineveh, is appalled that Jonah is asleep and rebukes the prophet: "How can you be sleeping so soundly! Up, call upon your god!" (Jonah 1:6). The narrator cleverly uses the same word to describe God's command to Jonah in 1:2 and the shipmaster's cry to the prophet in 1:6. In Hebrew the verb is קום, translated as "*Arise,* go to Nineveh" (1:2) and "*Arise,* call upon thy God" (1:6) in the 1917 JPS translation or "*Up,* call upon your god!" in the newer JPS version. The verbal echo is effective; both God and the sea captain demand that Jonah behave as a prophet should. The Almighty wants Jonah to help the ignorant people of Nineveh find salvation, and the captain wants Jonah to help save the innocent crew. Yet this foreign captain is not acquainted with God's merciful qualities and does not presume that Jonah's deity will assist those in peril at sea. The captain has no awareness of any special difference between the God of Jonah and any other deity worshiped by the heterogeneous crew. As the man in charge, the captain simply wants all potential avenues for assistance to be explored. Nonetheless, the captain expresses hope that Jonah's God can be convinced to spare the sailors: "Perhaps the god will be kind to us and we will not perish" (1:6). The captain, unlike the tight-mouthed Jonah, at least knows enough to ask for divine aid when trouble brews. The captain does not resist prayer; only Jonah does that. Ironically, the captain, a symbol of authority on the sea, acts as a foil to the silent prophet, symbol of authority on land.

In desperation to find the cause of the tempest, the sailors decide to cast lots, and of course the lot falls on Jonah (1:7), pinning directly on him blame for the ship's misfortune. Casting lots to determine action or end disputes has precedent in the Hebrew Scriptures (1 Sam 14:41; Prov 18:18; Esth 3:7). Generally thought to be an objective method of reaching a decision, casting lots is an ancient technique similar to drawing straws. In the book of Jonah, casting lots allows the sailors to find the guilty party, the one responsible for the howling storm. Now the sailors can make an incontrovertible cause-and-effect link between Jonah and the threatening tempest.

Readers may feel revulsion at the notion that a single sinner can cause the destruction of all aboard, yet the sailors behave admirably. Against all expectations, considering their heathen backgrounds, they do not immediately take Jonah's life and thus remove the danger from their midst. They are more inquisitive than bloodthirsty and act more like a group of lawyers than a lynch mob. The mariners immediately bombard Jonah with four questions: "[W]hat is your business? Where have you come from? What is your country, and of what people are you?" (1:8). "What is your business" is translated as "what is thine occupation?" in the 1917 JPS Bible. This Hebrew phrase, מה־מלאכתך, reveals aural similarity in the words for "occupation" (מלאכתך) and the word for "angel" or "messenger" (מלאכים), just as the earlier oral word play exists on "angel" and "sailor." Thus, "the sailors may be asking an 'innocent' question, but Jonah cannot help but hear in their inquiry the very thing he is fleeing, the task of being God's messenger to Nineveh" (Hoffer and Wright 147). Jonah responds, perhaps icily, only to the sailors' last query, "of what people are you?" He replies simply, "I am a Hebrew" (1:9).

Jonah and the Crew Spared

When Jonah calls himself עברי, a Hebrew, the tide begins to turn in favor of salvation. "Hebrew" is typically the name that foreigners apply to one who worships Yahweh, or an old term that Israelites use in describing themselves to foreigners (Gen 40:15; 1 Sam 4:6), but Jonah's answer is significant. By calling himself a Hebrew, he identifies himself with God's people — Abraham, Joseph, and the slaves in Egypt. This moment is pivotal in chapter 1. He further confesses that he worships "the LORD, the God of Heaven, who made both sea and land" (1:9). Jonah's use of the epithet testifies to the Lord's supremacy among the pantheon of deities worshiped in the region and is also reminiscent of Abraham's words in Gen 24:3 when the patriarch refers to "the God of heaven and the God of the earth." Unlike Abraham, who is more consistently obedient to divine will, Jonah is finally ready to take a first step toward accepting responsibility as a prophet of the Most High. Jonah acknowledges who he is — with brevity rather than zeal or enthusiasm. This change is not a small one for Jonah, however. Having previously sought to avoid his destiny, he runs no more. Jonah stands (bravely, one could argue) and faces those men whose lives he has endangered, telling them to throw him overboard so the sea will calm. Perhaps he has compassion for these strangers and wishes them not to die on his account.

At this point Jonah is willing to sacrifice himself so that others may live. He prophesies to his fellow travelers: "Heave me overboard, and the sea will calm down for you; for I know that this terrible storm came upon you on my account" (Jonah 1:12). He realizes that he is the cause of the sea's tumult, just as most of us tend to know deep down that we cause many of our own dilemmas. True, if he had not acted selfishly earlier when he boarded ship, there would be no calamity at sea now, but Jonah is at last awakened out of the "slumber" of irresponsibility and into nobility of action. Though he attempts for a time to abandon his fellow human beings, this act ironically puts his own life in danger too. Jonah begins to realize that no life exists outside obedience to God's will. Perhaps he now sees the foreigners as people, not just as unknown heathens; perhaps Jonah feels compassion for humanity. But Jonah's life is still at risk, for he asks to be thrown overboard into the raging waves that will surely drown him. Neither Jonah nor the narrator reveals the prophet's motive for asking the sailors to hurl him into the ocean, so the request may be more complex than altruistic self-sacrifice. The gesture may also represent his enduring stubbornness, his death wish, his desire to be removed from the presence of foreigners he hates, or even his belief that God will benevolently direct events.

Here again the sailors, supposedly representative of the pagan world, behave remarkably well. Perhaps Jonah's heroic gesture to be put overboard inspires them. They spurn Jonah's entreaty to heave him into the sea, despite the lot that has clearly implicated him as the cause of the storm. They refuse to forsake a fellow human being, even though Jonah is earlier more than willing to relinquish responsibility for them. Perhaps the men are reluctant to abandon Jonah because he identifies himself as an observant Hebrew and devotee to a powerful God. Whatever their reasons, the men "rowed hard to regain the shore, but they could not, for the sea was growing more and more stormy about them" (1:13). One proposed emendation to the text suggests that 1:13 should be transposed to follow 1:4, which first explains that God causes the tempest. This change might make for a better narrative flow in both parts of the story (Budde 227) by showing that the mariners immediately take action by vigorously pushing oars against a hostile sea.

As the text stands, however, the seamen exert all possible effort. They risk their own lives to avoid killing an alien passenger, for any attempt to reach shore during such a storm is surely futile and foolhardy. Seasoned mariners would know better than to head for the coastline during a terrible squall. Ancient sailing manuals contain dire warnings for sailors against the certain doom of trying to reach dry land during a raging tempest (Marcus 109). The fact that the sea grows rougher after Jonah confesses that he is the culprit signifies that identifying a problem is not the same thing as solving it. Owning up to a problem, under duress, will not negate it. In spite of awareness, which is a necessary first step, a heroic deed will still be necessary to correct the situation. Only after making every effort to find another way to handle the situation — casting lots, using their skill at rowing, praying — do the sailors succumb to the inevitable.

In midrashic tales the sailors first immerse Jonah only to his knees. The storm ceases, so they pull him back on board. When the storm immediately recommences, they plunge Jonah in the water up to his navel, with the same result. A third time the men lower Jonah in to his neck, finding once more that the sea calms and then rages again when he is removed from the water. Finally, the men realize that they have no choice and must release Jonah entirely into the ocean (*Pirkê de Rabbi Eliezer* 69). The point is that the crusty crew of "old salts" attempts moderate and conservative degrees of placating the forces of the deep before they give up on saving Jonah's life. The sailors' benevolent actions might even imply that they forgive Jonah, the cause of their current predicament.

Before capitulating to Jonah's suggestion and throwing him overboard, the sailors show that in their homelands they must have had some theological instruction. They offer up a prayer to Jonah's God, though their supplications seem based more on their desire to avoid punishment for executing Jonah than their wish to be his merciful companions: "Oh, please, LORD, do not let us perish on account of this man's life. Do not hold us guilty of killing an innocent person! For You, O LORD, by Your will, have brought this about" (1:14). The great irony here is that the prophet has yet to pray, but the heathens plead to Jonah's God to save their lives and spare them from the sin of murdering the prophet. The text does not indicate that the mariners are converted to the Yahweh cult on the spot, but they are convinced that Jonah's God holds men accountable for their deeds and sends huge storms. The mariners must figure that the more gods who are entreated, the better the chance of pardon from the plight. Offended gods could sometimes be placated with sacrifices and supplications in their varied experience, but their initial reaction is to balk at the notion of offering up Jonah as a human sacrifice to the powers of the deep.

The most obvious New Testament antithesis to Jonah's situation is found in Acts 27, when Paul of Tarsus demands that the entire 276-man crew taking him to Rome for trial not abandon ship during a violent storm. Staying with the vessel is essential, for Paul and his companions are symbolically aboard a ship of faith: "Paul said to the centurion and the soldiers, 'Unless these men stay in the ship, you cannot be saved'" (Acts 27:32). Like the sailors in the book of Jonah, Paul's crew throws cargo and tackle overboard after three days of the violent tempest (Acts 27:18–19), but the men persevere for many dark days before their ship hits a reef and runs aground. The ship breaks apart, but all the men swim safely to shore. We do not know what becomes of Jonah's companions in the days after they toss him into the sea; the narrator loses interest in the heathens after they complete their part of the plot by abandoning Jonah to the sea and its great fish.

When Jonah is dumped overboard and the sea stops raging, the men are further convinced of God's power over the ocean. "The men feared the LORD greatly; they offered a sacrifice to the LORD and they made vows" (Jonah 1:16). Rashi, an eleventh-century French biblical scholar, argues that the sailors promise to serve God forever (Hirsch 225), but the text offers no evidence that the mariners undergo a permanent conversion to Yahwehism or learn any lasting lessons from their brush with the Almighty. What they do understand is that Yahweh is to be taken seriously and that expression of gratitude is appropriate at this moment. After jettisoning Jonah from the ship, the Israelite narrator would not expect the sailors to do more than offer a sacrifice to God; he would not require them to give up their own gods. In much biblical thinking, non-Israelites are not responsible for worshiping the God of Israel. Nevertheless, the story of the sailors displays three elements seen in many stories, notably in the books of Samuel, Ezra, Esther, Jeremiah, and Joel. They include the "threat of disaster, acts of penitence, and eventual divine intervention to avert disaster" (Allen 223).

Only Elie Wiesel refuses to extol the sailors' superior ethics and comes close to calling them anti-Semites. Wiesel asserts:

> We may not choose life at the expense of another. Jewish law says that a community must never hand over one of its own members to the enemy even if refusal means death for the entire community. Although Jonah is not one of their own, he is their guest, their passenger. Don't they know that a ship's crew is duty-bound to

save the lives of the passengers before their own? And remember: Jonah is not a stowaway; he has, after all, paid his fare. (141)

As a Holocaust survivor, Wiesel understandably feels resentment toward collaborators and is the only scholar to make such a compelling argument against the sailors.

Whatever the motives of the sailors, the fact that the sea grows calm proves that they have acted rightly in dumping Jonah. The men also serve as divine agents in Jonah's story of gradually fulfilling his destiny as a prophet of God. When Jonah is thrown overboard, he undergoes a kind of baptism. The waters lap over him and wash away his former disobedient life. Thus, in the first chapter of the book, the narrator's positive characterization of the sailors suggests openness to non-Israelites, an accepting attitude in keeping with the book of Ruth and running contrary to the narrow and rigid thinking of Ezra and Nehemiah.

By the conclusion of chapter 1, Jonah makes a giant splash into the sea. But is it a leap of faith? He separates himself forever from the relative safety of the ship, from the companionship of other people, and (he must believe) from God. As he allows himself to be tossed into the fearful waters, surely he fears that his life is at an end and no divine forgiveness will come his way. The sea is wild and deadly, and the prophet has to think that it will overtake him. Nonetheless, with the help of the sailors, he plunges headlong toward duty. The mariners are essential to this part of the plot because seldom, if ever, does the ego allow itself to submit freely to the conscience. As soon as Jonah yields to the terrors of the waters and all they represent, they become peaceful and placid. With the sea at rest, Jonah is ready to commence the next episode in his struggle to become an obedient, forgiving human being and a loyal prophet of God.

CHAPTER 3

Jonah's Deliverance

O, hear us when we cry to Thee
For those in peril on the sea!
— William Whiting,
"Eternal Father, Strong to Save"

About to drown in the sea, Jonah is the recipient of a divine miracle that causes him to realize God's ability to deliver and forgive. "The LORD provided a huge fish to swallow Jonah; and Jonah remained in the fish's belly three days and three nights" (Jonah 2:1). The Lord is at the helm of Jonah's ship-of-life, the great fish, inside of which the prophet is simultaneously set adrift and kept secure. After three days the Lord will allow Jonah to come up for air on dry land, apparently transformed by his experience in the deep. Hardly a pleasure cruise, the sojourn inside the dark recesses of the fish's belly has the effect of an emotional tsunami. At its conclusion Jonah acknowledges the power of his deity and immediately sets off for Nineveh.

The fish is connected with revitalizing power because it lives in the ocean, the source of life. Thus the fish is associated with reproductive abilities, which partially explains the presence of so many fish gods in the ancient world — Vishnu in India, Dagon in Philistia, and so on — and why the story of Jonah uses the fish for its rebirth motif. In chapter 2 the narrator's role is less pronounced than in chapter 1, but he briefly provides a few salient details that form the frame of the chapter. In only three full sentences, two before a poem that composes the bulk of the chapter and one after, the narrator implies the completeness of divine control over natural events by introducing the seagoing method God employs to rescue Jonah, the length of time Jonah disappears from sight, and Jonah's eventual expulsion back onto dry land. The narrator provides minimal but essential exposition on both sides of the poem. For most of chapter 2, Jonah recites poetry describing his gratitude to God for rescuing him from death and his understanding that the Lord is responsible for deliverance. This is Jonah's prayer of thanksgiving

54

presented to God in verse, a poem offered up while Jonah is locked inside the life-sustaining confines of the fish.

The fact that Jonah's name means "dove" is significant in the discussion of the prophet's temporary stay inside the fish. The dove and the fish are sometimes connected in mythology. Beguiling Aphrodite, to whom doves are sacred, is born from the sea when she springs from the froth of the ocean, her name meaning "the foam-risen" (Hamilton 32). The dove and the water are also linked when they each play prominent roles in the Bible's story of Noah. Just as the fish represents water, the dove represents air. The air is another essential element of life, and in the Hebrew Scriptures, air is connected to spirit and soul, as in Gen 1:2 when a "wind from God" sweeps over the water. Wind, רוח, or moving air, may also be translated as the "breath" of God. Jonah, the dove who sojourns within the fish, is thus associated with two basic elements of life: air and water.

The trip into the belly of the fish is another descent, paralleling Jonah's first downward trek into the hold of the ship to sleep in chapter 1. Yet the huge fish is not simply a monolith of dread. It is also an instrument of salvation sent by God, who is in control of all the forces of nature. Because of this second descent, Jonah will emerge a changed man. That God causes a fish, whose natural home is far removed from the dry land required for human habitation, to swallow Jonah is significant (Wohlgelernter 132). In this isolated and watery abyss, completely alienated from humankind, Jonah will begin to regret his disobedience to the Lord. He will reform (temporarily) and recommit himself to the Almighty as a result of time spent inside the fish — inside his own conscience, inside himself. Jonah will repent of his disobedience, glimpse the glory of divine compassion, and receive the Lord's forgiveness.

The Belly of the Fish

Jonah is within the belly of the fish for a specific length of time, three days and nights. The only other place in the Hebrew Scriptures where three days *and* nights are discussed is in 1 Sam 30:12 when David revives an Egyptian found in the open county, a man who "had eaten no food and drunk no water for three days and three nights." On a literal level, anyone languishing for so long without nourishment would risk death. In this story of David's generosity, he aids a foreigner in danger of dying, death being associated with the magical number of three. Another example of the three days and nights ordeal involves a legend based on the Gen 37 story of Joseph, thrown into an empty pit by his jealous brothers. An extrabiblical story by Mirkhond claims that Joseph languishes for "three days and nights at the bottom of the well, during which time Jebrâil came every day to give him the consolation of the invisible world, and informed him of future hopes, which pacified Yusuf till time elapsed and his delivery took place" (Simpson 89). Joseph-in-the-well is a variation on the Jonah-in-the-fish story.

Three has always been considered a mystical, magical number and is frequently used in the Bible. *The Interpreter's Bible* suggests that the three days of Jonah's captivity allegorically imply a long time and correspond to the extensive period of Israel's exile in Babylonia (6:885). Three is also the number of the superlative (as in good, better, best). In the TANAKH three days are sometimes required to complete a journey (Josh 1:11, 2:16; 2 Sam 20:4). More importantly, the Hebrew Scriptures designates three days as the length of time required for divine salvation of errant Ephraim (Israel):

> Come, let us turn back to the LORD:
> He attacked, and He can heal us;
> He wounded, and He can bind us up.
> In two days He will make us whole again;
> On the third day He will raise us up,
> And we shall be whole by His favor.
>
> (Hos 6:1–2)

Three days symbolizes the relatively long duration of human suffering before God steps in to deliver sinners, a concept important to the book of Jonah. The Bible promises liberation from pain, even though humans may be afflicted for a dangerous amount of time. Three days also correspond to Sumerian and other national myths denoting the length of time needed for gods to make hazardous journeys to the underworld (Allen 213; Wineman 63).

What is the source of the three-days motif? The answer is unknown and probably unknowable, but one reasonable theory is that it corresponds to what the ancients saw when they looked into the night sky. For three nights when the new moon is in its dark phase, it is not visible and seems to vanish. Jonah "disappears" inside the great fish for three days and nights, is presumably lost, and undergoes a type of spiritual death. Yet he miraculously is brought back to life at the end of this symbolic time period.

No wonder, then, that the three-day motif is continued in the New Testament. Jesus dies on the cross and is buried in the tomb for three days before being resurrected (e.g., Luke 24:21). From a mythological point of view, this period is the same three days that Jonah is in the fish's belly before being returned to the land of the living, and Christians view Jonah's story as prefiguring Christ's time in the grave. In this standard mythological motif, "the novitiate [was placed] in a grave or coffin, out of which he was raised to new life" (Simpson 35). Often such stories, as the one in the gospels, include a descent into the underworld and thus demonstrate the hero's triumph and power over death. The initiated person is reborn as a changed individual, purified in body and soul. Both Jesus and Jonah undergo a kind of physical death and spiritual resurrection. Jesus himself compares the two of them when he scolds scribes and Pharisees who desire to see a "sign." Jesus rebukes them, saying: "An evil and adulterous generation asks for a sign, but no sign will be given to it except the sign of the prophet Jonah. For just as Jonah was three days and three nights in the belly of the sea monster, so for three days and three nights the Son of Man will be in the heart of the earth" (Matt 12:39–40).

Though Jonah is in the belly of the fish for the relatively long time of three days and nights, the fearsome animal actually serves as a sort of rescue craft at sea. Old translations of the Jonah story indicate that a whale (not a fish) ingests him. Admittedly, the sea monster is an odd type of conveyance, an entirely different sort of vessel than the ship from which he has just been hurled. Landlubbers like the ancient Israelites might be hard pressed to describe any sort of sea creature in convincing detail — shark, porpoise, whale, whatever. That Jonah is gobbled by an oceangoing animal certainly stretches credulity, as George Gershwin's song from *Porgy and Bess* states: "he made his home in / that fish's abdomen. It ain't necessarily so." The first Greek translation of the Hebrew Scriptures, the Septuagint, states that "the LORD commanded a great whale to swallow up Jonas" (1095). The fanciful whale-of-a-tale idea stuck throughout the centuries, and even today the story of "Jonah and the Whale" is much better known worldwide than the more accurate translation of Jonah and the big fish (דג גדול).

Translation arguments aside, debate remains as to how hospitable or hostile the huge fish really is. God appoints it, but does it function as a benevolent savior or a malevolent sea dragon? Is it friend or foe? Is Jonah entering the innermost recesses of his own soul or what Ps 23 calls the "valley of deepest darkness"? While the fish's gigantic size makes it appear more ferocious than any creature inhabiting the ocean, the book of Jonah never portrays it as a predatory animal that combs the surface of the ocean searching for innocent prey. This fish is no seafaring garbage disposal, shredding trash that litters the ocean. The fish contains no stinging tail or poisonous tentacles, as would a stingray or Portuguese man-of-war. The narrator mentions no razor-sharp rows of teeth, found in carnivorous sharks. The fish does not tear Jonah limb from limb or chew him to pieces. The prophet is apparently swallowed whole and remains otherwise uninjured. The story-teller remains cool and matter-of-fact as he describes Jonah being engulfed by what several critics have described as a benign "sea taxi." If, however, the fish is a Leviathan-type monster, the message of the book of Jonah is that our threatening, internal demons can be transformed into saving graces. A hero must undergo a maturation process, a rite of passage. Typically, the challenge is to defeat the monster that represents the unconscious. The fish is thus awesome but not horrific. It represents our internal struggles, our daily battles that we are capable of overcoming.

As he enters the fish's gaping maw, Jonah passes through a kind of "magical threshold" and into the beast's body (Campbell, *Hero* 90). The midrash suggests that the mouth of the fish is comparable to the portals of a large synagogue (*Pirkê de Rabbi Eliezer* 69). Jonah's passing into this strange dungeon is thus like a pilgrimage to a holy place. Threshold im-agery is found throughout literature, from the majesty of heaven's "open door, which no one is able to shut" (Rev 3:8) to the absurdity of the rab-bit hole through which Alice falls into Wonderland. When characters pass through a threshold, they enter another plane of consciousness, a new realm of existence, and the reader can bet that wondrous, cataclysmic events are about to transpire. In chapter 2 of the book of Jonah, our hero does not exactly "go gentle into that good night" (as poet Dylan Thomas suggests one should never do). But neither does the monster annihilate the prophet. The dark, unknown fish does not harm Jonah, as it would if it were meant to punish the prophet for his transgression of heading for Tarshish. Sink-ing into the fish's mouth, Jonah leaves behind the light-filled world, albeit one that has recently grown black with thunderclouds. Jonah knows and understands the upper world, but he is now banished from God's sight into a netherworld that the prophet has heretofore never experienced, compared to Sheol in Jonah 2:3. When he disappears into the mouth of the great fish, those still onboard ship must think Jonah has died. The mariners would log-ically deduce that Jonah is no more, but their conclusion is mistaken. Jonah is alive and though perhaps not entirely well, he is on the mend. Jonah's passing through the fish's threshold is a form of self-annihilation, a journey inward after which the prophet can be reinvented, his holy spirit rekindled, his sacred mission reborn. By "dying" to his physical self, as represented by his captivity in the fish's belly, Jonah has an opportunity to be reawakened spiritually to life and duty, to love and forgiveness.

Metaphorically, Jonah's sojourn inside the fish symbolizes that an in-dividual can indeed survive an examination of the unconscious. In a sense, our bodies and souls benefit from such strenuous water aerobics. From this perspective, the fish represents a safe haven, not a penalty, for the prophet who needs time to reevaluate himself carefully. One need not fear the voyage within, though the potentially overwhelming impact of such a journey should not be underestimated. This will be no easy jaunt. Jonah's world is about to be turned upside down, to disintegrate so that a new one can emerge. Allegorically, Jonah being ingested by the colossal beast parallels Israel being overrun by the Babylonians at the time of the exile, certainly one of the most painful of national experiences. Jonah could have avoided the confrontation with the huge fish and the Israelites could have avoided exile (according to Lamentations and other biblical works) if they had been obedient and pleased God. Jonah's inability to avoid the fish and Israel's inability to escape the second slavery show that God has special plans for the chosen people who cannot circumvent their election. During the awe-inspiring ordeal inside the fish, Jonah must come to terms with his anguish and small-mindedness. He will face his demons and emerge, as does any character who encounters a fearful monster, as one who is somehow transformed, at least temporarily.

The Bible does not mention which direction the fish swims while it carries Jonah. One may assume, however, that it heads easterly, the direction where the narrator would expect to find land. The east also carries with it important symbolism. It is the direction of the rising sun, the new beginning, the fresh start. Most important, east is the direction leading back toward God's holy city of Jerusalem, the destination of the faithful.

Since the fish provided by the Lord is arguably headed in the right direction, there is no reason to assume that it is anything but an instrument of divine deliverance and that God is always closer than we imagine, ready to grant forgiveness. This fish is the opposite of the sea serpent of Amos 9:3, created by God to search out sinners wherever they may try to hide: "And if they conceal themselves from My sight / At the bottom of the sea, / There I will command / The serpent to bite them." On the contrary, this fish is a "beneficent device for returning Jonah to the place where he may reassume the commission he had previously abandoned" (Landes 12).

In 2:1 of the book of Jonah, the fish (דג) has a masculine gender, but in the very next verse, 2:2, the fish is feminine (דגה). Its femininity has led modern scholars to associate the sea with amniotic fluid, the fish with the womb, and Jonah with an embryo. At the very least, the fluctuation in gender reveals the author's ambivalence about the nature of the fish (Zimmerman 582). The text itself indicates that the great fish is female, thus protective and sheltering of the "new" being inside it. In the womb the little life can grow because it is safely held and nurtured.

Since the earliest days of biblical exegesis, people have imagined elaborate supplements to the scant detail provided by the narrator concerning Jonah's experience. The midrash suggests that at the beginning of time, God created this fish that would someday swallow Jonah (*Pirkê de Rabbi Eliezer* 69). One commentary is especially provocative:

> With everything that was created during the six days of creation, God made certain stipulations, about which Scripture says, "I, even My hands, have stretched out the heavens, and all their host have I commanded" (Isa. 45:12). I commanded the Red Sea to split apart for Israel; I commanded heaven and earth to be silent before Moses; I commanded the sun and the moon to stand still before Joshua; I commanded the heavens to open before Ezekiel; I commanded the fish to spew out Jonah; I commanded the fire to do no hurt to Hananiah, Mishael, and Azariah; I commanded the lions not to harm Daniel. (Bialik and Ravnitzky 16)

In other words, at the moment the universe was created, God ordained the marvels later recorded in the Hebrew Scriptures and considered the prophet Jonah among the worthy men who would deserve divine salvation and forgiveness.

Other ancient embellishments to the book of Jonah, referred to by Simpson (101) as "rabbinical rubbish," propose that the immense creature has eyes as large as windows allowing the prisoner Jonah to look out, or that lamplight dots the dark interior so that Jonah can see while he is inside. According to others, a giant pearl is suspended within the fish's intestines and illuminates the whale's innards so the prophet is not plunged into total darkness (*Pirkê de Rabbi Eliezer* 69–70). The Zohar contends that when Jonah is dumped into the ocean, he instantly dies of fright. His soul leaves his body and is transported to heaven where it is judged by God and returned to the sea. When Jonah's soul reverts to its former earthly abode and touches the mouth of the fish, the marine animal dies but is miraculously revived after three days (Hirsch 227). Thus the Zohar provides commentary on the soul's relation to the body and to the Lord's salvation.

The most fanciful and complex story claims that the great male fish tells Jonah that he is to be consumed by Leviathan, the Bible's ocean-dwelling symbol of chaos. Jonah bravely asks the fish to take him directly to Leviathan and promises the fish to save both their lives. Upon meeting the dreaded sea monster, Jonah flashes the seal of Abraham, causing the terrified creature to dart quickly away. As a reward for this valorous service, the fish then gives Jonah a ride around the world to show him its wonders — the route taken by the ancient Israelites across the Sea of Reeds (also called the Red Sea), the pillars holding up the earth, and so on (*Pirkê de Rabbi Eliezer* 70–71). Thus pass three days and nights, the time the Hebrew Scriptures say that Jonah spends in the fish's belly. In other traditions the ornate story continues and parallels what the book of Jonah reveals in 2:1 and 2:2 — the fish's gender change (from a large male to a smaller female). The extrabiblical story further suggests that Jonah is then transferred from the belly of a male fish to the body of a female carrying many unborn fry. (A hint for this idea is first suggested in the Talmud, Nedarin 51b: "perhaps he was vomited forth by the large [male] fish and swallowed again by a smaller [female] one.") In this cramped, uterine environment Jonah is uncomfortable, so he finally decides to pray to God for forgiveness. After his prayer, Jonah is spit up on dry land, a sight witnessed by the sailors who originally throw him overboard. The crew is so overcome with the splendor of the event that they discard their idols, return to Joppa, continue to Jerusalem, undergo circumcision, and become Jews (Hirsch 227; Bialik and Ravnitzky 134).

A final, rather humorous sidelong note to all these myths about Jonah is the way many critics bend themselves into pretzels in order to explain away Jonah's experience when he is trapped inside the great fish. Those who find the biblical story too fantastical concoct rational explanations about what happens to Jonah. For instance, some theorize that Jonah is picked up in the water by another ship called the "Big Fish" or that he spends three nights at an inn named "At the Sign of the Whale." In *Moby Dick* Melville's fictional crewman, Sag-Harbor, doubts the veracity of the Bible story. He conjectures that "when Jonah was thrown overboard from the Joppa ship, he straightway effected his escape to another vessel nearby, some vessel with a whale for a figure-head ... possibly called 'The Whale,' as some craft are nowadays christened the 'Shark,' the 'Gull,' the 'Eagle'" (Melville 392). Faithless Sag-Harbor also suggests that the whale is merely "a life-preserver ... which the endangered prophet swam to, and so was saved from a watery doom" (Melville 392). Another explanation for those who find the miracle too hard to swallow is that Jonah dreams the whole incident while asleep in the hold of the ship (Bickerman 4), not so unlikely an interpretation, given the Bible's penchant for heroes having important dreams. If Jonah's experience is a dream, he awakens with stronger intentions to obey God's call.

The early biblical commentators are not the only ones who carefully craft stories of men in peril on the sea. Variations on Jonah's engulfment tale are found in myths told worldwide throughout the centuries. Joseph Campbell explains why:

> The story of Jonah and the whale is an example of a mythic theme that is practically universal, of the hero going into a fish's belly and ultimately coming out again, transformed. The whale represents the power of life locked in the unconscious, and the creature in the water is the life or energy of the unconscious, which has overwhelmed the conscious personality and must be disempowered, overcome and controlled. (*Power* 147)

Jonah and heroes of other mythical tales are given the opportunity to emerge as changed individuals. Psychologist Beth Hedva reflects on the "archetypal pattern of growth and change found in ancient and indigenous cross-cultural rites of initiation. Initiatory rites of passage may show us how to find our way through pain, separation, alienation, and shock of betrayal — to feel fully alive again" (5). Mythological stories from all over the globe mirror Jonah's experience. Jonah needs to learn obedience and compassion before he can practice forgiveness. As is evident from his tale and many others wherein a person is plunged into the sea of unconsciousness, lessons of forgiveness or bravery or whatever the protagonist needs to learn are internalized. Yet despite the trauma of initiation via watery ordeal, characters from the myths of ancient Greece to the films of George Lucas have trouble achieving sustained perfection when they return to their routine lives.

Sometimes early church fathers found it helpful to cite, "for the benefit of unbelievers" (Bickerman 11), Greek and other mythological parallels to the story of Jonah, fights between a deity and a monster. The envelopment theme speaks to humanity's most universal and profound fears concerning introspection and/or death, but they also fascinate us because they show human beings tending to the everyday business of conquering big fears. The engulfment theme is found in antique tales belonging to Eskimos along the Bering Strait, Mexicans, Indians, Japanese, Chinese, Australians, New Zealanders, Polynesians, and Africans, among many others. The details change with the environment of the primitive storytellers. Sea coastal people spin yarns about gruesome sperm whales, poisonous sea serpents, giant clams capable of devouring people, or octopi with strangling tentacles. In the stories from landlocked societies, sea creatures disappear and are replaced by large land animals such as elephants or wolves. Typically, the hero is alone when the monster overtakes him, and the beast must be defeated so the story can end happily.

Many Greek and Roman poets, including Simonides of Ceos (556–468 B.C.E.) and Ovid (43 B.C.E.–17 C.E.), tell and retell the tale of Perseus, which is analogous to Jonah's story in several ways. King Acrisius fears a prophecy that his newborn grandson, Perseus, would grow into a man and commit regicide. The king constructs a great chest, places the infant Perseus in it, and casts it onto the sea. Saved by the gods who take an interest in his case, another detail corresponding to Jonah's situation, Perseus survives pummeling waves and later slays the frightful Medusa (Hamilton 141–48). Also in Greek mythology is the story of Hesione, daughter of Laomedon, King of Troy. Hercules rescues her from a sea monster that swallows the mighty Hercules, but he kills the beast by hacking up its innards. Perhaps the most impressive engulfment myth involves Greek Titan Kronos (called Saturn by the Romans). Kronos, son of Uranos (sky) and Gaia (earth), is the father of Zeus. Learning that his son is plotting to dethrone him, Kronos swallows many of his children, including Demeter, Hera, Hades, and Poseidon. Zeus escapes his father's wrath only because his mother rescues him, whereas Jonah escapes death because of a fish provided by a benevolent, forgiving Lord. What all these tales share is the common motif of a protagonist's engulfment that results in his changed outlook and role.

Another famous connection to the Jonah story concerns Jason and "The Quest for the Golden Fleece," the title of a popular classical Greek poem by third-century B.C.E. poet Apollonius of Rhodes. Jason and his brave collection of companions aboard the ship *Argo* face many disasters at sea while they attempt the nearly impossible assignment of obtaining the Golden Fleece to please evil King Pelias. Almost all their challenges involve raging winds and ocean storms. First, Jason and his men go ashore at Lemnos, where only women live. All the men are dead, except one who is saved when his daughter puts him inside a chest (reminiscent of Jonah's helpful fish) and sets it adrift on a rough sea. Next, a handsome crewman named Hylas is lost at sea because a water nymph desires to kiss the youth and drags him down to a watery grave. Also, the men encounter the Clashing Rocks, which perpetually careen into one another and smash to pieces all ships trying to sail through them. Jason sends a dove (recall that Jonah's name means "dove") to test the bird's ability to navigate safely through the Clashing Rocks. When the dove succeeds, Jason realizes his men will also be able to row through the giant rolling stones and escape the sea's mischief (Hamilton 117–22). Whether a deliberate parallel or not, Jonah's Hebrew name, "Yônah," can be transliterated into Greek as "Iônas," a metathesis of Jason or Iason (Hamel 344). The book of Jonah may have been one of the first stories of seafaring woes, but it certainly is not the last. In the Greek version of the trial by water, Jonah's counterpart must bravely pass the initiation test to emerge as a braver, more confident leader of people.

Sometimes sea animals are friendly and save human beings in trouble. For example, Arion, a poet and musician, was apparently a real person (c. 700 B.C.E.) but led an almost mythic life. Although none of his poetry has survived, stories about him endure to this day. He travels from Corinth to Sicily, enters a music contest, and wins. On the voyage home, jealous sailors covet the prize and plot to kill Arion by throwing him overboard. His last request is to sing and play his lyre. After Arion is flung into the ocean (shades of Jonah), dolphins that are enchanted by his sweet music safely give Arion a ride back to dry land (Hamilton 289). By comparison, the psalm composing much of chapter 2 in the book of Jonah could parallel mythic songs concerning congenial animals that appreciate good music (Hamel 346), and the helpful dolphins can easily be compared to Jonah's salvational fish. In both cases sea creatures save the protagonists from disaster.

Many well-known novels of more modern times have nautical themes connected to Jonah. For example, Daniel Defoe's *Robinson Crusoe* (1719) tells of a man who, like Jonah, runs away to sea. Crusoe is shipwrecked and lives a solitary life for many years. In fleeing to sea, one could argue that Crusoe and Jonah are both running from themselves and what their lives have become. In Melville's *Moby Dick*, the fictional minister, Father Mapple, compares the whale's ivory teeth to prison bars (Melville 51), and Captain Ahab's crew comprises a mixture of races and religions, just like the mariners on Jonah's ship. Vengeful Ahab is on a kind of sacrilegious quest, pursuing the whale at the cost of the crew and his own soul. A few years later, in his 1870 novel, *Twenty Thousand Leagues under the Sea*, French writer Jules Verne creates another megalomaniacal character, Captain Nemo. The captain captures ocean explorers investigating marine disturbances, and the novel is noted for its prognostication of the submarine in which Nemo lives. Submarines had yet to be invented in Verne's time, but Nemo's strange craft functions rather like Jonah's whale in the Talmudic story about the animal giving Jonah a tour of the undersea world. More recently filmmaker George Lucas uses "standard mythological figures" (Campbell, *Power* 145) in his *Star Wars* movies. For instance, in the first film to be released in the series, the trash compactor scene where the walls close in and threaten to crush the characters is a modern-day retelling of Jonah's perils in the belly of the fish. Again, the characters emerge with renewed dedication to carry out their mission, and Han Solo discovers that he is less mercenary and more moral than he had imagined.

Inlanders before and after biblical times developed animal engulfment myths about bears and other large land creatures. The Zulus of interior Africa have a story about a mother and her two children who are ingested by an elephant. Imprisoned inside this largest of land mammals, the mother sees the whole world reflected in microcosm, as Jonah does inside the great fish. Perhaps best known of the engulfment legends is the children's fairy tale of Pinocchio (1883) by Carlo Collodi, pen name of Italian writer Carlo Lorenzini. Pinocchio, a puppet who comes to life, has many adventures designed to teach him (and his youthful audience) the difference between right and wrong. When swallowed by a fierce Dogfish, Pinocchio meets his real father, who has also been captured by the beast. The two of them compare adventures and later walk out of the asthmatic creature's mouth. One of the most memorable scenes, immortalized by Walt Disney in a 1943 full-length animated cartoon, is Pinocchio's harrowing experience and lessons learned after being swallowed by a whale. Also, most children know the fairytale of Little Red Riding Hood, adapted in the nineteenth century by the brothers Grimm but well known before their rendition. It is another tormenting tale of engulfment. A pleasant little girl visits her grandmother and is devoured by a wolf disguised as the old lady. The fairy tale ends when a hunter cuts open the wolf and releases the imprisoned girl. Yet another example is legendary Irish hero, Finn MacCool (whose character may be based on a historical person). Finn, leader of a band of warriors, has countless adventures with giants and hags. In a vestigial echo of the Jonah story, an amorphous monster swallows and then releases Finn. Across the ocean Mishe-Nahma, the great sturgeon and king of fishes, swallows Native American Hiawatha, immortalized by Henry Wadsworth Longfellow's epic poem. Hiawatha delivers a deathblow to the fish's heart, and its body is consumed by helpful birds of prey that release the hero. All these stories are initiation rituals wherein the main character, like Jonah, faces a serious dilemma and emerges changed by the experience. Engulfment, whether on land or sea, is a universal mythic experience symbolizing spiritual death and resurrection.

In many mythic tales, "the novitiate went through rites that implied a simulating of death, which was followed by a new birth, — often this was symbolized by pretending to descend into the underworld" (Simpson 12). The *Book of the Dead* is a collection of magic incantations and prayers used in ancient Egypt as a guidebook for the dead on their journey to the underworld, but it differs dramatically from the Jonah story because the initiate is not allowed to return to the visible world. Yet the Egyptians did have resuscitation stories, as in the raising of Osiris, ruler and judge of the dead, in a rite that the Egyptians reenacted annually. Similarly, the Babylonians celebrated the yearly awakening of Tammuz, a Mesopotamian underworld deity. Stories of death and rebirth are found in so many countries that it is hard to account for the similarities. Patterns of migration do not adequately explain the degree to which people who have never had any contact with one another tell the same types of stories, including those resembling the book of Jonah. A possible explanation is the existence of a collective human consciousness, a worldwide awareness of the same fundamental principles of life. Whatever the reason, initiation, death, and resurrection stories have existed from the earliest stages of human civilization.

In all these myths and legends, forgiveness is seldom sought or achieved by the main characters, but many of them have something in common with Jonah. They often learn from their ordeals, and at the end of Jonah's experience in the fish's belly at chapter 2 and beginning of chapter 3, we see how much the prophet has gleaned from his fantastical sojourn. Yet among all these myths from around the world, the story of Jonah remains unique. Its four small chapters explore, in more depth and with more power than other myths, theological issues including human fallibility, divine compassion and forgiveness, and how human and divine personalities interact.

The Psalm of Thanksgiving

In the book of Jonah, something almost miraculous occurs and speeds the moment of Jonah's deliverance. The rebellious prophet, locked inside the fish in a simulated death, launches a go-for-broke offensive and decides to pray: "Jonah prayed to the LORD his God from the belly of the fish" (2:2). Allegorically, as Jonah cries to the Almighty from within the abyss, he stands with generations of believers who have faced disaster and called to God for help (Landes 23), yet Jonah does not directly ask God to release him from his present calamity or to forgive his trespasses. Instead, he acknowledges that deliverance, akin to forgiveness, lies squarely within the domain of divine providence (2:10).

Ironically, as he is alone and sinking into the depths of the fish's innards, Jonah at last attains the height of his spirituality and achieves a degree of religious maturity not previously seen in the sailor episode of chapter 1. In contrast to the mariners' public supplications at 1:5 and 1:14, Jonah's prayer in chapter 2 is a private matter between the prophet and God. It is not designed to impress or please the ship's captain or anyone else. When Jonah finally petitions God, he is by himself, seeking the approval of no other humans and not within earshot of anyone who might judge his motives. In the Jerusalem temple, psalms were sung publicly in the presence of the entire congregation. Yet here, confined inside a dark enclosure where the light of day and humanity are eclipsed from his sight, Jonah discovers a higher morality than he previously exhibited on the ship. The forces of nature, at

God's behest, return Jonah to his master. In the "aqua psalm" (Sherwood 238) that composes the bulk of chapter 2 (verses 3–10), Jonah seems to be reborn to his higher self, and the audience's sympathy for the prophet is rekindled. The prayer is a way to psyche out and wipe out Jonah's internal monster.

Many of the prophet's adventures invite controversial reaction in readers and critics, but none so much as the poem in chapter 2. This psalm presents textual problems that have plagued Bible scholars for centuries and make it hard to insist that the poem was originally part of the story. Historically, critics have argued that the supplication of chapter 2 is a later interpolation, penned by someone other than the original author and inserted into the prose narrative. Perhaps a poem already in circulation at the time was lifted and placed near the middle of the book of Jonah. It was not added willy-nilly but deliberately introduced at this moment by a pious editor who found it unthinkable that a man facing danger would not stop to pray or would be saved without petitioning God.

The earliest sources of the book of Jonah — the Dead Sea Scrolls and the Septuagint translation — offer the poem in basically the same form and location as current Bibles (Landes 9–10; Perkins). Would it make a difference if Jonah's petition to God in chapter 2 were in the form of prose rather than poetry? In those moments when the soul seeks God, prose is sometimes insufficiently inspirational, and the "higher" technique of poetry is preferred. Through imaginative images, sensory impressions, and rhythmic outpourings of the human heart, poetry can reach aesthetic heights and elevate the reader's soul in ways that elude pedestrian prose. Whenever a prose narrative stops and a poem is inserted into the biblical narrative, something very special is happening and the reader should take note. For instance, the wilderness experience of the Israelites is framed by poems on both sides of the adventures in the desert. After the parting of the Sea of Reeds, as the children of Israel stand safely on dry land and watch Pharaoh's soldiers drown, they pause and sing a victory song, a poem recorded at Exod 15:1–18. Then the prose recommences and continues virtually unbroken until the end of the wanderings in the desert at Deut 32:1–43. The two poems serve as bookends to support the prose narrative of liberation from Egypt, and they are beautiful additions to the story. Also, the song of Deborah (Judg 5) provides a poetic variation on Judg 4, enhancing the prose story and adding interesting detail. The poem in Dan 2:19–23 and many other poems within prose narratives in the Hebrew Scriptures all have the same general salutatory effect. Similarly, the poem inserted into the book of Jonah adds immensely to the aesthetics of the work. The poetry lifts the tale out of the realm of ordinary storytelling and into the region of the sublime.

The appearance of poetry in the midst of prose is not unique to the book of Jonah. Poetry does, in fact, represent a convention of ancient Hebraic literature (Watts 135). The poem within the narrative of Jonah is neither an accident nor a literary whim, but a recognized technique used by writers and/or editors. (Practically all biblical writing was edited, either by the original author or by someone else.) The book of Psalms was probably the hymnal of the Jerusalem temple. If scribes, who had ready access to those preexisting hymns, inserted this one into the book of Jonah, they chose it for its aptness to the theme of Jonah's obedience/salvation/forgiveness dilemma.

Today at New York's Broadway and London's West End theaters, a convention marks an apt analogy to the psalm's insertion into the book of Jonah. Most of a modern musical comedy is composed of dialogue that the actors speak to each other (or occasionally direct to the audience). Frequently, however, the action is suspended to insert a vocal number (and perhaps a dance) into the play. Strictly speaking, the song is not always essential to advancing the plot, but is an enjoyable interlude that draws in the audience and complements the dialogue. The audience is so engaged by these musical compositions that they are generally followed by applause, further halting the drama's action but also enhancing its effect. The consequence of the psalm in the second chapter is similar for an audience today, and that result would have been even greater in ancient times when the story was read aloud and performed dramatically (Watts 139–40). More importantly, though the poem halts the narrative momentum, tension in the plot results. The poem intensifies audience awareness that an ethical story is being told. This strategy of including the poem directs the reader to an undeniable moral interpretation, especially in the poem's last lines (2:10).

Jonah's flight and his stiff-necked refusal to pray in chapter 1 make the poem of chapter 2 seem inconsistent with the prophet's character and thus create tension in the plot. The psalm may be appropriate to his situation now that he is at the point of death, but it seems inappropriate to the narrator's prior characterization of Jonah as rebellious, disobedient, angry, selfish, and sullen. Among the psalm's most astonishing features are that it fails to acknowledge Jonah's previous rapscallion behavior onboard ship and does not reference Jonah's current precarious position inside the fish. These omissions are glaring and are perhaps further evidence that the psalm was written by someone else and grafted onto the book of Jonah. The poem certainly highlights Jonah's denial of his obligation to obey God promptly.

Perhaps a change in Jonah is beginning to take place, and the poem is used to create a climate where the audience must review its opinion of Jonah as a narcissistic prophet. We do not really have enough information about Jonah's personality to understand yet whether his prayer is an expression of rock-solid faith that God will emancipate him, ambivalence about God's ability and willingness to help, or certainty that his cause is now totally lost. We must read further for a clearer picture of the chameleon prophet.

Josephus accepts the notion that the poem was uttered after Jonah is redeposited on dry land (Salters 31). By the time of twelfth-century Ibn Ezra, the poem was typically seen as a hymn of thanksgiving for aid already rendered rather than a plea for help to come. Ibn Ezra disputes this assertion and claims that chapter 2 is prophecy anticipating Jonah's future restoration to God's good graces (Cohen, *Twelve* 142). Another view is that because the fish saves Jonah from drowning, the prophet already has adequate reason to express gratitude, even though he is still in crisis. He remains in deep water, but he is alive and protected by the divinely appointed fish.

A little poem entitled "Jonah" by Aldous Huxley (1894–1963) advances the notion of how the prophet's beautiful prayer resonates within the fish's inner cavity and fills the great creature with music. When Jonah prays he chants "canticles and hymns" that resonate within the fish's empty insides. The prophet's song touts divine glory and mystery, and the beast "spouts music as he swims" (Huxley 102). In this poem, Jonah's song magically transforms the frightful beast into a kind of floating symphony.

Jonah's prayer has inspired other artists who adapt and retell it. One especially poignant example is in *Moby Dick*. Herman Melville's fictional preacher, Father Mapple, leads his congregation in a hymn reminiscent of Jonah's plight:

> The ribs and terrors in the whale,
>   Arched over me a dismal gloom,
> While all God's sun-lit waves rolled by,
>   And lift me deepening down to doom.
>
> I saw the opening maw of hell,
>   With endless pains and sorrows there;
> Which none but they that feel can tell—
>   Oh, I was plunging to despair.
>
> In black distress, I called my God,
>   When I could scarce believe him mine,

> He bowed his ear to my complaints —
>   No more the whale did me confine.
>
> With speed he flew to my relief,
>   As on a radiant dolphin borne;
> Awful, yet bright, as lightning shone
>   The face of my Deliverer God.
>
> My song for ever shall record
>   That terrible, that joyful hour;
> I give the glory to my God,
>   His all the mercy and the power. (45–46)

Everyone in Father Mapple's church joins in the singing. Just as Huxley's "Jonah" suggests that the prophet's hymn fills the fish with music, Melville's hymn fills the church and is loud enough to drown out the sounds of a storm raging outside. Melville's plot-stopping poem is a moving variation of the one found in the second chapter of the book of Jonah, entirely appropriate to the novel's storyline and a fitting tribute to its ancient counterpart. Chapter 2 thus becomes a paradigm of prayers to God, a model for others to come.

But Jonah's prayer is hardly unique within the Bible. His psalm bears striking resemblance to several others in the TANAKH. Line-by-line analysis reveals blatant borrowings from more than a dozen psalms (including Pss 18, 24, 30, 31, 42, 69, 88, 107, 116, 120, 124, 142, 143). Chapter 2 of the book of Jonah is a "cento, picking verses from other psalms . . . and 'reinterpreting' them, adapting them to the present situation" (Daube 41). In fact, chapter 2 is "a pastiche of psalms of deliverance. One recognizes formulae that are almost clichés in the psalter. . . . Only two verses have no identical phrases borrowed from other psalms, and these two verses also have equivalent counterparts" (Lillegard 25). The poem is thus highly derivative, duplicating a pattern of familiar musical language contained in representative specimens dotted throughout Psalms. Nevertheless, while Jonah's poem contains lines that are familiar to avid Bible readers, Jonah's poem also remains unique. Comparisons to other poems remain superficial. No other psalm in the Bible so directly depicts Jonah's plight; few others so specifically reflect his need for forgiveness and his change of heart.

Though psalms fall into several categories, hymns of thanksgiving are the sort most frequently found in the book of Psalms. Typically, they pay tribute to the Lord for healing the speaker from illness or disease, preserving the speaker from enemies, or guiding the speaker out of trouble. Poems of thanksgiving are not entirely joyful, however. They often lament that God is slow to respond to the plaintiff's cry of pain, angrily insist that life is unfair, and present an ill-tempered outlet for the poet's darkest emotions. Yet God is also praised in thanksgiving poems, indicating that when we feel like hell, we sing anyway. Regardless of our current afflictions, we acknowledge God's justice and promise of deliverance.

Jonah's psalm fits well into this category of thanksgiving poems, but herein could lie the beginnings of satire. If Jonah, face-to-face with his own mortality, is merely parroting the words of others, reciting by rote phrases that have become meaningless prattle to him, then his repentance is insincere and he remains fundamentally unchanged. Some believe that a profound incongruity exists between Jonah's dire plight at sea and the psalm's expression of gratitude for liberation. The author of Lamentations writes of his foes:

> They have ended my life in a pit
> And cast stones at me.
> Waters flowed over my head;
> I said: I am lost! (53–54)

Perhaps Jonah's poem should contain a similar cry of despair in addition to its thanksgiving.

The argument is also made that the psalm in chapter 2 is a diversion or perhaps a pleasant ornament, but certainly superfluous to the plot. Some critics reject outright the poem as later accretion. Regardless of what skeptics say, the poem is an indispensable part of the story. It is even possible that the poem came first. It might have originally been written by the eighth-century prophet named Jonah, son of Amittai, who is mentioned in 2 Kings, and the prose story was a later addition (Landes 3). Other critics prefer the notion that a postexilic redactor wrote the poem (or borrowed a preexisting one) and inserted it into the original prose story. Either way, the poem is a brilliant literary stroke. With echoes of the storm motif from the previous episode and imitations of popular psalms, the poem fits right into the story and is an especially artistic component of the overall work. A prose narrative that goes directly from 2:1 to 2:11 and excludes the poem would miss the opportunity for Jonah's moving transformation. Without the poem, Jonah would lack the chance to grow, to make the deliberate change of heart he will need when he again walks on dry land.

Jonah does not straightforwardly ask for forgiveness in the poem, although Josephus adds at v. 7, "O Lord my God, let my ruined life be restored." In the Bible, Jonah's plea for help remains indirect. He is contrite throughout chapter 2, and the act of saying a prayer should be interpreted as an act of repentance. Jonah's passivity in chapter 1 is now replaced by the action of composing and reciting the poem (Emmerson 87).

Without doubt, the poem in chapter 2 adduces the notion of divine forgiveness and is therefore a fulcrum, a crucial ingredient to the prophet's major dilemma. Regardless of who wrote it or when it was placed into the narrative, seeing the psalm as vital to the story makes a significant difference in the way the overall messages of human repentance and God's power of forgiveness are made manifest in the book. At the very moment when all appears lost, all is gained. New growth emerges from the stump of Jonah's old life, just as new plants spring forth from the remains of fallen trees in the forest. The efficacy of prayer is shown, for prayer is essential to the resurrection theme of the book. Jonah enters the jaws of the fish as a lost and condemned man, but his prayer grants him the opportunity to start afresh, offering the hopeful message that from the depths of the netherworld's despair, repentance is possible and forgiveness will surely follow. Jonah may now reaffirm his subservience to God.

Jonah's psalm is also a kind of interior monologue, a literary technique similar to stream of consciousness in a novel, which records directly the innermost emotions of a character. An interior monologue allows the story's narrator to disappear completely so that the prophet himself can present his feelings and thoughts. The psalm offers a much-needed opportunity for Jonah to take the time he needs to reevaluate his life and make peace with his God. Arguably, every prayer offered by a human being is a kind of interior monologue.

Yet right from the start, this interior monologue presents critical conundrums. Verbs are one of the first anomalies that one notices, for they appear in the past tense:

> In my trouble I called to the LORD,
> And He answered me;
> From the belly of Sheol I cried out,
> And You heard my voice. (2:3)

The text offers no evidence that Jonah prays in chapter 1 when the captain of the ship wakes the sleeping prophet and begs him to call upon his deity. While the mariners offer up petitions to the Lord, Jonah remains silent. So the past tense of the verbs in 2:3 cannot refer to Jonah's previous behavior. (Alternatively, if Jonah does utter a prayer in chapter 1, our omniscient narrator chooses not record it.) To make more sense in the context of the psalm's present location within the overall story, the present tense should be employed, for Jonah is currently inside the fish's belly. Perhaps the Scripture

should logically begin, "In my trouble I call (or am calling) to the LORD."
A shift from third person "he" to second person "you" is typically found in
poems throughout the book of Psalms and often simply implies the speaker's
increasingly personal connection to the Almighty. But the shift to the past
verb tense is stranger, considering the circumstances that lead a stubborn
Jonah to alight inside the fish.

Church father St. Jerome (c. 342–429), baffled by the verb tenses of
chapter 2, points out that the psalm, as constructed, is not a prayer for
rescue but a praise for deliverance and forgiveness already bestowed (Bickerman 12). In the year 386 Jerome made a pilgrimage to Bethlehem and
settled there, where he completed his Vulgate version of the Bible, the first
translation of the Scriptures from Hebrew into Latin. In the Vulgate Jerome
changed the original text's past tense, so concerned was he by the peculiar
verb problem.

Others, more committed to maintaining the integrity of the original Hebrew's past tenses, were faced with interpretational difficulties. Quite often,
as far back as medieval times, critics found meaning in the poem by viewing
the prayer as a flashback, spoken by Jonah as he remembers his ordeal after
he is spewed back onto shore. Flashback is a device employed by many authors to rearrange or collapse time dramatically and achieve a literary effect,
usually exposition. Perhaps the psalm in the book of Jonah is intended as
a deliberate jumbling of time, allowing the prophet to relive and thus reor-
ganize the point when his life was endangered. A redeemed Jonah from a
later time period could thus be recalling the hazards of his previous situation, which would account for the past verb tenses of the poem (Gunn and
Fewell 133). Furthermore, when we remember the past, we can recover the
present (Lacocque and Lacocque, *Psycho* 95).

Jonah's prayer to God indicates at 2:3 that he cries out from Sheol,
the ancient Hebrew term for the underworld to which souls of the dead are
consigned. Sheol is neither heaven nor hell nor purgatory, and it corresponds
directly to no Christian concept of the afterlife. It is not a place of eternal
reward or punishment; it is simply a repository for dead spirits. Sheol's
location in most TANAKH passages is downward (Gen 37:35; Isa 14:9, 15;
Amos 9:2; Ps 30:4); it is dark (Job 17:13); it is devoid of learning or wisdom
(Eccl 9:10). Jonah's indication that he is in Sheol indicates that he probably
already numbers himself among the dead, for Sheol is synonymous with
the grave (Isa 28:15, 18). Ironically, Jonah cries "from the belly of Sheol,"
מבטן שאול, which also carries the connotation of "from the womb of Sheol"
(Simpson 99), with all its rebirth meanings clearly evident. At this early
juncture, Jonah does not seem to realize that the fish is the instrument of

his salvation that saves him from downing. Soon, however, the poem will become a psalm of thanksgiving for his deliverance.

The Koran's treatment of Jonah's reaction inside the fish is simpler than the Bible's. The Koran does not mention Sheol directly but alludes to "the depths of darkness." Surah 21:87 refers to Allah in the plural and states Jonah's confession of sin:

> And remember Dhu al Nun [the man of the Fish]
> When he departed in wrath:
> He imagined that We
> Had no power over him!
> But he cried through the depths
> Of darkness, "There is
> No god but Thou:
> Glory to Thee: I was
> Indeed wrong!"

This passage is the Koran's closest equivalent to Jonah's psalm in the Bible's chapter 2, and in it the speaker avows his misdeeds — a necessary step in the process of obtaining forgiveness.

In the biblical prayer we begin to learn more about Jonah, what motivates him and what characterizes his relationship to God. In Jonah 2:4 a forlorn prophet accuses God of being responsible for present woes: "You cast me into the depths, / Into the heart of the sea, . . . / All Your breakers and billows / Swept over me." Jonah blames God for all misfortunes and conveniently forgets that the sailors are the ones who hoist Jonah overboard at his own request. He does not yet understand that the huge fish equals a huge debt of gratitude that Jonah owes to God, but the past tense of 2:5 makes sense as a flashback: "I thought I was driven away / Out of Your sight." In earlier days Jonah mistakenly believed that he and God were separated; now he is beginning to comprehend matters more clearly.

Verse 2:5 continues with Jonah's lament that he may never again see the holy city of Jerusalem: "Would I ever gaze again / Upon Your holy Temple?" The Lord's presence, which Jonah has deliberately avoided since fleeing to Tarshish at 1:3, is associated with the masterful Jerusalem shrine, located in the southern kingdom of Judah. The temple was, quite simply, the center of Jewish spiritual and religious life for over a thousand years, first constructed by King Solomon on sacred Mount Moriah. The Torah dictates that every able-bodied Israelite should make a pilgrimage to the temple three times a year for festivals. The temple was the symbolic home of Yahweh on earth and the centralized focus of the religion. There sacrifices were made, services held, and rituals conducted. It is no wonder that Jonah, though he is a northerner, hopes that his prayer will be acknowledged in God's dwelling place. Jonah mourns the notion that he may now forever be separated from the Zion temple. His earlier flight notwithstanding, as Jonah faces death he longs to stand again at the temple, his eternal spiritual home base, the center of his universe.

The author of the psalm seems thoroughly conservative, an adherent to orthodoxy as it was practiced in Jerusalem. The poem alludes to many temple rituals. If the author were more liberal, he could also be satiric — less enveloped in and dedicated to strict interpretations of Torah and not so adamant about observing laws and traditions. A liberal author may be deliberately trying to humiliate the prophet. By making him a bellicose northerner and having a fish become nauseated over swallowing him, the author may be satirizing the Sadducees, the most traditional party in power in Jerusalem (Lacocque and Lacocque, *Psycho* 99).

As he contemplates perpetual separation from God, Jonah's thoughts return to his experience in the sea: "The waters closed in over me, / The deep engulfed me. / Weeds twined around my head" (2:6). This passage vividly recalls that Jonah was in great danger of drowning when the sailors threw him overboard. The ocean's natural vegetation threatened to strangle him. Earlier translations make the situation seem even more desperate. The King James Bible, for instance, first published in 1611 and sometimes containing different verse numbers, states: "The waters compassed me about, / even to the soul: / the depth closed me round about, / the weeds were wrapped about my head" (2:5). The King James translation, almost identical to the JPS 1917 version, is supported by the 1985 JPS translation of the text at 2:8, which uses the Hebrew word נפש, meaning soul, but translates it as "life": "When my life was ebbing away." The King James and 1917 JPS versions rightly indicate Jonah's feeling "that more than his body is submerged" (Warshaw 192). A growing realization of his need for divine forgiveness emerges as Jonah finds the vine-infested, seaweedy deep engulfing him.

Verse 2:7 brings to a nadir the startling imagery of just how low Jonah has sunk. Like Gilgamesh and others who move downward into the darkness of the underworld, Jonah plummets "to the base of the mountains." This descent motif is first used when he goes down into the bowels of the ship to sleep at 1:5 and continues when he sinks into the sea at 2:4. The ancients believed that subterranean pillars supported the world, so Jonah has now dropped as far as humanly possible, to the very foundation of the earth. Prison imagery completes v. 7, as "the bars of the earth closed upon me forever." He fears that his disobedience will serve as prison irons, jail him, and continue to separate him from the land of the living. Jonah could at this point respond affirmatively to Yahweh's query to Job: "Have you penetrated to the sources of the sea, / Or walked in the recesses of the deep? / Have the gates of death been disclosed to you? / Have you seen the gates of deep darkness?" (Job 38:16–17). Jonah indeed has fully experienced the bleakest regions the soul can know.

Yet at this instant when Jonah has sunk to the nether regions of the universe and in a continuation of the same verse describing prison bars, a change in the psalm's tone occurs. The long descent concludes and an ascent begins. At the moment of his greatest despair comes a confident affirmation: "Yet You brought my life up from the pit, / O LORD my God!" (Jonah 2:7). The next verse elaborates upon this triumph:

> When my life [נפש, soul] was ebbing away,
> I called the LORD to mind;
> And my prayer came before You,
> Into Your holy Temple. (2:8)

Jonah's previous fear of being separated from God, as symbolized by exile from the holy temple in Jerusalem, vanishes. Ibn Ezra interprets "holy Temple" to mean God's abode in heaven, rather than the building in Judah's capital city, but the midrash and most commentators prefer to consider it to be a concrete reference to Jerusalem (Kahn 91).

Verse 8 offers textual problems, however, for the prayer to which it refers seems to have been uttered at an earlier time and is not given in the narrative. Nonetheless, the main point is that Jonah now believes he will survive because his prayer has been answered. This stanza is therefore pivotal to the issue of forgiveness. For forgiveness to occur, the sinner's petition for God to bestow divine grace must precede it. This concept, certainly not unique to the book of Jonah, will become the foundation of the religious idea of forgiveness. Its significance cannot be overstated.

The psalm continues by expressing pity for those, either ignorant foreigners or Israelites who have abandoned the ancient covenant, who are not yet reassured concerning divine grace: "They who cling to empty folly / Forsake their own welfare" (2:9). A 1985 JPS TANAKH footnote indicates that the meaning of this Hebrew verse is uncertain, and it has received various translations. Earlier versions, including the 1917 JPS, say, "They that regard lying vanities / Forsake their own mercy." Protestant theologian and reformer John Calvin (1509–64) defines "lying vanities" as "all inventions with which men deceive themselves" (Cohen, *Twelve* 144). Cohen also equates "their own mercy" to God's lovingkindness, for God is the originator of all mercy (144). The NRSV says, "Those who worship vain idols / forsake their true loyalty." Bowing to idols is the height of foolishness, for they can offer no help. All of these translations point to the inevitable conclusion that people who do not embrace Yahweh are only hurting themselves.

The psalm concludes with an open proclamation of Jonah's newfound fidelity to God. Jonah will manifest (future tense, not past tense) his devotion through action — vociferous praise, penitent sacrifice, and committed vows:

> But I, with loud thanksgiving,
> Will sacrifice to You;
> What I have vowed I will perform.
> Deliverance is the LORD's! (2:10)

Thus the prayer ends with Jonah's reflections on salvation. The future tense makes it clear that Jonah believes he has been saved, for he makes promises to be kept in days to come. He pledges to worship — to sing loudly of God's glory and to accompany his grateful homage with offerings, presumably when he returns to the Jerusalem temple. The Bible often reminds readers to enter God's house with praises on our lips, as in, "Enter His gates with praise, / His courts with acclamation" (Ps 100:4). Praise equals warfare against demons within and without. At the moment of the prophet's greatest despair, God accepts Jonah's sacrifice. In ancient times animals were sacrificed at the temple, but Jonah's offering will be different. It is what the New Testament book of Hebrews refers to as "a sacrifice of praise" (13:15). The Lord accepts heartfelt offerings: "True sacrifice to God is a contrite spirit; / God, You will not despise / a contrite and crushed heart" (Ps 51:19). Jonah, crushed almost to the point of death, surrenders an extremely valuable commodity — his humbled self-esteem — and places it on a metaphorical altar. The prophet concedes his dependence on Yahweh's compassion.

The vow that the prophet promises to fulfill at Jonah 2:10 parallels the one made by the mariners in 1:16, at last bringing Jonah up to the moral level of the foreigners. Ironically, he has heretofore trailed in the wake of the heathen crew's religious action. Chapters 1 and 2 both end with promises to sacrifice to God, first made by the sailors and now by Jonah. When in jeopardy, foreigners and native-born Israelites must finally acknowledge their own need to pray and accept God's ability to establish sovereignty.

Jonah's prayer climaxes in 2:10 as he meditates on God's power to rescue and redeem. This conviction that salvation belongs to God sums up one message of the book of Jonah: deliverance "is neither a reward for merit nor a tempering of justice with mercy. It is, instead, a free and gracious act of divine love" (Cooper 144). Furthermore, Jonah's previous complacency appears now displaced by a firm commitment to reform. Greek and other mythological heroes overcome their problems by acts of physical prowess (such as slaying a dragon) or by mental maneuvers (such as answering a riddle). Jonah, on the other hand, is not a Giant Killer. He is released from the great fish because of repentant prayer. A similar path to liberation is found in the tale of Daniel, a prophet frequently in trouble because Babylonian kings resent his prayers to God. Just as Jonah's newfound faithfulness results in his delivery from the jaws of the huge fish, Daniel escapes the lions' jaws by displaying his faithfulness, admittedly far more unwavering than Jonah's. By affecting this change of heart, Jonah fulfills the notion of passing from death to life (Lacocque and Lacocque, *Complex* 53). Continuing with the fish as a womb image, God now prepares to cut Jonah's umbilical cord, delivering the prophet from fear and psychological immaturity. Because of God's compassion, Jonah may again join the land of the living. In fact, the Hebrew word for "compassion," רחמים, has the same root as "womb," רחם. Forgiveness requires a kind of death, the death of hostile feelings and the rebirth of compassionate ones. The death and resurrection motif in the book of Jonah, understood by Christians to prefigure the crucifixion and rising of Jesus, represents a dying of our old selves and a reawakening to a new life.

In 2:11 Jonah is restored to human society: "The LORD commanded the fish, and it spewed Jonah out upon dry land." Mirkhond states that Jonah is expelled "like an infant wrapped in swaddling-clothes" (Simpson 86), which is certainly a gentle way to think of Jonah's removal from the fish's belly. "Spew" in English is generally defined as "gush" or "eject," but a more forceful elimination is not implied in "spew." Older Bibles, including the 1917 JPS version, give an alternative, also accurate translation of the Hebrew transitive verb קיא (printed for grammatical reasons as ויקא in the text) as "vomit" and say that the fish "vomited out Jonah upon the dry land." In English "vomit" is typically defined as an undignified regurgitation or violent expulsion. To vomit out Jonah is shockingly brutal. It naturally leads generations of critics to point out the potential hypocrisy of Jonah's metamorphosis at the end of the prayer. They see humor, irony, "audacious parody" (Mather 284), and even satire in the fish's allergic reaction to the belatedness of Jonah's sincerity in the psalm he has just uttered. After what could be regarded as the prophet's self-righteous, facile, or perfunctory proclamations in the belly of fish, the beast gets sick to its stomach and throws up. An alternative interpretation of "vomit" is that a fierce expulsion is necessary to remove Jonah from the fish so that he is encouraged along his way to Nineveh. Without such ferocious prodding, the prophet might have been willing to stay inside the great fish's belly until God forgets about him or has a change of heart about the assignment to Nineveh. The biting commentary of James Crenshaw is typical of yet another explanation: "This entire psalm is a devastating mockery of Israelite piety as it is exemplified by the dubious prophet whose sole concern was ... a restriction of divine compassion to Israel" (381). Such stinging criticism is predicated partly upon קיא being translated as the repulsive word "vomit" with its extreme negative connotations in English.

But "spew out" is also an accurate translation for קיא, and though it may have coarse connotations of spitting up from the mouth, it does seem gentler than "vomit" and does not necessarily point so directly to satire as an essential feature of the episode. This verb is used in the Hebrew Scriptures at Lev 18:24, 28 and at 20:22, referring to sinful Israel being expelled from the promised land. Once again, the older translations use the term "vomit," but the newer JPS version prefers what some may regard as the kindlier "spew out" when the broader context suggests the Israelite people. The only exception comes in the new JPS version at Isa 28:8, when God gathers the remnant of the chosen people and pronounces judgment on the wicked of Judah by vomiting them out. The 1985 JPS version consistently uses "vomit," however, when referring to God's disgust with Egypt (Isa 19:14), Moab (Jer 48:26), and Job's false friend Zophar (Job 20:15). Given that both the terms "vomit" and "spew out" are accurate translations, the choice may depend upon connotations of the word and upon the translator's interpretation of God's attitude toward Jonah, the Jewish people, and the enemies of the Jews.

A loving God who is in charge of the fish commands it first to ingest and then to expel Jonah. Both times the fish's actions are crafted by Yahweh to save the prophet's life. Allegorically, engulfment by the fish represents Israel's forced exile at the time of the Babylonian captivity, but even that punishment is a result of God's loving desire to bring the people back from their errant ways. Chapters 3 and 4 of the book of Jonah show that God clearly has not yet finished trying to mold the prophet. Jonah is recalcitrant, but God desires to teach him more lessons about love, mercy, and forgiveness. Therefore, that God intends to satirize the prophet beyond all hope of redemption is doubtful. After all, Jonah is to be an instrument of God in Nineveh. True, the Almighty has had more stalwart prophets, but that does not mean the Lord will easily give up on Jonah. Humor is present for those who want to see it, but satirizing Jonah is not the main point of the episode.

The Koran contains no vestiges of satire. Surah 68:49–50 declares:

Had not Grace
From His Lord
Reached [Jonah], he
Would indeed have been
Cast off on the naked
Shore, in disgrace.

Thus did his Lord
Choose him and make him
Of the company
Of the Righteous.

In the Koran, Jonah's sincere repentance restores him to Allah's favor and releases him from physical and psychological pain.

The fish and the poem/psalm, as they appear in chapter 2 of the book of Jonah, have many positive functions. They engage readers, reawaken our sympathy for the wayward prophet, give him time to reflect upon his perilous situation and to have a change of attitude, and advance the book's implied theme of divine forgiveness. They also provide closure for the episode begun in chapter 1 on the deck of a ship headed to faraway Tarshish. Finally, the poem's concluding phrase, "Deliverance is the LORD's" (2:10), causes the reader to celebrate Jonah's salvation. We will soon discover, however, that our celebration is premature. Resurrection from deathlike disobedience is not necessarily a once-in-a-lifetime event. Life may figuratively be a series of passages from "life" to "death" and back again. For Jonah the song sung inside the fish of chapter 2 is a false climax to the symphony of his psyche. Plenty more cacophony is to come. The narrative's major tension has yet to be truly solved. Now that God appears to have forgiven the prophet, one would think that Jonah would eagerly, enthusiastically extend that same forgiveness to others. But Jonah will encounter the forgiveness dilemma in chapter 3, and he will face it with characteristic ambivalence.

CHAPTER 4

Nineveh's Disobedience

If you pardon, we will mend.
— Shakespeare,
A Midsummer Night's Dream

A second chance is a blessing from God. How many times have we wished that we could unsay something we have said, undo something we have done, redo something we have failed to complete properly? Who among us has not disobeyed our own conscience and capitulated to selfish desires? When we give in to our wants and ignore our duties, we may fear that we have forfeited any special relationship we have tried to create with the Lord. The book of Jonah teaches otherwise. Blown by the winds of promise, Jonah is wafted back onto shore. When "the word of the LORD came to Jonah a second time" (3:1), the prophet is indeed fortunate. While Jonah calls to the Lord (2:3) and pledges to make sacrifices (2:10), nowhere is he actually shown to ask forgiveness for his previous refusal to obey God and preach to the Ninevites. Yet Jonah has another opportunity to right a wrong, to correct a misstep, to solve a dilemma, to reconcile with God. Because our egos are strong and our flesh is weak, service to God necessitates that we be forgiven for past mistakes and allowed to begin again. Jonah does not remain in the womb, in the grave, or in the belly of the huge fish. He passes into a new stage of development, analogous to moving from infancy to adolescence.

When the commission comes for the second time, Jonah realizes that he must accept the job he previously refused. "The word of the LORD" is also the "soft murmuring sound" or "still, small voice" (1 Kgs 19:12) from within, the voice of conscience. As suggested earlier in an interpretation that goes well beyond the scope of the biblical text, what Carl Jung calls the "Shadow" is that darker portion of Jonah's self. According to Jung's theory, Jonah's reluctance to minister to the Ninevites may be seen as a wish to preserve this piece of himself, a piece that he would know needs punishment. Perhaps he even believes that receiving divine retribution would signal his deeper connection to God. On the other hand, his disobedience and desire

81

not to go to Nineveh could represent his attempt to deny and run from his Shadow, those aspects of his personality he desires to reject. In agreeing at last to go to shadowy Nineveh, Jonah implicitly acknowledges his need to confront his murky side and repent. Earlier he fled the word of God. Now he is well on his way to defeating the inner enemy and becoming his authentic self.

There is an old Jewish story about a man who looks around and sees the plight of the world. At every turn he detects human misery — starvation, poverty, war, and heartache of all kinds. In anger and desperation, he shakes an angry fist at God and rails, "How can you allow your people to suffer like this? What kind of God are you? Don't you care about humanity? Why don't you do something to help?" The clouds part and a voice from heaven patiently replies, "I did something. I sent you." The story does not go on to reveal the man's response, but it is not hard to imagine his shock at being selected by God to help others in time of crisis. Few of us would feel worthy; few of us would see it as our responsibility to solve society's problems. Whether he likes it or not, Jonah is the one being called, and he has to receive the message twice before understanding his obligations.

In the Hebrew Scriptures several cities are synonymous with sin, including Sodom, Gomorrah, Babylon, and Nineveh. For centuries the Israelites would remember the atrocities committed by citizens of these cities. Linguistically, Nineveh is linked with the tales of Sodom, Gomorrah, and Babylon, for the "wickedness" of all four towns is repeatedly mentioned. This establishes a theme of evil that begins in Genesis and continues to the days of Nineveh when Assyrian hordes destroy Israelite land. Ninevite values are the opposite of Israelite values, and going to the evil city would be the same to Jonah as going again into the belly of Sheol. Having just won his deliverance by claiming devotion to God in the huge fish, Jonah must have been simultaneously astonished and resigned to the fact that divine will is immutable. He has to travel to the huge city as originally ordered. God has saved Jonah and now expects to be served in return.

Nineveh is one of the most ancient cities in the world. In 721 B.C.E. the powerful Assyrian empire, commanded by King Shalmaneser, swooped down and annexed the northern kingdom of Israel (2 Kgs 18:10). The southern kingdom of Judah continued to exist independently, though the people lived under the Assyrians' shadow and were forced to pay heavy tributary. Eventually, in 612 B.C.E., Nineveh was overthrown by Babylon, but most biblical references continue to reflect the Jews' animosity toward their vanquished enemy. Nineveh became the capital of Assyria at the time of powerful King Sennacherib (705–681 B.C.E.). Sennacherib launched an impressive building program and constructed a magnificent city, extending and beautifying Nineveh to become the showplace of its day, a veritable ancient Versailles with a palace, temple, gardens, and administrative buildings (Allen 221). From the capital city, wars were launched, and the Ninevites established a reputation for brutality. Even if the book of Jonah were composed long after the days of Shalmaneser and Sennacherib, the Jews would not have forgotten the humiliation and ill treatment they received at the hands of Nineveh's leaders and citizens. The Assyrians invaded surrounding territory repeatedly as they burned and plundered cities and deported the inhabitants. To the Israelites, the immorality and criminality of Nineveh would be self-evident, and they would have good reason to continue fearing Ninevite rapine. The town is associated with political deceit, military savagery, violent plunder, and blasphemous anti-God practices.

Nineveh, "like Rome in the days of the rabbis, imposed its yoke upon the Holy Land and the holy people" (Bickerman 16). In the New Testament's Revelation to John, Babylon is personified as the "great whore" (17:1), but to the Israelites of Jonah's time, the evil lady is Nineveh. Nahum and Zephaniah foretell the city's destruction. For the Israelites, the day could not come too soon. Nineveh, with its perfidious history, richly deserved its reputation for wickedness. Modern-day people can perhaps understand the degree of Jewish antipathy toward the Ninevites by comparing them to the Nazis of the twentieth century. Though it may be unwise to compare the evil of any other empire to that of the Third Reich, Chaim Lewis's hyperbolic description is apt for those who remember the horrors of the Holocaust when the ashes of murdered Jewish victims blackened the sky:

> What Nineveh meant in the mythology of Israel can be understood only by our generation who carry the searing memory of Auschwitz. The Assyrians were the Nazi stormtroopers of the ancient world. They were a pitiless power-crazed foe. They showed no quarter in battle, uprooting entire peoples in their fury for conquest. They extinguished the northern Kingdom of Israel to leave us only with a tender memory of the yet to be revealed lost ten tribes. For Jonah, Nineveh then was no ordinary city; it carried doom-laden, tragic memories; it stood as a symbol of evil incarnate. (162)

Tarshish represents distance from God, but Nineveh represents blackest depravity. To ancient Israelites the name Nineveh, Assyria's capital, would have had similar connotations to Berlin when it was Hitler's capital from 1933 to 1945. Forgiving hideous crimes would cause no small dilemma for the Jews of either era.

Archeological evidence substantiates the Bible's claim that Nineveh was a great city of Mesopotamia. The name of Nineveh is associated etymologically with the Assyrian "nunu," a fish (Simpson 141). Water, so important in chapter 2 of the book of Jonah, is one of the essentials of life, both animal and vegetable. The sea is the reservoir of water; out of it comes ancient, life-giving deities. The fish, living within the sea, is therefore associated with the ocean's creative power, for the water is seen as the primal source of all things. Leviathan and Behemoth are variants of Jonah's great fish. It is also possible to think of the city of Nineveh as being connected with the fish. In cuneiform the representation for Nineveh is a two-story building with a fish on the bottom floor (Simpson 157). Thus, the name of the city to which Jonah is sent is expressed in writing from the earliest times by combining the symbols for house and fish, which has led some commentators to the theory that Jonah was never in the sea at all, as a literal reading of chapter 2 would suggest. Instead, he was in Nineveh the entire time (Simpson 158).

According to Gen 10:8–11, the first great king mentioned in the Hebrew Scriptures, Nimrod, founded Nineveh. Nineteenth-century British explorer and political advisor to the Shah of Iran, Henry Rawlinson, discovered the ancient city's site in the early 1850s (Gabel et al. 47). For a couple of millennia its strategic location along the Tigris River, near present-day Mosul in northern Iraq, allowed Nineveh to maintain its bloody stranglehold on the region. The Bible's labeling of Nineveh as "that great city" is potentially hurtful to the Jews, since the same term is applied to Jerusalem when its destruction is predicted in Jer 22:8. Jerusalem is supposed to be the antithesis of Nineveh, but ironically the Bible employs the same epithet to describe them both.

God's command for Jonah to go to Nineveh is now repeated, perhaps to indicate that divine will has not changed and perhaps to show God's determination in saving the worst of sinners. Jonah is told, "Go at once to Nineveh, that great city, and proclaim to it what I tell you" (Jonah 3:2). This decree is not entirely new, but a partial repetition of the directive given at 1:2. The language of the recommissioning is slightly different. The first part of 3:2 is an exact duplicate of 1:2: "Go at once to Nineveh, that great city," but the second section modifies chapter 1's edict.

Though the evil city of Nineveh is named as Jonah's destination in both chapters 1 and 3, the nature of the command is different when God gives it a second time. In chapter 1 Jonah is told to "proclaim judgment upon it" (וקרא עליה), but in chapter 3 Jonah must "proclaim to it (וקרא אליה) what I tell you." The 1985 JPS translation suggests that God originally commands Jonah to condemn the city. The wording of 1:2 has a harsh, threatening tone.

Jonah's role is clear: to announce the city's doom. (If Jonah and all Israel hate the enemy Ninevites, the prophet would likely relish the opportunity to preach their demise to their faces. Jonah's flight in chapter 1 makes little sense if he indeed despises the people and wants them dead.) In chapter 3 God seems to retreat somewhat and suggests that the exact nature of the message will be entrusted to Jonah later. For the present, only God knows the content of the forthcoming command. If the Lord plans to dictate the precise language of the oracle, then Jonah has no room for personal maneuvering or altering of the message. The text at 3:2 reveals that God intends to provide a script and prompt the lead actor, but the Lord is cryptic and vague about what Jonah will soon be directed to say. The more God is involved with determining the message, the more difficult it will be for Jonah to stray from the script, no matter how he feels about it.

"Without a revelation there can be no prophet" (*Interpreter's Bible* 6:875). Jonah must now wait for the revelation. Chapter 3 of the Bible story does not clarify what Jonah already knows about the message to be delivered in Nineveh. Yet the prophet's experience in the belly of the huge fish has turned him to submission, for "Jonah went at once to Nineveh in accordance with the LORD's command" (3:3). Why does Jonah now leave without murmuring a single syllable of complaint? Has he learned that he cannot escape God's gaze? Does he fear punishment if he tries to flee again? Is he sincerely grateful for deliverance provided by the huge fish? Are praises of the poem in chapter 2 still on Jonah's lips as he heads for Nineveh?

What the Bible omits is sometimes as important as what it includes. In this case, it does not suggest that Jonah proceeds to Nineveh with happiness in his heart. It does not indicate that he joyfully embraces his extraordinary opportunity to become more obedient, denounce wrongdoing, correct social injustice, or reverse the fate of a doomed people. The Bible simply states that Jonah goes. After his experience in the big fish's belly, Jonah defers to God at last, but it is to be a grudging obedience. The ancient words from Horace's *Epistles* apply: "Those who cross the sea, change the sky above them but not their souls" (Book I, xi, line 27). Human nature sometimes causes individuals to avoid unpleasant tasks, especially when they involve overcoming bad habits from the past. Jonah does not burn for a chance to serve God or yearn to cross the desert like a sandstorm, but his problem is more serious than mere laziness. From start to finish, his story is about a person who tries to circumvent divine will. Jonah's compliance will soon be vitiated by his continuing antipathy toward the Ninevites.

Jonah sets out to the big city: "Nineveh was an enormously large city a three days' walk across" (3:3). The past tense may indicate that the actual city had passed into myth and memory by the time the story is written down. In other biblical passages, however, it is simply used as a narrative past tense of the verb "to be" and carries no special connotation of "once was but is no longer." Then we see that the same adjective for "great," גדלה, is used to describe both the monstrous fish and the monstrous city, giving the impression that they are similar in their size and fearsome character. Nevertheless, the Hebrew for "enormously large city," עיר־גדלה לאלהים, can be literally translated as "a large city of God," which implies more precisely that the Lord considers Nineveh to be part of the divine kingdom. The literal translation foreshadows where the plot is eventually headed — toward God's love and forgiveness of Nineveh. It is also possible, however, that עיר־גדלה לאלהים means "a large city of myriad gods." For now, the reader only knows for certain that Jonah is entering a big metropolitan area.

Nineveh's exact size is a controversial issue. The author had probably never been to Nineveh and knew its vastness only by reputation. Perhaps the author gives the city's dimensions, "a three days' walk across" (3:3), to convey the enormity of Jonah's job. The three days it takes to traverse Nineveh correspond metaphorically to the time-consuming process of dealing with our darker fears, as Jonah does during his three days inside the great fish. Three days need not be interpreted literally. The population of the city, not specified until the end of chapter 4, is said to be 120,000 people. This may or may not be an accurate estimate of size, but it certainly underscores the book's numerous claims that Nineveh is a "great city."

At least one ancient Greek historian, Diodorus Siculus (first century B.C.E.), records that Nineveh's splendid walls were approximately fifty-five miles long, and if we apply Herodotus's estimate of seventeen miles as a reasonable day's walk, then the city would have been just over fifty miles long (Allen 221). Another interpretation is that it would require three days to meander through the city's maze of winding streets. It is also possible that the city comprises Nineveh plus a composite of smaller, nearby towns. Biblical evidence at Gen 10:11 states that the city and its suburbs (Nineveh, Rehoboth-ir, Calah, and Resen) are collectively grouped and designated as "the great city" (Cohen, *Twelve* 145–46). A 1920 study of Assyrian provinces includes a map of the Nineveh general administrative area circa 750 B.C.E., showing it to be about a three-day walk at its longest stretch. To biblical scribes, "city" and "province" were indistinguishable terms (Ferguson 306–7). Archaeological surveys dating back to the mid-nineteenth century indicate this four-city area to cover approximately sixty miles (Craigie 229), though excavations show that the single city of Nineveh was far less grand, perhaps having a circumference of eight miles. Alternatively, the magic number three may be employed by the author to exaggerate size. Comedy results from the author's deliberate hyperbole concerning colossal Nineveh. No ancient city could be so huge, and even the largest present-day city could be traversed on foot in less time. Today, for instance, the Old City of Jerusalem with its crenellated walls can be traversed on foot in about twenty minutes. The proportions of Nineveh seem abnormally magnified, but the reader is supposed to be astonished, not to get out a calculator and figure acreage. Nineveh is a city of epic proportion; its actual size is beside the point. Metaphorically, the challenge awaiting Jonah is mammoth.

After the huge fish spits Jonah out, we know not where, he still probably has a lot of walking to do before reaching Nineveh. As the prophet finally approaches the city (Jonah 3:4), the size of his task must become apparent. Though the Bible give us no account of a bustling Nineveh, its environs, or what the prophet thinks as he approaches, it is easy to imagine what his eyes behold and his mind projects. The surrounding countryside is lush and green along the Tigris River. Olive and citrus groves and fertile cultivated fields lie just outside the city walls. The dusty road to Nineveh meanders along the river and is crowded with merchants, farmers, and pilgrims having secular and sacred business in the big city. Once inside the city gates, Jonah roams past countless overcrowded homes. Adobe dwellings are packed in close proximity along the labyrinth of streets. Jonah feels lost as he wanders the narrow and winding streets. Some enormous houses have lovely gardens and elaborate wooden carvings, painted brightly to ward off evil spirits. Suddenly, without warning, tiny alleys give way to larger, straighter boulevards. A panoply of people appears. Jonah might see a person accidentally get trampled by a cart laden with vegetables or textiles. Some people look at him with curiosity or suspicion; others ignore him altogether. Women balance baskets on their heads and wear colorful embroidered caftans, shell or ivory jewelry obtained from traders, and leather sandals with bright beadwork. Children play games in the streets as the adults barter for goods and gossip with friends. Holy men look askance at the unruly, disrespectful youngsters. Soldiers in full military uniform march around with an air of official importance. Jonah eventually approaches the impressive palace adorned with marble, gold, and gemstone decorations. The imposing government buildings cause the prophet to contemplate this city rich in history but flowing with blood. Perhaps he senses the teeming streets as an excellent breeding place for hatred toward Israelites, and his own potential for hostility toward foreigners wells up inside him. Jonah is indeed a stranger in a strange land. As he walks, he prefers to fade into the miasma. Deeper into the city, which seems to reproduce right in front of his eyes and grow by the minute, the crowds thicken as he continues to walk. Dogs roam the streets, and animals are everywhere — mule-drawn pushcarts, goats with tinkling bells, sheep bleating for their food. As he attempts to act with outward calm, his heart races. Now that he is about to become God's mouthpiece, Jonah's impressions of the city are more immediate than they were when he was in his native land. All the Bible relates, however, is his brief prophecy.

The Prophecy

Though Nineveh is a three-days' journey across, the Bible says that Jonah only walks one day before proclaiming his message. He does not procrastinate and gets right down to business. At this point in the narrative, he deserves our admiration and affection. Going into the heart of the alien city, he boldly denounces it: "Forty days more, and Nineveh shall be overthrown!" (3:4). We know not what language Jonah speaks as he delivers the message; the author does not bother with such frivolous detail. It is miracle enough that Jonah reports for duty and that his audience understands; how they are able to comprehend the prophet is a question seldom posed.

In Hebrew Jonah speaks a mere five words at 3:4:

עוד ארבעים יום ונינוה נהפכת.

Though not the only prophecy in the book of Jonah, for he predicts at 1:12 that the sea would calm down if the sailors throw him overboard, this is an especially curt utterance and has no parallel anywhere else in the TANAKH. Jonah does not introduce himself to the people, get to known them, offer any credentials, or repeat his warning. He is the opposite of Cassandra, the Greek prophetess who cannot stop reiterating her message, even though no one listens. The Bible offers no suggestion that the Ninevites know of Jonah's success as a prophet in his homeland or his experience inside the belly of the fish. Perhaps most important, Jonah does not tell the Ninevites that his God is the source of the oracle. Instead of a salvo, he issues a single bombshell. Those experienced with Hebrew literature may recognize in the five-word prophecy the rhythm of the lament, found also in Amos 5:2 and Lam 1:3a (Limburg 80). This pattern would have been unfamiliar to the Ninevites, however. Maybe Jonah's lone pronouncement would have greater impact upon the people than an often-repeated, elaborate address, but Jonah's simple prediction seems mean-spirited and stingy. The author does not show the prophet wooing the people, winning their hearts and minds, and pleading with them to reform.

In forty days, says Jonah, Nineveh will be no more. Why the wait? The annihilation of Sodom comes immediately. Lot and his family have less than one day's notice to flee or be destroyed. The Sodomites are given no warning at all, no chance to change their ways. Yet in the book of Jonah, between the announcement and the impending destruction is a rather large amount of time. The text indicates (3:2) that God will author the message, so the deity has apparently built in a grace period, plenty of time for repentance. But why is the number forty selected? Forty, a number familiar to Bible readers, appears often in Scriptures. In the TANAKH, forty is an idiomatic expression signifying a long time and is not necessarily meant to be taken literally. Noah's flood lasts forty days and nights; Moses is instructed by God on Mount Sinai for forty days and nights; the Israelites wander in the desert forty years. If the forty days and nights appointed in the Synoptic Gospels for Jesus' temptation in the desert are added to the list, forty looks like the duration of a test that a hero or nation must undergo. In the Noah, Moses, and Jonah narratives, forty is associated with destruction delayed. God wipes out most of the world but spares Noah, his family, and the animals carried on the ark for forty days. When Moses leaves the children of Israel for forty days, they build a golden calf, causing God's threat to destroy them. Moses intercedes for his people, and when he again ascends the mountain for a second forty days with God, the people are subsequently forgiven. Forty is thus the number linked to divine compassion. In the forty days given to Nineveh, the people will also repent and receive God's mercy.

The Septuagint's prophecy has the same wording but reduces the forty days to three. Thus the three days of Jonah's sojourn in the fish's belly and the three days needed to cross Nineveh are repeated in the length of time before the prophecy comes to fruition, forming a nice aesthetic and literary touch. With a mere three days to decide how to respond, the tension is heightened, the length of the fast is plausible, and the entire city's quick reversal of attitude is more dramatic (though perhaps less believable).

The warning to the Ninevites implies that they will be punished if they do not repent, but Jonah preaches no such message. He is not a missionary trying to convert the heathen. He does not intercede with God on behalf of the Ninevites, and he does not urge them to mend their ways. What Jonah says is more in keeping with God's original demand that the prophet "proclaim judgment upon" the city (1:2), rather than God's 3:2 command to "proclaim to it what I tell you" (Angel 62). The Bible's forty days is a literary necessity in order to teach the lesson that God will grant mercy to those who ask forgiveness.

God delivers the content of the prophecy to Jonah in private. The narrator does not record the scene, so readers can only assume that Jonah obediently repeats the message as God reveals it to him. An alternative possibility is that unfriendly Jonah sabotages the prognostication (Lubeck 38) by changing God's conditional oracle to an unconditional one promising overthrow in forty days. Given that Nineveh is not demolished within that time frame, ascribing a message alteration to Jonah exonerates the Lord from lying to the Ninevites, toying with their emotions, and terrifying the people without ever intending to follow through on the threat.

One of the most frequently voiced objections to Jonah's prediction, even if delivered in wording that emanates from God, is that it is too brief and directly offers the Ninevites no alternatives. The people's fate is inescapable, and Jonah offers no hope of survival. Nevertheless, the brevity of the prophecy may actually conform to expectations among people in ancient Assyria, where "factual statements and predictions were always given in brief form and presumably elaborated by the Chief Secretary and interpreted orally" (Wiseman 46). The Ninevites may not expect the prognostication to be lengthy. It is an edict, and edicts give information, not explanations (Walton 44). The Greek term for a prediction that implies but does not state an alternative is "conditional fate," as opposed to "declaratory destiny," which operates like an unstoppable magic incantation (Bickerman 30–31).

Today weather forecasters do much the same thing as Jonah when they predict a tornado. Meteorologists cannot prevent the storm from happening, but they can foretell the approximate time of touchdown, and people can decide independently what precautions they should take to avoid loss of property and life. Sometimes Hebrew prophets declare an immutable truth to their audiences; at other times, they proclaim a softer scenario that can be altered by changing behavior. In Jonah's mind, Nineveh is like Sodom and Gomorrah. Destruction is imminent and sure. In historical fact, Nineveh's destruction *is* sure. The King James version of the Apocrypha expresses confidence in Jonah's prediction: "Go into Media, my son, for I surely believe those things which Jonas the prophet spake of Nineve, that it shall be overthrown" (Tob 14:4), but the NRSV changes the prophet's name from Jonas to Nahum. Destruction does not literally come in forty days, but if the symbolic meaning of a long time is recalled, Jonah's prophecy is accurate. Nineveh is eventually destroyed in 612 B.C.E., a fact probably already known to the original author and audience. The temporary reprieve won in the book of Jonah does not overrule God's inevitable plan to annihilate the wicked city, for the people's repentance and the Lord's forgiveness granted today cannot ensure pardon of future misdeeds.

The Koran corroborates the Bible's story and suggests that when the people demonstrate their faith, God forgives them and allows them to live for a time:

> When they believed,
> We removed from them
> The Penalty of Ignominy
> In the life of the Present,
> And permitted them to enjoy
> (Their life) for awhile.
>
> (Surah 10:98)

The Koran's assertion that the Ninevites live "for awhile" reflects the historical fact that their nation is later destroyed. It also may show the limits of prophecy when it varies with history. The reprieve found in the book of Jonah eventually passes away. Yet for the present, God is willing to allow the people to continue.

The prediction is that Nineveh will be "overthrown," נהפכת, from the verb הפך, the same term used in the Hebrew text and in the 1917 JPS translation to describe what happens to Sodom and Gomorrah, towns leveled by raining fire and brimstone (Gen 19:24). Nevertheless, הפך does not necessarily mean physical destruction. (In Hebrew "destroy" is quite different, אבד.) Instead, הפך can signify a spiritual overthrow of inappropriate worship and behavior, a "moral revolution" (Warshaw 201). The medieval French Jewish commentator Rashi (1040–1105) was the first to suggest that there is a paronomasia in the word "overthrown" and that Jonah does not comprehend his own prophecy. Jonah believes the city will physically collapse, whereas the story demonstrates a spiritual crumbling instead. In this sense, Jonah's prophecy is accurate immediately. Nineveh's familiar pagan ways are vanquished, at least temporarily (Jonah 3:5). Jonah's five-word prediction of overthrow is therefore deceptively simple. Actually, it contains two alternative renderings: that Nineveh will be wiped off the face of the earth or that Nineveh will be transformed. Because the latter is what transpires right away — the Ninevites experience a change of heart — it is reasonable to assume that transformation is what God intends the message to inspire. The author of the book of Jonah is revealing divine characteristics not presented by the author of the story about Sodom and Gomorrah. Nineveh's overthrow, of which Jonah speaks, occurs on a spiritual level, thus protecting him from becoming a false prophet when God later decides to spare the city. The Bible warns against false prophets, whose predictions are recognized as charlatan rantings when they do not come true: " 'How can we know that the oracle was not spoken by the LORD?' if the prophet speaks in the name of the LORD and the oracle does not come true, that oracle was not spoken by the LORD; the prophet has uttered it presumptuously: do not stand in dread of him" (Deut 18:21–22). There is no false prophecy in the book of Jonah, if הפך refers to a spiritual overthrow. Additionally, God's reputation as loving and forgiving is also guarded.

The Repentance

One of the book's most astonishing statements comes next: "The people of Nineveh believed God" (Jonah 3:5). *En masse* a city of colossal size undergoes colossal change. Without even a whisper of doubt, the entire city is transformed into a bastion of faithful penitents. The scale of their faith in God is epic and miraculous, involving everyone and everything, from the highest to the lowest, from the royal household to flocks of sheep. The city's size and reputation make the sudden switch hard to believe, even farcical, and the text is always accused of containing satiric hyperbole. The quick-thinking sailors in chapter 1 are now seen to foreshadow the Ninevites' abrupt transformation, but their speediness and efficiency strain credulity. Their instantaneous conversion stands in stark contrast to Jonah's stubborn refusal to obey God. Even under duress, Jonah is a reluctant prophet, yet the Ninevites quickly become believers.

The text does not indicate that the people believe Jonah. They believe God. The prophet has done nothing to ingratiate himself to the crowds, but they nonetheless acknowledge their sinfulness and show faith that Jonah's deity has the power to overthrow the city in forty days. Thus the sailors and the Ninevites are persuaded that the God of Jonah is supreme. Yet no biblical indication is available that they become Jews, accept Torah, undergo circumcision (though *Pirkê de Rabbi Eliezer* suggests that they do), give up idols, or make peace with the Israelites. How deep the Ninevites' belief goes remains legitimately open to question. Perhaps they are willing to do enough to save their lives in the present crisis but are not interested in becoming God's devotees forever. Their belief could be nothing more than a desperate, one-time attempt to stave off an emergency and avoid death.

In the New Testament, the citizenry of Nineveh is praised for its belief: "For just as Jonah became a sign to the people of Nineveh, so the Son of Man will be to this generation" (Luke 11:30). In the gospel of Matthew, the sign of Jonah relates to his three days in the belly of the fish, seen as a prophecy of Christ's three days in the tomb. Luke, however, offers a different twist to the Jonah reference. Luke points to God's power to forgive wickedness, for there is no direct evidence that the Ninevites know of Jonah's ordeal inside the great fish. Therefore, in Luke, Jonah does not become a sign to the Ninevites because of the miraculous delivery from the tempest at sea. Rather, Jonah becomes a sign of deliverance because the Ninevites are not destroyed, as Jesus becomes a sign of deliverance because of the resurrection (Swetnam 76). "The people of Nineveh will rise up at judgment with this generation and condemn it, because they repented at the proclamation of Jonah, and see, something greater than Jonah is here!" (Luke 11:32). The Ninevites are examples of faith and repentance that the gospel writer wishes his contemporaries would emulate with belief in Jesus. Therefore the mission of Jesus is related to that of Jonah. Both of them are called upon to preach to their generations (Brown 21). Scholars debate whether Matthew or Luke has the proper interpretation of the enigmatic sign of Jonah (Chow 53). In each gospel, the sign is linked to the Jews' not accepting Jesus as the Son of God. Matthew compares Jonah's sojourn in the fish to Christ's three-day burial in the earth, and Luke connects the Ninevites' repentance for wrongdoing to the Jews' failure to repent and acknowledge Christ's divinity.

The Koran ironically refers to the foreign Ninevites as the "People of Jonah" and also lauds them: "And We sent him / (On a mission) / To a hundred thousand / (Men) or more. / And they believed" (Surah 37:147–48). Why do they believe? Perhaps they thought the message fulfilled omens already received — a solar eclipse, an earthquake, or some other natural phenomenon. Reading the skies was commonly practiced in Assyria, and perhaps Jonah's pronouncement was just a matter of good timing, coinciding with other cataclysmic warnings from the Ninevites' own soothsayers and seers (Walton 45). Assyrians would certainly be familiar with the concept of placating an offended deity by offering sacrifices and supplications, but the story mentions no celestial or seismic event near the time Jonah is in Nineveh.

Given the immediate belief of the Gentiles at Jonah 3:5, the book is frequently cited for anti-Semitic purposes. According to this view, it is Jonah, more than the sailors or Ninevites, who needs to mend his relationship with God. The prophet's flight from God, refusal to pray when the sailors make supplications, and laconic utterance against the Ninevites have all been seen as implicit proof that Jonah hates outsiders. From there the gigantic leap is made about the xenophobic and ethnocentric Jews not wanting to share their status as God's people with any group of Gentiles. Yet the book of Jonah is clearly Jewish literature. Its author is an ancient Israelite who is telling the story to others of his own religion. The salvation that foreigners receive comes to them because of the act of an Israelite man, fallible and imperfect, but certainly a Hebrew. The sailors learn that Yahweh is the originator of the storm only because Jonah tells them. The Ninevites discover that they are marked for overthrow only from Jonah's prescience. Yes, the foreigners seem more active and devout than Jonah. The prophet is sometimes the object of irony, humor, and even satire. Yet the overall message remains that God has elected Jonah (Israel) to bring the message of divine salvation to the Gentile world. Originally, the author's intended audience is Israelite, not Assyrian. To interpret Jonah's message as being anti-Jewish, showing the Gentile world how to hate the Jews for their stinginess, is unfair and inaccurate. One of the book's purposes is to be a scolding of sorts to Jews, a reminder that God loves all people and that an intolerant attitude is not acceptable, but the message is given by Jews to Jews. Despite good reasons to discard an anti-Semitic interpretation, some critics revisit it in chapter 4 when they excoriate Jonah's anger over the Ninevites' salvation as an example of ongoing Jewish refusal to forgive the Gentiles.

Though the anti-Semitic interpretation should be rejected, when the people of Nineveh believe God, they do serve as an object lesson to Israel. If wicked foreigners can believe, so should God's chosen people. The Ninevites' sudden and complete reversal is in noticeable contrast to the continuing inattention that Israel pays to its prophets. In many stories of the Hebrew Scriptures, Israel is prosperous and idolatrous. Numerous prophets declare the need to reform and repent. Hearing about the Ninevites proclaiming a fast and donning sackcloth (3:5) would indirectly urge Jonah's countrymen to do the same thing. Furthermore, the book challenges all people, Israelite and non-Israelite, to be as submissive to Yahweh as the sailors and Ninevites.

The Ninevites, like the sailors, attempt to save themselves. The city's inhabitants fast and wear sackcloth. Fasting accompanies praying, whether a Bible passage explicitly says so or not. The Hebrew Scriptures frequently mention fasting, and the audience would be reminded of this tool of self-abasement as a traditional sign of penitence, especially effective when the whole community participates (Jer 36:9; Joel 2:15–16). The fast refers not only to abstention from food; it also designates an official period of mourning required by Israelite law (Wolff 151). The self-humiliation and irritation associated with donning sackcloth are an outward sign of inward piety. The scratchy mourning garments symbolize the wearers' willingness to make themselves uncomfortable before God and to put aside their previous life. The Ninevites' acts of denial and self-humiliation could indicate an acceptance of the judgment that God has rendered or an attempt to defer the punishment and sway God's opinion about the people. Fasting and wearing sackcloth are not commonly found in Mesopotamian literature (Walton 52), but they are ordinary acts of contrition in ancient Hebraic writings. The author is using penitent measures familiar to his own people, not necessarily recording what foreigners would normally do.

The miracle of the Ninevites' fasting and wearing sackcloth equals the miracle of Jonah being saved by the big fish. Rabbinic text claims that four groups of people are special to God: Israelites who have not sinned, Israelites who have sinned and repented, proselytes, and Gentiles who fear heaven (Bickerman 28). Jethro, the Gentile father-in-law of Moses (Gen 18:11); Ruth, the Moabite who accepts Yahweh (Ruth 1:16); and all the faceless and nameless people of Nineveh are examples of Gentiles who learn to revere God. Jonah's prophecy opens the Ninevites' eyes to the possibility of serving the Lord.

As the people of Nineveh do, so does their king. It is indeed curious that the king belatedly dons traditional Jewish mourning garb (sackcloth and ashes, Jonah 3:6) and declares, along with his nobles, that every person and animal must fast. Though only a tiny percentage of the population would hear Jonah's single-sentence prophecy, their grassroots repentance is already under way by the time the message reaches the sovereign and he springs into action. There is evidence that in the ancient world, alien visitors bearing medical, political, or religious news appeared before the local magistrate, or their information was brought to the attention of local authorities (Wiseman 43). When countries organized foreign delegations to conduct political business, seers would typically be part of the negotiating team. After double-checking for other omens to verify Jonah's claim, perhaps constellation readings made before Jonah's prognostication, the Assyrians would have little hesitation in accepting the foreigner's forecast (Walton 46). Therefore Jonah's prophecy would likely have come to the king's attention, provided that Jonah could present a letter of introduction or some other credentials. The narrator skips the superfluous details about how the king comes to receive the news. Considering the people's spontaneous belief and action, the king's proclamation seems unnecessary. It does, nevertheless, grant the added dignity and authority of royal power and parallel the repentance of King Hezekiah and all Judah in Jer 26:19.

In ancient times there was probably no such title as the king of Nineveh, just as today there is no title for the king of Madrid. Several studies have attempted to ascertain who this monarch of Nineveh might have been (e.g., Lawrence, Ferguson). Regardless of the truth concerning the character's actual existence, the narrator's point is clear. Readers would expect so mighty a monarch to resist vigorously the predictions of a foreign prophet, but here the king's action parallels that of the sea captain in chapter 1. Both characters are men in authority who instantly pay heed to Jonah's God. Just as the captain appears after the seamen to play his part in the narrative, so does the king appear after his subjects. The book of Jonah thus achieves parallel structure, and the readers are inclined to transfer their friendly feelings for the mariners and their captain to the Ninevites and their king. The ruler of Nineveh considers Jonah's dire warning to be leveled against himself as well as the people under his charge, just as the captain realizes that all aboard his craft are in danger.

A king's command cannot be ignored, no matter how outrageous. When he declares that "No man or beast — of flock or herd — shall taste anything!" (Jonah 3:6) and also "they shall be covered with sackcloth — man and beast — and shall cry mightily to God" (3:8), he invites smiles from many readers. It is funny, even ludicrous, that cattle are expected to fast, wear mourning clothes, and pray aloud. Surely the narrator jests with this overblown, repetitive portrait of spontaneous acceptance. Surely the readers are supposed to be incredulous. At the very least the narrator relishes hyperbole. The oft-held contention that the book of Jonah is satire rests, in part, on the assumption that it is ridiculous for animals to participate in repentance rituals.

Perhaps the stubborn Israelites are being mocked for refusing to put aside their sinfulness when numerous prophets urge them to mend their ways. Yet in the Apocrypha's Jdt 4:10, the Israelites cry to God for protection, and animals are included: "They and their wives and their children and their cattle and every resident alien and hired laborer and purchased slave — they all put sackcloth around their waists." Though odd, the custom is therefore not unheard of in Israelite culture. Furthermore, Herodotus (9:24) tells the story of a Persian military unit that cuts its horses' manes and tails as a sign of human grief when the commander is killed (Wolff 153). In the book of Joel only the priests fast and pass the night in sackcloth, but the cries of bewildered beasts are also interpreted at Joel 1:18 as petitions to God. Perhaps the idea in the book of Jonah is not that cattle are sinful and need to repent but that it is extra penance for the Ninevites to withhold food and drink from their livestock. Repentance must be sincere among the Ninevite community if the people are determined to include king and commoner, man and beast in the attempt to sway God. The act of the animals fasting and wearing sackcloth would bring all living things into sync and serve as an example of "the organic unity seen as pervading all of life, and the reality of animals comprising part of the basic topocosm of all life" (Schochet 53). The solidarity of all God's creatures, begun on the sixth day of creation when "every kind of living creature" (Gen 1:24) is formed, is thus reenacted in the book of Jonah.

The king also decrees that "everyone turn back from his evil ways and from the injustice of which he is guilty" (Jonah 3:8). In the beginning of chapter 1, the "wickedness" of Nineveh comes to God's attention, though the exact nature of the evil is not specified. The king, in a startling admission, acknowledges the sinfulness of his people. In the 1917 JPS translation of the same verse, the sin is now directly mentioned, as the people are urged by their sovereign to turn away from "the violence that is in their hands." The 1917 edition makes the same case for the corruption of the antediluvian world of Noah: "the earth was filled with violence" (Gen 6:11). Yet the rough people of Noah's time are given no opportunity to repent and are destroyed. The narrator of Jonah has a different purpose. "Violence" suggests that the Ninevites are domestically cruel to one another and excessively brutal with battlefield soldiers and civilian captives. The Ninevites are guilty of inhumanity. While discussing a 1992 Academy Award–winning film starring Clint Eastwood, *Unforgiven*, Gregory Jones posits that the movie's theme is an "unrelenting depiction of a world where forgiveness is assumed to be impossible or, at most, ineffective.... Violence is the inescapable reality that persistently tears at the fabric of people's lives until everyone is diminished, if not destroyed, by it" (*Embodying* 73). The violence of the Ninevites is rooted in the basic tendency of humankind; Jones contends that we are ontologically ruled by our violent nature. To overcome it we must, along with the ancient Ninevites, deny the dark forces their power over us.

The violent sins Nineveh commits against Israel receive no special attention in the narrative. Nineveh is not doomed for any specific crimes that have been done against the chosen people. Furthermore, idolatry, which one might expect God and Jonah to condemn, does not appear to be the charge against these foreigners or the crime to which the king confesses on behalf of his community. In biblical thinking, non-Israelites are not usually expected to worship the God of Israel. They are not punished for idolatry but for breaches of morality, as in the case of Sodom and Gomorrah.

The king's next lines are fascinating. He clearly has no real knowledge of Yahweh and no assurances from Jonah that the people's repentance will have the desired effect. The monarch muses, "Who knows but that God may turn and relent? He may turn back from His wrath, so that we do not perish" (Jonah 3:9). Any tenderhearted reader would have pity for the king's humility. Aware of their offenses and willing to mend their ways, king and subjects remain unsure that a vengeful God, who cannot be dissuaded, has not already sealed their fate. The sea captain utters the same lack of confidence in his statement, "Perhaps the god will be kind to us and we will not perish" (1:6). These foreigners do not know God the way Jonah does. They have no guarantee of divine clemency and entertain only the smallest glimmer of hope. Yet they acknowledge the sovereignty of Jonah's deity and throw themselves on God's mercy. The sparing of Nineveh is chapter 1 retold in a different setting and with different characters. The sailors and their captain are exchanged for the Ninevites and their king. And in chapters 1 and 3, Jonah's experience is repeated. He tells the people about his God and they believe.

Little do the Ninevites know that they have good reason to wonder whether God's judgment is immutable. At other points in the Bible God asserts divine sovereignty and does not relent when petitioned. For example, King David hopes that God would spare his first son with Bathsheba, so he fasts, prays, and utters similar pitiful words, "Who knows? The LORD may have pity on me, and the child may live" (2 Sam 12:22). When the child dies, David expresses understandable (though not admirable) anger toward the Lord. In Joel 2:14, the prophet also expresses doubt: "Who knows but He may turn and relent." It seems that even those more fully acquainted with God's ways often wonder what will become of them when God is displeased. Jonah offers no guidance to the people; the text includes no hopeful message of forgiveness that he preaches to the Ninevites. Regardless of their inability to predict the outcome and Jonah's possible suspicion of their sincerity, the Ninevites appear to engage in earnest repentance. It may save them and it may not.

The Ninevites' heartfelt confession of sin and improved conduct are necessary before forgiveness occurs, but they cannot guarantee it. Their prayers imply right words and honest remorse, but the Ninevites also turn away from their evil actions. The first part of v. 10 indicates that God is aware of the Ninevites' behavior: "God saw what they did, how they were turning back from their evil ways." It is interesting that the text says God "saw what they did" or "saw their works" in the 1917 JPS version. "Saw their works" could imply that wearing sackcloth does not convince God to relent. Though fasting and praying are deeds, additional benevolent acts could also cause God to alter the outcome of the story. Penitent words and humble clothing may not be efficacious.

In the second part of Jonah 3:10, the narrator answers the question uppermost in the reader's mind. God forgives the Ninevites and thus firmly establishes the concept of divine universal love. How could the people escape God's wrath? Isn't it too late for the Ninevites? No, divine pity is evoked when they turn from their evil ways. Having created humankind with free will and the ability to choose good or evil, God also provides repentance as the means for all people to escape the punishment that otherwise accompanies wrongdoing. This sentiment is expressed in the writings of the prophets. For example, "And if a wicked person turns back from the wickedness that he practiced and does what is just and right, such a person shall save his life. Because he took heed and turned back from all the transgressions that he committed, he shall live; he shall not die" (Ezek 18:27–28). In other episodes God has a change of heart but punishment follows anyway. In Gen 6 God saves Noah, his family, and many animals but floods the rest of the wicked world. Exodus 32 finds the Almighty sending a plague at the conclusion of the golden calf story after deciding not to kill all the people. In Amos 7:1–9 the Lord does not send a plague of locusts but does apply a metaphorical plumb line, with its implied judgment, to the people of Israel. In these examples God repents of total annihilation but institutes lesser punishment, perhaps at a later date (Bolin 142–43). God may forgive and then later revoke the pardon. Retribution may come at any time.

God is so eager to save humankind that even the wicked Ninevites can repent and be saved: "And God renounced the punishment He had planned to bring upon them, and did not carry it out" (Jonah 3:10). The more literal 1917 JPS translation says, "And God repented of the evil, which He said he would do unto them; and He did it not." Whether the Hebrew נחם is translated as "renounce" or "repent," the message is clear. In this case the Ninevites themselves hold the key to unlock God's divine mercy. The act of repentance neutralizes the forces of darkness and renders punishment unnecessary. The Talmud (Pes. 54a) indicates that repentance was among those seven commodities (including the Torah and Paradise) fashioned by God at the time of creation.

Yet if the older translation of 3:10, "God repented," is allowed, it raises serious questions. Does the Bible story imply that the Almighty has committed a sin that necessitates repentance? Typically, divine action is justified as a by-product of divine prerogative. Synonyms used instead of "repented" include "regretted," "was sorry," "retracted," "changed His mind," "thought better of," and relented" (Fretheim, "Repentance" 50–51). All these terms reveal a deity prepared to reverse a decision, reconsider a judgment, respond to a changing reality. In order to implement salvific priorities, the Lord may choose to "repent" of a previous verdict against humanity. Arguably, God hopes to find cause for such a reversal so that people experience forgiveness and salvation instead of punishment, but the book of Jonah puts no words to that effect in the Lord's mouth. This episode implies "that the future is genuinely open" (Fretheim, "Repentance" 65), an idea that fits with the open ending presented in the book's final chapter when Jonah and God have a choice of behaviors.

In other passages, notably in the book of Micah, God does have a change of mind and tenderly bestows to the Israelites the same forgiveness freely given to the Ninevites. Here God cannot forsake the chosen people, however sinful they may be. God also points out that divine compassion is superior to human:

> I have had a change of heart,
> All My tenderness is stirred.
> I will not act on My wrath,
> Will not turn to destroy Ephraim.
> For I am God, not man,
> The Holy One in your midst:
> I will not come in fury.
>
> (Hos 11:8–9)

The Lord's methods of dealing with sin are likely to be more merciful than human inclinations. In fact, "we are called to forgive each other, but God's forgiveness is of a wholly other order. The difference lies in the decisiveness of God's forgiveness" (Sponheim 322). The profound imbalance between divine and human pardon leads Danish philosopher and religious thinker Søren Kierkegaard (1813–1855) to conclude, "As sinner, man is separated from God by the most chasmal qualitative abyss. In turn, of course, God is separated from man by the same chasmal qualitative abyss when he forgives sins.... There is one way in which man could never in all eternity come to be like God: in forgiving sins" (122). The Jonah narrative certainly supports this view.

God's change of mind, at the crux of the book of Jonah's meaning, is not always found in the Hebrew Scriptures, as has already been suggested in the example of the death of David and Bathsheba's first son. The Lord also refuses to relent in the story of Saul, perhaps because the narrative reflects a historical succession of crowned heads. God promises to take the monarchy away from King Saul when he sins. Though Saul pleads to God for mercy and forgiveness, the prophet Samuel emphatically announces to the king, "the Glory of Israel does not deceive or change His mind, for He is not human that He should change His mind" (1 Sam 15:29). Desperate for approval, Saul grasps Samuel's robe and rips it, symbolizing the tearing asunder of the king's relationship with God. For Saul, there will be no remission of punishment. David is anointed in his place. Furthermore, God refuses to revoke punishment in Jeremiah's visions wherein the earth is to be returned to a primeval condition of darkness and chaos (4:28). In Ezekiel's apocalyptic oracles God promises not to relent. Israelites will be judged according to their behavior: "I will not refrain or spare or relent. You shall be punished according to your ways and your deeds" (24:14). These narratives relate God's ability to decide who will be forgiven; "it is just as erroneous to say that God *cannot* reverse his decree as it is to say that he *must*" (Cooper 162). Different biblical passages have different purposes. When the storyteller desires to conform to the facts of history or to elucidate divine power, a harsher tone may emerge than when the narrator focuses on a divine penchant for mercy and forgiveness.

Allegorical interpretations can also easily be applied to Jonah 3:10. The book educates Israel and its prophets. Perhaps Israel will learn a lesson from its enemy to the east. If the story is told to preexilic Israelites, they are reassured that if they follow the Ninevites' example, the pronouncement against and punishment of the chosen people will become unnecessary (Dennison 34). Messages of doom are conditional, or so the story suggests. Meanwhile, postexilic Jews are challenged to overcome their antipathy toward the Assyrians and to see the whole world through the loving eyes of the Creator. Yahweh has the power and the compassion to grant clemency to all who seek it. For the Israelites the pitfall in accepting their role as the chosen people is the potential for exclusiveness that it may foster. A more universal interpretation "is that God be seen as the centre, and that [Jonah] see himself as chosen to serve God's wider purposes" (Magonet 94). In other words, a broader view is that "Israel was chosen to serve as the carrier of faith in order to disseminate it among all nations" (Simon ix). The human predilection to restrict God's power to one people or geographic location is reductive.

God's mercy is bestowed upon the Ninevites, and Jonah's prediction about the city's destruction is laid aside. While the Lord blesses the prophet Samuel so that "none of his words fall to the ground" (1 Sam 3:19, 1917 JPS translation), Jonah seems to be overridden. Several psalms carry out this theme of God's universal love. For example, Ps 65:6 praises God, "our deliverer, / in whom all the ends of the earth / and the distant seas / put their trust." Psalm 66:4 asserts that "all the earth bows to You," and Ps 67:5 maintains that "nations will exult and shout for joy, / for You rule the peoples with equity, / You guide the nations of the earth." If readers assume that Jonah does as he is told and proclaims exactly what God tells him to say, then Jonah is not a false prophet who deliberately leads people astray with wrong teachings. Jonah must have assumed that though the world is full of error and falsehood, God's word is eternally reliable. What a shock it would be to him when Yahweh's word appears to remain unfulfilled, for Jonah is concerned to protect God's credible reputation. The Lord does not seem to share Jonah's concerns for maintaining credibility.

In biblical stories, God and Israel are originally conceived as belonging exclusively to one another. In Exod 4:22 God proclaims, "Israel is My first-born son." The author of the book of Jonah presents the more highly evolved thinking that though Israel is the first child, it is not the only one. Divine love extends to the entire human family. It knows no territorial limits, no boundaries found on maps. Nineveh is a Gentile metropolis full of depraved people, whose sins are stacked up like dry, combustible kindling. But the city matters to the Lord, especially when its inhabitants turn away from evil. The Israelites, the Jewish author maintains, will have to put aside any prejudices they have against foreigners, for everyone is dear to God. This story, originally told by Jews to other Jews, suggests an exalted vision of a world governed by grand universal compassion.

In some passages the book of Jonah suggests that God's salvation is predicated upon human action. In chapters 1 and 2, it is prayer. In chapter 3 it is fasting (which would include prayer), donning sackcloth, and turning from evil — indications of repentance and reformation. Though signs of contrition move God to feel compassion and to renounce the planned punishment of Nineveh, God remains free to decide when and how to administer justice (Landes 28). People cannot control or manipulate the Lord, who is free to deal with Nineveh according to divine wishes and not those of the Ninevites or Israelites (Trible 269). While Nineveh's deeds may be a necessary component in God's recanting of punishment on the city, they alone are not sufficient to guarantee the Lord's change of mind. The decision will finally depend upon God's sovereign decree (Fretheim, "Theodicy" 231). God has license to choose, but one of God's attributes is that divine decisions are not unalterable, though they may be "beyond human categories of justice or logic" (Bolin 147). God's will defies superficial analysis and easy classification, and one crucial lesson is that mortals are often incapable of comprehending, let alone judging, their deity (Sasson 351). God is shown as an ever-present, active participant in human affairs, but that participation does not guarantee our understanding of what God does. Other passages (notably 4:2) will suggest that God does not act only according to whim or caprice, however. The Almighty behaves in ways consistent with a magnanimous nature, but people's confessing or turning from evil cannot be elevated to a dictatorial, prescriptive formula of what God must do. In Exod 33:19 God insists upon divine prerogative: "I will be gracious to whom I will be gracious, and will show mercy on whom I will show mercy"

(1917 JPS translation). Even if Israelites do not like or understand why divine mercy is extended to those who seek to destroy Israel, they must accept the reality of it.

Nevertheless, the Talmud reiterates how precious a contrite heart is to God and states that "the place which the penitent occupy the perfectly righteous are unable to occupy" (Ber. 34*b*). Those wayward people who sin greatly but realize their mistakes and deliberately change are perhaps more precious to God than those who consistently resist temptation more successfully. "Better is one hour of repentance and good deeds in this world than the whole life of the World to Come," says the Talmud (*Abot* 4:22). God declares to the House of Israel: "it is not My desire that the wicked shall die, but that the wicked turn from his [evil] ways and live. Turn back, turn back from your evil ways, that you may not die" (Ezek 33:11). That sentiment applies to foreigners too and is not meant for Israel exclusively. Most of the Hebrew Scriptures stories focus on Israel, but repentance is a gift given to most who would take it. God looks to the entire family of humanity and hopes people will be gathered in under divine protection and love. Ironically, in chapters 1 and 3 of the book of Jonah, the only penitent people are foreigners — the sailors and the Ninevites. They separate from the part of themselves that is offensive to God. Repentance implies that people reevaluate their past life and endeavor to reshape their future.

The repentance of the Ninevites has huge consequences for the Lord. In the TANAKH God repents twenty-seven times and does not repent nine times (Willis 156). Stories that are early and late, northern and southern, prose and poetry all refer to God and this anthropomorphic quality. Beginning in Gen 3:8 when the Lord walks through the Garden of Eden, as if Yahweh were a person with two legs and a pair of silent tennis shoes, the deity is given many human qualities in Scripture. Nevertheless, the idea of God changing "his" mind presents problems. Divine repentance is a metaphorical use of language indicating a turning away from a previous decision because God is profoundly moved. Technically, God can repent in a way that either preserves or destroys human lives. The Ninevites' repentance causes the repentance of God, but herein lies a controversy. If God is omniscient and infallible, then how can God make a mistake that requires rectification? Surely only an inferior god would ever need to author change. A transcendent being would know in advance what would happen and thus be above any need to overturn a decision. A deity exempt from error could not be swayed by strong emotion. Yet biblical stories, such as Abraham's binding of Isaac and many others, may show that God responds to specific, changing circumstances. The notion of God repenting contradicts fundamental conceptions about the deity's eternal perfection and completeness. Perhaps for this reason the 1985 JPS translation alters the traditional "God repented" to "God renounced."

In the Jonah narrative, God's mind is changed but not God's nature. God's character is to forgive those who seek mercy and compassion rather than to remain unyielding. The Ninevites help God to act according to divine nature when they repent of wicked ways. The book of Jonah reminds readers of how freely God, contrary to the laws of logic and earned punishment, readily reverses a prior resolution when presented with an opportunity. God's will is done when prophecies of gloom and judgment are rendered unnecessary and discarded. Flexibility and changeability are part of the divine character. This is the immutable truth of God.

God's forgiveness of the Ninevites shows that human beings are in a genuine relationship with God. In real relationships there is always give and take. Besides, why cannot God know in advance that the punishment will be renounced? As one critic states, "God's foreknowledge does not mean that history is written in advance, or that human will is not free to choose and to decide without prior divine predetermination. Instead, it means that from the viewpoint of faith, nothing happens by chance or arbitrarily, but according to God's sovereign and prevenient purpose" (Willis 169–70).

The goal of many prophetic books is to demonstrate that divine oracles must be fulfilled, often because the people do not listen. The book of Jonah breaks that tradition and shows the conditional nature of prophecies of doom. It is profoundly ironic that Jonah, perhaps the most successful of all prophets, is the one whose prophecy fails to materialize. The words of Isaiah, Amos, Hosea, and others fall onto deaf ears. The Ninevites listen to Jonah and thus make him appear successful because they heed him, yet ineffectual because his words do not strictly come true. God's most important gift is continued life. A benediction from the Mishnah praises God's mercy and says, "May he that answered Jonah in the belly of the fish answer you and hearken to the voice of your crying this day. Blessed art thou that answerest in time of trouble!" (*Ta'an* 2:4). Forgiveness is extended throughout the wounded world.

CHAPTER 5

Jonah's Lessons

And through all eternity
I forgive you, you forgive me.
— William Blake,
Poems from MSS

Old paint on canvas, as it ages, sometimes becomes transparent. When that happens it is possible, in some pictures, to see the original lines: a tree will show through a woman's dress, a child makes way for a dog, a large boat is no longer on an open sea. This is called pentimento because the painter "repented," changed his mind. Perhaps it would be as well to say that the old conception, replaced by a later choice, is a way of seeing and then seeing again. (Hellman 309)

So begins Lillian Hellman's memoir. With a reflection upon artistic repentance, the author sees her work and then sees it again. Even the best of creators sometimes has a change of heart. And so it is in the book of Jonah.

After God forgives the Ninevites, the biblical scene abruptly shifts. Jonah has been absent from the narrative since 3:4, but he now sullenly re-enters the story. Jonah's dilemma is most profoundly and clearly expressed in chapter 4 and so are the lessons to be learned from it. The story might have ended just after the pivotal episode when divine salvation is bestowed upon Nineveh, but it does not. It cannot. Meaning would be seriously altered if the tale concluded at 3:10. The Lord and the prophet have unfinished business, for the sparing of Nineveh "displeased Jonah greatly, and he was grieved" (4:1). The 1917 JPS translation of "was grieved" (וַיִּחַר) is that Jonah "was angry." The audience begins to conclude that the story's climax does not, after all, come in chapter 3 when the Ninevites turn from their evil ways; God and Jonah must still work things out.

Success has come to Jonah, or so one would think. He has delivered his message of doom, and a guilty people have repented and been saved from punishment. Mission accomplished. Congratulations all around. Surely Jonah would have to struggle to remain humble, for pride could easily plague anyone who so completely fulfills the missionary task. Once again, however, Jonah does not behave as the modern reader expects. Instead of applauding himself and praising God, Jonah is "grieved" or "angry" about what God has done. When God's irritation with the Ninevites ceases, Jonah's begins. If readers have a traditional concept of the Old Testament God as the deity of wrath and harsh justice, they must now reconsider. The Lord's mild compassion is contrasted to the prophet's burning indignation.

The Lord's salvation, bestowed upon Jonah in the great fish episode, does not seem to have made the prophet any less dour. Examples of three other men who become angry with God appear in the Hebrew Scriptures, yet Jonah is perhaps the most irate of them all. In these other cases, the Hebrew word for anger "indicates that in Biblical times there was an intuition of an important finding of modern psychology, that depression involves, or resembles, anger turned inwardly, against oneself" (A. D. Cohen 171). For example, when God pays no heed to Cain's gift and accepts Abel's, "Cain was much distressed [ויחר] and his face fell" (Gen 4:5). As a result of his jealousy, Cain is unable to control his murderous emotions and kills his brother. By contrast, Jonah is ready to kill off an entire city of people, not just a single individual, as Cain does. Next is the prophet Samuel who "was distressed [same Hebrew word] and he entreated the LORD all night long" (1 Sam 15:11) when God rejects Saul after instructing Samuel to anoint Saul as king of Israel. King David is also "distressed" because God strikes down Uzzah as he reaches out to steady the Ark of the Covenant as it is being brought into Jerusalem (2 Sam 6:8). The ark is sacred; touching it is like touching God, and no one can be allowed so close, but Uzzah probably does not know this and is well intentioned as he handles the holy relic. All these cases are similar to Jonah's in that Cain, Samuel, and David also have hurt pride. They feel that Yahweh has promised one thing and delivered another. Cain invents the concept of sacrifice, for he is the one who first brings an offering — the fruit of the soil he tills. Yet Abel outdoes his brother and brings "the choicest of the firstlings of his flock" (Gen 4:4), and God prefers the second gift. Cain is understandably enraged at God for what appears to be unfair favoritism. Similarly, Samuel is obedient to God when told to proclaim Saul the first monarch of a united Israel. Almost immediately, God finds Saul unacceptable, so Samuel must anoint another king. Samuel's annoyance is very human, for he must have wondered why God made the wrong choice at the start. Samuel now looks incompetent, and no prophet wants to appear foolish, indecisive, or mistaken. David is angry because his marvelous victory procession into his new capital city is marred by what must appear to human eyes as harsh divine justice. David's moment of glory is tarnished by the sudden death of Uzzah, which may have seemed startlingly unjust to onlookers. All of these cases mirror Jonah's. The men become angry when they do not fully understand or approve of God's behavior. From the limited human perspective, there is cause for displeasure at the Lord's execution of sovereign will. Yet in each case human behavior actually results in a reaction from the Lord. When the Ninevites repent, God forgives, but Jonah is like Cain, Samuel, and David. The prophet is "grieved" over what God does.

Loving one's enemies, perhaps the antithesis of Jonah's approach to the Ninevites, has challenged peacemakers throughout time. While speaking about his white oppressors, Martin Luther King Jr. said in a Christmas 1967 sermon that African Americans could not win people to their side through hatred. He said he felt fortunate that Jesus had not told us to like our enemies because there were some individuals that he could not possibly like: "I can't like anybody who would bomb my home. I can't like anybody who would exploit me. I can't like anybody who would trample over me with injustices. I can't like them. I can't like anybody who threatens to kill me day in and day out" (Johnson 47). Yet King could love them. Arguably, the oppression the Israelites experienced at the hands of the Ninevites was somewhat comparable to what blacks suffered at the hands of whites. In church basement gatherings of the 1960s, blacks (and some whites) congregated to repent their anger and hatred and to commit themselves to nonviolent change. These meetings are reminiscent of Jonah's sitting in the belly of the great fish and later, because he still does not comprehend the concept of loving his enemies, also recall his sitting under the ricinus plant until he could begin to hear that God loves all people. Jonah is a slow learner, and whether he really bends and finally accepts the divine message while he is seated in the searing sun of Scripture is never clear (Hampl 299). At times Jonah seems to be a man devoid of love, unsympathetic toward the Ninevites. He wants God's law and order, not mercy. Jonah does not comprehend the primary message that there is a value higher than justice. Yet these notions remain speculative, for nowhere does Jonah directly state that he begrudges the Ninevites their salvation or finds them undeserving. Jonah's explanation is that he knew all along that a forgiving God would not carry out the punishment.

Jonah's sizzle turns to fizzle when he reveals his motive for fleeing to Tarshish:

He prayed to the LORD, saying, "O LORD! Isn't this just what I said when I was still in my own country? That is why I fled beforehand to Tarshish. For I know that You are a compassionate and gracious God, slow to anger, abounding in kindness, renouncing punishment." (4:2)

Perhaps Jonah first refuses the denunciatory mission because he objects to so cruel a threat against the Ninevites and wants no part of it. Yet more probable is that Jonah prefers divine justice to divine mercy. If so, the prayer at 4:2 reveals much significant information about Jonah's character.

Jonah does not need to learn that the possibility of repentance is open to all. He knows that fact as he boards the ship in Joppa. Chapter 4 is not about what the Ninevites do; it is about Jonah's reaction. The fact of God's universal lovingkindness is already established. What remains to be demonstrated is whether Jonah, himself delivered by the divinely appointed fish and then from the fish back into human society, accepts God's plan for the whole universe. Only now, using the element of surprise, does the narrator reveal Jonah's motive for fleeing to Tarshish. We learn that Jonah never doubts God's authority and mercy. The prophet implies, however, that outside Israel there is an ongoing lack of respect for God's word. Jonah understands that the Almighty will pardon the Ninevites in the short run, but the prophet does not know who will continue to guide them to righteousness.

The "grace formula" (Willis 166) of 4:2 is one of the fundamental conceptualizations that Israel has of its God. It is also an echo of other biblical passages that are the spiritual antecedents of Jonah. The Bible highlights God's merciful character, even as Jonah inveighs against it, and the language piles up phrases to emphasize God's loving nature. The reader now realizes that though God has blustered again and again, no one in the story has died, no ships have been lost at sea, no cities have been laid ruin. God has threatened, but no harm has yet come to anyone or anything. The passage at 4:2 most strongly resembles Exod 34:6, the Torah's liturgical fragment that suggests attributes describing God's nature: "The LORD! The LORD! a God compassionate and gracious, slow to anger, abounding in kindness and faithfulness." In Jonah 4:2, the prophet hurls before Yahweh a standard summary of divine attributes that are controlling metaphors for the Hebrew Scriptures' portrayal of the Almighty and are well known to Israelites, but now the meaning is subtly yet significantly changed. The creedal statement of Exodus, coming at the end of the golden calf episode, shows that the Lord's mercy is available to the chosen people. In the book of Jonah, that view is expanded.

Seven passages in the TANAKH contain similar anthropathic language affirming God as "slow to anger" and "abounding in steadfast love": Exod 34:6, Ps 86:15, Ps 103:8, Ps 145:8, Joel 2:13, Neh 9:17, and Jonah 4:2. Of these, only the Joel and Jonah verses indicate that God renounces previously prescribed punishment. All six of the other verses are deliberate restatements of the original Exodus analysis of God's personality, placed within other poems and prose passages because of their beauty and power and to remind readers that God's basic character does not alter with time or circumstance. In fact, Jonah 4:2 may be an exegesis on Exod 34:6. The Jonah verse repeats key words but expands upon their meaning by broadening the population to which they refer and showing God's response to intercessory prayers of all nations.

Scholars who interpret Jonah to be midrash point to the whole story as an explanation not only of Exod 34:6 but also of Num 23:19:

> God is not man to be capricious,
> Or mortal to change His mind.
> Would He speak and not act,
> Promise and not fulfill?

Ezekiel 18:23 also needs amplification: "Is it my desire that a wicked person shall die? — says the Lord GOD. It is rather that he shall turn back from his ways and live." In all three of these passages, the question arises of what divine traits predominate. Does God prefer mercy to justice? Is God truly willing to repent — to see and then see again? Does God's love extend beyond Israel? Which of the traits of God, repeated at Jonah 4:2, dominate? The book is a homily to explain the preferences of the ancient God of the Israelites. Here God's conduct is a model for human beings, encouraging us to the same mercy and flexibility as the deity (Rogerson 513). In origin the formula of Exod 34:6 is valid for the Israelites, but there are always signs that protection is applied to all of God's creatures, as early stories indicate. For example, God allows no harm to come to the Egyptian slave woman, Hagar, when Abraham and Sarah cast her out into the wilderness of Beer-sheba (Gen 21), showing that all of God's creations are objects of providential care. The narrow, nationalistic tendency to believe that the Lord's kindness is reserved for the chosen people is, by the literature of those very chosen ones, shown to be unworthy and ungodly.

In 4:2 God is "abounding in kindness." The Hebrew word for "kindness" is חסד. It is connected to "pity" (חום), which Jonah seems to lack toward the Ninevites. "Early readers would connect חום with חסד, pity with steadfast love" (Warshaw 198). Joel's language, though similar to Jonah's, illustrates the special status of Israel. God's pity for the chosen people is aroused when they ask for help in the book of Joel. Though the similarities in the two books bespeak a connection between them, "Joel and Jonah present distinct anthological interpretations of the initial account of covenant renewal in Exod 32–34, where the formula of Yahweh's gracious and compassionate character is first introduced in the Torah" (Dozeman 209). While Joel focuses on Israel, Jonah expands God's pity to reach beyond the boundaries of a single nation. In other words, the tale of Jonah represents the Jewish people's spiritual quest to interpret Torah as bearing essential revelations to the formation of the remainder of the Jewish Bible. God has free will, just like humankind, and God can freely extend pity to anyone. Therefore, that the book of Jonah postdates the book of Joel seems likely, for Jonah amplifies God's character in a way not known in Joel. God is more godlike in the book of Jonah (Miles 178).

In 4:2 Jonah thinks he knows God and what to expect from the divine character, and the view of the Lord as a forgiving father is surely supported in other biblical passages. Yet even in the book of Jonah, God remains a powerful and independent force capable of choosing to behave in a variety of ways. While we may like to believe that God saves the helpless (as the sailors), rejects punishment for the repentant (as the Ninevites), and is patient and compassionate (as Jonah asserts), these divine traits are rendered problematic by the text and historical outcomes (Cooper 149). The sailors are experienced and resourceful, not helpless in storms to which they are fairly accustomed; Nineveh is eventually destroyed because the repentance of one generation does not redeem a people for all time; and in many biblical episodes God angers quickly, not slowly, and punishment is swift. In the book of Jonah, Yahweh exercises divine prerogative to save or destroy at any time, eliminating the worm (4:7) just after preserving the Ninevites (3:10). Human beings cannot dictate to God who will be sheltered and who will be shelled; we cannot control or manipulate God with our behavior, for the Lord remains free to make decisions about who and what to save. The story shows that we do not live "within an environment peacefully circumscribed by the predictability of tradition and the guaranteeability of God" (Sherwood 234). Through Jonah we recognize our own powerlessness in light of divine mastery. No formula can require God to be mechanically magnanimous, for that would negate what it means to be the Almighty.

Jonah's affirmation of God's perfection comes within a prayer, yet the tone of this second prayer is vastly different from the petition offered up in the belly of the fish. Instead of declaring again that "deliverance is the Lord's" (2:10), Jonah now asks for death: "Please, Lord, take my life, for

I would rather die than live" (4:3). Jonah has just witnessed the rescue of an entire people, but the expected crisis → deliverance → rejoicing literary pattern is replaced by the surprising crisis → deliverance → death-wish structure of the story. As Jonah desires to die, his "wishbone" is greater than his "backbone." Other prayers appear in the book of Jonah, but this is the only one to which the Lord responds verbally, causing the prophet to reemerge as the center of attention for the rest of the book while discussion of the Ninevites ceases.

Jonah is not the only man of God to ask for death. Moses (Num 11:15) and Job (Job 6:8–9) request to die rather than to continue living with their problems and afflictions. Samson asks to die with the Philistines (Judg 16:30). Even the mighty Elijah prays to perish in the wilderness, but for a far different reason than Jonah: " 'Enough!' [Elijah] cried. 'Now, O LORD, take my life, for I am no better than my fathers' " (1 Kgs 19:4). Elijah fears that Queen Jezebel will kill him and laments his inability to squelch her polytheism. Jonah, on the other hand, longs for death after his success with the polytheistic Ninevites. Elijah's noble reason for seeking an end to life, "for I am no better than my fathers," is replaced by Jonah's puny "for I would rather die than live." Elijah is weary of battling unrepentant infidels; Jonah is fatigued by unwanted success. Elijah seeks escape from the humiliation of his continuing conflict with the unyielding monarch; Jonah wants to die when sinners switch their allegiance to God. In these episodes, Jonah is no Elijah.

What has happened to the resolve Jonah shows in the uplifting prayer he says within the fish's belly? Human nature is fickle. We are likely to have many about-faces in our lifetimes. Once we have seen the light and reformed, we can never rest assured that we will not slip again and need another reformation. We may go along in the right direction for years, then suddenly make a mistake and return to our previous ways of thinking and acting. In chapter 4 of the book of Jonah, the all-too-human prophet again fluctuates between noble and ignoble attitudes and actions. His pious resolve of chapter 2 dissipates, leaving Jonah with his deeply ingrained, baser emotions. However contrite Jonah becomes while inside the great fish, his spiritual outlook now darkens as he contemplates his own future after Nineveh's salvation. Either the prophet does not fully believe what he says while inside the sea monster — an idea that seems unlikely given the sincere tone and elegant diction of that prayer — or he lapses and needs further amelioration. Jonah is shown again to be Everyone, the average human being who shapes and reshapes himself in order to maintain a connection to the divine. Jonah certainly knows about God's love, but Yahweh and the prophet must continue the dialogue in order for Jonah to become his authentic self. Sometimes, even God fails to reach us. Thus Jonah is ironically cast in the role of anti-hero who seems to prefer death to God's universal forgiveness. The worse the prophet looks, the stronger is the message that his story presents. An unflattering interpretation of Israelite prophecy casts Jonah as unrepentant in the end, yet if this analysis of his character is correct, his stubbornness is precisely the characteristic that teaches the Israelites to reject Jonah's philosophy and embrace superior ethics.

Why is Jonah hostile to people he does not really know? The Talmud states, "Whoever is compassionate toward his fellow-creatures (and forgives wrongs done to him), compassion is shown to him from Heaven; and whoever is not compassionate toward his fellow-creatures, compassion is not shown to him from Heaven" (*Šabb.* 151*b*). Is Jonah so frustrated with God's soft touch toward Israel's enemies that the prophet longs for death? Proverbs 24:17 warns, "If your enemy falls, do not exult; / If he trips, let your heart not rejoice." The passage goes on to declare that the Lord will be displeased if we rejoice in the misfortune of enemies. Perhaps Jonah rightly mistrusts the expediency of the Ninevites' repentance and sees it as a superficial dalliance with God, motivated only by momentary fear. Jonah might believe that the Ninevites are experiencing a mortification that will prove ephemeral when the immediate danger passes, rather than a genuine reversal and lifelong commitment to the God of Israel. Jonah may even project in the Ninevites a temporary attention to Yahweh, a situation similar to the short-lived devotion of the sailors, repeated and writ large. Still, though the Ninevites may not be the most sincere or pious people on God's earth, Jonah cannot know for sure how they will behave in the future. Yet he seems ready to condemn them all. They do not know the God of Sarah and Abraham, for never before has there been a prophet to tell them. In the name of justice, abstract and cold, the prophet will soon indirectly voice his preference for their collective demise. Jonah may have difficulty trusting their remarkable belief, but this interpretation is mere speculation not supported by Jonah's direct statements or an omniscient narrator's comments. He expresses no outrage at God's pardoning the Gentiles. Perhaps Jonah's distress arises from the fact that despite being God's chosen messenger, he is excluded from God's thinking about the city's fate (Bolin 175–76). Perhaps he feels confusion about why God would not be completely forthcoming with him concerning the destruction of Nineveh.

So a despairing Jonah begs God for death. When Jonah prays to die and God rhetorically inquires, "Are you that deeply grieved?" (Jonah 4:4), Jonah departs the city to wait and see what will happen. Unhappy, unlucky Jonah finds a spot east of Nineveh to sit passively and wait in his self-imposed exile, just as Cain leaves Paradise and goes "east of Eden" (Gen 4:16). Jonah the anti-hero takes no further action, hatches no more schemes, makes no other decisions. He does not lead the Ninevites in prayer, encourage them to continue and deepen their commitment to God, or share with them the Torah of his own people. Instead of working to shape events, Jonah is content to find a secluded place, pout, and watch events unfold. His experience as a Jew causes him to know in advance the positive outcome of the Nineveh case. What Israelite prophet could tolerate the thought of being a harbinger of ill tidings to a foreign people, knowing full well that God's nature will not allow destruction of the repentant? Jonah may have suspected that the Ninevites would believe his message — he is a seer, after all. Yet he must transcend the self and accept the mission, though it makes him appear to be a false prophet in the eyes of the world when his prediction of (physical) destruction does not immediately materialize. No longer God's herald, Jonah is now like a night watchman waiting for disaster to strike but knowing it probably will not. The heathen are converted and secure in divine protection.

Just as Jonah waits to see what will happen, so does the Jewish audience. Why doesn't he just return to his native Israel, they must wonder. He seems compelled to see the mission through to its end. At the time the book of Jonah was written, the issue of God's forgiveness of enemies was not settled for the audience either. Though the people's intuition and learning of Torah told them to expect universal compassion from the deity, the concept was sometimes hard to accept. Many Israelites must have found untenable the forgiveness of a brutal and dangerous people who were sure someday to bring about Israel's very destruction. They would wonder if mercy should have limitations. Verse 4:2 of Jonah demonstrates that the Israelites have never believed in an authoritarian God who lacks pity, and this book even demonstrates that the deity has been correct all along in bestowing forgiveness to almost everyone who seeks it. God is right to force Jonah to go to Nineveh and deliver a message of doom that would ultimately make the punishment unnecessary. Jonah may have been correct to resist the calling, for by fleeing to Tarshish, he is not simply a coward who seeks to avoid danger. The sea voyage and the mission to Nineveh put Jonah at great risk. Through his personal ordeals, we learn just how valuable all God's creatures are. The message applied to Israel in Mic 7:18, "Who is a God like You, / Forgiving iniquity / And remitting transgression," is thus expanded to cover a broader spectrum of people.

God certainly treats the Ninevites well, but what of God's behavior toward the prophet? At times the portrait of God is not flattering. Sometimes the Lord seems to intentionally mock Jonah. God knows what readers may suspect but cannot know for sure: that Nineveh will not be destroyed as Jonah is told to predict. How humiliating that must be for the prophet. Jonah is concerned because he has made a divinely decreed prediction that appears to go unfulfilled. Surely God's word ought not be irrevocable. At other places in the book of Jonah, the Lord is not as charitable as Jonah 4:2 indicates. For instance, God readily puts not only Jonah but also the sailors in harm's way. God humiliates the prophet in front of the enemy Ninevites by sparing the city for which Jonah is told to forecast overthrow. Whatever God does to the prophet is done for his own good, however, and Yahweh is not yet finished with Jonah's education at the beginning of chapter 4. God leads Jonah away from stinginess, nationalism, and abstract absolutes and toward a model of goodness and holiness. Actually, God's question to Jonah at 4:4, "Are you that deeply grieved?" is very gentle. In chapter 4 Jonah is perhaps now the recipient of undeserved grace. The Lord could conceivably be angry with a vacillating, stubborn prophet. Yet God's words to Jonah are soft and even a touch humorous. A stern rebuke might lead to more serious rebellion by Jonah, but a mild reproof would leave the prophet some dignity and thus allow him to engage in self-examination. The particulars concerning Jonah's grudge against the Ninevites are not stated in the text, but plausibly he believes their culture to be brutal and their repentance to be fleeting. Nowhere does the book indicate that the Ninevites give up their idol worship, and history proves that they did not. Jonah may therefore judge their repentance to be insincere. The fact that God does not take decisive action against Jonah, demoting him from prophet to private citizen or even killing him for disobedience, indicates a measure of divine tolerance for Jonah's position.

If Jonah were a villain, at the very least an ethical narrative would have to end with his formal submission to God's will. If Jonah were a moral reprobate, the Lord would surely discipline the prophet severely. Others (Uzzah's example at 2 Sam 6:6 remains poignant) have been killed for what are arguably less serious infractions. As chapter 4 opens, Jonah has technically done his job: Nineveh is saved and a happy ending is possible, except for the sad prophet's lingering bad mood. The amiable tone of God's reproach is a concession to Jonah's viewpoint, and "despite all Jonah's failings, God still chooses and uses him, and is prepared to reason with him to the end" (Magonet 86). As Jonah is kindly led by the Lord's lenience, so are readers, and herein lies the philosophical and religious dilemma that is the central purpose of the book. Walter Crouch, alluding to language from the New Testament (e.g., Rev 2:7) takes the prophet's side and, perhaps foolishly, offers a response by Jonah to God's concluding exclamation about caring for the Ninevites:

> O Yahweh, do you have eyes to see but cannot see and ears to hear but cannot hear? Nineveh has not repented. They, as I in the belly of the great fish, are only afraid of dying at your hands. They have manipulated your soft heart just as I have. I remain unrepentant and so do they. O great and mighty Elohim, you have thought nothing about destroying countless cities through the ages — are you, in this circumstance, really that gullible? (112)

Rabbi Joseph ben Akiva (c. 50–c. 132) criticizes the prophet because "Jonas was jealous for the glory of the son (Israel) but not for the glory of the father (God)" (Bickerman 17).

People learn from the divine model, and God's punishment usually helps to educate the people. God is angry at the sinner in the way a parent is annoyed with a disobedient child. Parents desire for their progeny to behave well, and so does God. Another lesson comes at Jonah 4:5. The booth or sukkah that Jonah builds for himself as shade while he waits is somewhat reminiscent of the cave at Mount Horeb where Elijah finds shelter in the wilderness beyond Beer-sheba (1 Kgs 19), though of course Elijah does not construct the cave. The sukkah is a temporary dwelling, the kind used for overnight lodging in the fields during harvest time. From inside it Jonah is perhaps still full of hopeful expectation that Nineveh will be destroyed. It serves as a temporary house, private and protective, but ultimately inadequate. The booth functions as a haven, a "substitute temple" (Gunn and Fewell 141) that cools his body and temper. Sukkah (סכה) is the singular form of the Hebrew word used to commemorate the harvest festival, סכות, and the booth (also translated as "tabernacle") symbolizes God's wondrous providence and covenant with Israel.

Jonah's cover, probably made of tree branches with leaves, would soon wither and offer insufficient protection from the elements, especially the searing sun. Its appearance in the story is more symbolic than functional, for as Jonah sits under the shelter, he is also under God's protective care. Though secure Ninevite homes might provide more adequate lodging, Jonah constructs a temporary dwelling — one that connects him to the history of his people and represents their mobile sanctuary in the wilderness at the time of the exodus from Egypt. The Festival of Booths is designed to commemorate the forty years of wandering in the desert when the Israelites were totally dependent upon God for all life-giving sustenance. Furthermore, prophetic writings refer to God's apocalyptic judgment as a harvest, a time when the good crops are gathered in and the chaff is weeded out.

Textual problems with chronology cause interpretation difficulties in Jonah 4:5, however; the verse seems to violate the time sequence in the remainder of the book. Jonah has been absent from the narrative since uttering his famous five-word Hebrew announcement: "Forty days more, and Nineveh shall be overthrown" (3:4). God's forgiveness occurs while the prophet is off stage, so to speak, meaning that Jonah might not realize what has transpired. When Jonah builds the booth and sits down "until he should see what happened to the city" (4:5), the narrator suggests that Jonah does not know the outcome of events. The place where he waits is "east of the city" (4:5); he views Nineveh from an exquisite remove. Yet 4:1 says that "This [God's renouncing of punishment for Nineveh] displeased Jonah greatly." Jonah's anger is so strong that he prefers death to life, which contradicts the idea that he lacks information when he constructs the booth and waits. Furthermore, in the very next verse, God creates a plant to shade Jonah, though he already has a booth to shield him from the sun. From this point, no further mention is made of the booth. Jonah has only the plant, adding to the confusion about the booth and its efficacy as a shelter from sweltering weather. One explanation is that the booth verse has been preserved out of its original order. If Jonah goes out of the city, builds the temporary dwelling, and awaits the outcome at an earlier point in the story, immediately after the 3:4 destruction proclamation, then the booth construction makes more sense, as does the need for the plant in chapter 4. Transpose 4:5 to follow 3:4, and the logical temporal sequence is reestablished. One can assume that the east wind of 4:7 destroys the booth. In forty days (a long time, in biblical parlance), the leafy booth would naturally wither, and Jonah would need more covering. The booth and the plant would thus be separated in the narrative's time sequence, but this is only a partial solution to the question of the two sources of shade. Alternatively, the booth is deliberately placed in chapter 4 but should be read as a flashback (Craig 53) or "an absurd attempt [on Jonah's part] to reverse time and undo a historical event (the forgiving of Nineveh), which has already taken place" (Elata-Alster 51). Another explanation is that in the long oral history of the book of Jonah, two traditions arose — one of the booth and one of the plant — and both are preserved in the written version of the tale (Wolff 163; Salters 36).

Perhaps the booth/plant episode can be explained by misplacement or scribal error, but sloppy integration work seems unlikely. A reasonable assumption is that the two shading elements are inserted deliberately into the original story to underscore the extra lengths to which the narrator goes to discuss Jonah's sources of comfort. The booth and the plant are not contradictory because Jonah builds the booth for his own purposes, and God creates the plant for divine purposes. Though Jonah has already constructed the booth to screen the sun, a loving God — who also needs to teach Jonah further lessons about compassion — nevertheless appoints a plant to provide additional shade. In other words, God gives us more than we need to be at ease. Hence, the booth and plant are purposely juxtaposed to advance the theme of God providing for Jonah's solace. This is yet another example of God's mercy: first, God rescues Jonah via a great fish; second, Jonah prays in the belly of the fish and God causes it to return Jonah to dry land; third, the Ninevites pray and are forgiven by God; fourth, God provides Jonah with shelter from sun and wind.

In v. 6 the plant grows over Jonah's head: "The LORD God provided a ricinus plant [castor oil plant or gourd], which grew up over Jonah, to provide shade for his head and save him from discomfort. Jonah was very happy about the plant." This is a strange reaction for a man who claims to want death. Castor oil plants grow rapidly to a height of ten to fifteen feet and produce plenty of leafy shade, but in the very next verse, God causes a worm to kill the plant. The prophet's happiness fades as quickly as the gourd itself, evidence of Jonah's shifting attitudes throughout chapter 4. The prophet presents an odd juxtaposition of life force and death wish.

The ricinus plant is almost like a tree, and when God creates it, Jonah misinterprets God's actions once again. He had initially seen the storm and great fish as a threat, his Sheol, whereas God sends the fish to rescue Jonah when the storm would have killed him. Jonah learns to be gladdened and grateful while in the fish, and now he is pleased about the plant. He does not yet comprehend that God intends to destroy the gourd to teach the prophet a lesson about the transitory nature of life and the power of a "God Who engineers Providence through His established laws of nature" (Zlotowitz 136). As in previous passages, a parallel exists to the great Elijah's journey to the wilderness outside Beer-sheba. Elijah "came to a broom bush [juniper tree] and sat down under it" (1 Kgs 19:4). There he prays for death. Neither prophet receives the immediate release he seeks, for in both cases, God still has theophanies to reveal.

The revelation will come to Jonah through hardship. The heat tortures him when God provides a worm to attack and kill the shade plant. In classical terminology, the huge dragon guarding the Golden Fleece has been reduced to a paltry worm. In biblical analogy, the worm is similar to the maggot that destroys the manna of the Exodus or the trouble-bringing serpent in the Garden of Eden.

Gunn and Fewell state:

> For a brief moment the plant is the tree in the Garden, the tree of knowledge of good and evil. Jonah partakes of its fruit — its shade. The tree delivers him from evil. The question is, what knowledge of good and evil will he learn from it? ... This tree, like the one in the Garden, has a worm. (142)

Jonah has always been protected by God's enclosures. First the fish, then the booth and plant cause Jonah to rejoice, but both the fish and the plant ultimately leave Jonah on his own once more. Jonah must go beyond the security of divine enclosure and face the world on his own. There is no perfect Garden of Eden where we may sit out our days in comfort and peace. The snake approaches. Here it is reduced to the size of a worm — same shape, different dimensions — that eats its way toward Jonah's heart. Life is the worm that God sends to roust us out of our comfort zone. Its tribulations and demands that we help one another will not allow us to sit idly by and wait to see what will happen. The ricinus plant or gourd that brings Jonah happiness is in Hebrew קיקיון; it is a hollow vegetable. Through its destruction, God intends to rattle the empty heart of Jonah and provide him with yet another lesson.

Although he expresses no direct gratitude to God for the plant, Jonah loves it because it gives him what he needs and asks for nothing in return. When God takes away the gourd, Jonah lapses into deep depression and asks to die (Jonah 4:7–8), revealing that the prophet feels nothing for the vulnerable plant itself. He simply regrets that it is no longer there to provide comfort for him. The text makes it clear that the gourd dies by the hand of God who sends רוח קדים חרישית, a "sultry east wind" (4:8) to destroy the plant. The exact translation of the *hapax* "sultry," חרישית, is debated, however, and the 1917 JPS translation calls it a "vehement" wind. The word likely derives from the Hebrew verb חרש, which means "to be deaf," and Spanish commentator Ibn Ezra suggests "deafening" as the appropriate adjective to describe the oppressive, wilting sirocco heat (Cohen, *Twelve* 149). In the absence of the plant, the sun is so overwhelming that Jonah faints and begs for death again. Ironically, he is angrier about the loss of the plant than the loss of an entire city. The destruction of the gourd becomes a parable, similar to the one Nathan tells to King David (Gunn and Fewell 143). When David condemns the parable's rich man who steals a poor man's ewe and "showed no pity" (2 Sam 12:6), the Israelite monarch also unwittingly castigates his own behavior for stealing the wife of another man. So it is with Jonah's anger over the plant's demise. The angry and judgmental prophet unknowingly causes the audience to judge him. At least David confesses to Nathan, "I stand guilty before the LORD!" (2 Sam 12:13) and receives pardon. Jonah never confesses his sins.

It must appear to Jonah that God is persecuting him, first with a tempest and now with a relentless and unbearable heat. Meanwhile, a historically bloodthirsty metropolis escapes unscathed. Serving such a deity would seem like a dubious honor at best, and when God inquires if Jonah is "so deeply grieved about the plant," Jonah responds affirmatively: "Yes," he replied, "so deeply that I want to die" (4:9). Jonah does not actually contemplate suicide; he simply entreats God to let him perish, as the plant does.

The far-fetched Freudian interpretation of Jonah's anger offers a different insight into his death wish. This view focuses on the prophet's struggle with incest taboos and goes something like this: Jonah is furious because his mother loves her husband more than she loves her son, Jonah. This situation is unjust, he believes, and is represented by Nineveh's wickedness that Jonah must denounce. The prophet's ego causes him to rebel against both parents, and the saving of the city symbolizes Jonah's overcoming of his sexual longing for his mother and his wishes for her destruction (Fingert 55–65). Another psychological study suggests that the prophet's desire is to obtain for himself alone the love of God. Nineveh represents "the bad mother whom [Jonah] wants to destroy because she mothers others" (More 7). Jonah is jealous of his siblings in Nineveh because they, too, receive parental love. Consequently, Jonah flees to Tarshish to avoid the murderous impulses that his id thrusts upon him. There is conflict on the psychological and the theological levels. Jonah's psyche fights with his religious piety. His fidelity to his martyred people and his knowledge that God is "compassionate and gracious" (4:2) to all peoples are at war within Jonah. No wonder the prophet despises his dilemma and longs for death.

Jonah's current death wish is different from the one at 1:12 when the prophet tells the sailors to heave him overboard, willingly sacrificing himself in order to save the crew and stop the sea from raging. In the scene with the sailors, Jonah has not yet reached the depth of despair that he attains toward the end of the book. He does not say to the sailors, "Hurl me overboard, for I want to die." In chapter 4 Jonah is angry and depressed. He has watched the result of the Ninevites' faith in God and knows that he has reluctantly been the instrument of their salvation. He may even realize that he is living at odds with God's divine mercy and love. This causes the prophet to become despondent and wish for his own death along with the plant's.

Jonah invests too much in things of this world. The gourd becomes overly important to Jonah, almost a kind of idol (Goodhart 52), and Jonah's joy comes and goes as quickly as the plant itself. God appoints a worm to kill the plant in order to teach Jonah a lesson. Losing the plant is a matter of personal inconvenience for Jonah, nothing more. In a sense, the gourd is a sacrificial offering. It dies for Jonah at the behest of God. With its death, it tries to open Jonah's heart to healing mercy. Jonah is "deeply grieved" (4:9) when the gourd dies, not because he values the gourd but because he values the cooling shade its palmate leaves provided him.

God controls the life and death of the plant. Just as God is the proven sovereign of the sea in the great fish episode, so the Lord has dominion over the plants of the earth. Yet God's natural world is unreliable, as far as human comfort is concerned. The weevils are at work. Here we are shown that their destructive power is the will of God, though the image of a worm eating a gourd appears nowhere else in the Bible. As a symbol, the castor oil plant is peculiar to the book of Jonah, a literary device used to show the transitory nature of the natural world ruled by God. Yahweh hopes that the destruction of the plant beloved by Jonah will cause him to reconsider his attitude toward the city's destruction. In the final verses of the book, the Lord will show that forgiveness is preferable to harsh judgment. The great fish comes to save Jonah the prophet, but the gourd appears and disappears to save Jonah the man. Its creation offers Jonah the opportunity to repent, forgive, and be forgiven.

The Hebrew name for the deity who brings forth the gourd is different in this verse than at any other place in the book of Jonah. It is impossible to prove that the original narrator employs specific names for God for theological purposes, so as to underscore the unfathomable aspect of God's character within the story, but a pattern does seem to emerge in the Hebrew text. Twice what appears to be a deliberate pattern is broken, at 4:2 and at 4:6. God is referred to once as אל (El), the primitive, generic word for God in Semitic languages. "El" appears only at 4:2 when a venerable passage from Exodus is alluded to and the ancient deity of the Hebrews is acknowledged. At 4:6 when the deity creates the plant, a different term for God is employed for the only time in the story. Here God is called יהוה־אלהים (Lord God), which could advance in the mind of the insightful reader a thematic connection to Genesis's Garden of Eden where the same term, Lord God, is first applied to the Creator. While the variations may be accounted for merely as the artistic license of the narrator, the reader begins to wonder if terms for the deity reveal a deeper meaning. In English (and in the entirety of the analysis of the Jonah story put forth in this book), the terms "Lord" and "God" and "Lord God" may be used interchangeably, but this is not necessarily the case in the Hebrew Scriptures.

Distinct terms for the Almighty's name sometimes designate aspects of divine nature or varying relationships between the deity and other characters in a story. As a general rule, the most frequently used Hebrew word for God, Elohim (אלהים), is employed in the book of Jonah when a heathen god is referred to by foreigners (e.g., the sailors and captain at 1:5–6) or when foreigners call upon Jonah's God (e.g., the Ninevites and their king at 3:5–10). On the other hand, the Tetragrammaton היוה (Yahweh) is the name Jonah himself uses for the deity throughout much of the book (e.g., 1:1 and 3:1 with the Lord's commissions to Jonah, 2:1–11 in Jonah's prayer, and 4:10 with the final admonition). In three places variations on the composite name of Lord God are found, such as "LORD, the God of Heaven" (1:9), "LORD his God" (2:2), and "LORD my God" (2:7). Yet only at the gourd's formation in 4:6 is the compound name יהוה־אלהים (LORD God) seen without modifiers. F. D. Kinder explains general thematic and aesthetic reasons for using different terms for the deity:

> On the whole . . . the theme of Israel and the Nations closely controls the choice of one term or the other as appropriate to the more intimate or the more general relationship of God to man. But the purely aesthetic impulse towards variety of language also asserts itself, freeing the narrator from undue bondage to his rules, and at the same time reminding the reader that the names are in the last resort interchangeable, common to the one Yahweh Elohim. (128)

The narrator may just be seeking variety of language. Still, the singular use of "LORD God" at the point when the gourd is created has thematic significance as the story draws to a close and Jonah grapples with his deity's unique creative character.

The LORD God brings forth the gourd, which may also represent the first Jerusalem temple, God's sheltering sanctuary that will be destroyed by the Babylonians. Jonah's story suggests that nothing is permanent in this world, except perhaps God's wondrous love and mercy. Both the booth and the plant offer only temporary havens. Ironically, the more substantial shelter is spiritual, an understanding of God's lovingkindness. Jonah will soon see that God's "mercy is not merely a capricious and negative suspension of law and order, but is an affirmative act of love" (Warshaw 94). Human beings, created in the divine image, should model God's compassion. Jonah's initiation continues.

Though Jonah is primarily concerned with his own comfort and grieves for the loss of it, perhaps the prophet's feelings are more complicated than a reader might originally think. On the surface it appears that the broad vision of God's grace is contrasted to the pettiness of man's selfish desires and fleeting pleasures. Yet anyone who feels such compassion for a plant must, theoretically at least, be able to muster up genuine concern for people too. One so sensitive to the plant world would surely respond to the needs of human beings. It is doubtful that Jonah's concern over the withered plant and the summer heat would suffice to cause one of the most earnest death wishes in literature. At 4:9 Jonah asks to die a second time. God never directly accuses Jonah of not caring about the Ninevites, though the prophet does seem to express more intense concern over the death of the gourd than the demise of 120,000 people. When Jonah pities the plant, he pities himself. Jonah does not burst into another psalm when the plant appears, as he does when the big fish saves his life, but his mood does change from glum to joyful and back again with the plant's appearance and demise. When God's benevolence benefits Jonah, he responds with adulation. When God removes the comfort from Jonah's life, his anguished death wish quickly returns.

The swift, overnight destruction of the gourd is designed to teach Jonah the unacceptability of Nineveh's destruction. God demonstrates to Jonah through an *a fortiori* argument that the great, evil city is just as necessary to the totality of creation as a single gourd (Zlotowitz 144). Yet the death of the plant also represents the death of Jonah's lost hope that the city will indeed be overthrown. The plant's demise is supposed to bring with it a breakthrough in Jonah's understanding of the sanctity of all life, but the plant perishes in record time and Jonah's comprehension may be stillborn too. The gourd is the only thing that dies in the story, though other things are threatened with death.

Jonah's relationship with the ricinus plant is the antithesis of God's relationship to Nineveh (Butterworth 32), and the Lord points out this difference to the contrary prophet. The last two verses are critical to the meaning of the book as a whole because they originate in the mouth of God and reflect the concluding issue, God's freedom to express concern in whatever way the deity chooses. Yahweh gently chastises Jonah and asserts divine authority at 4:10–11 in a splendid *coup de grâce*:

> You cared about the plant, which you did not work for and which you did not grow, which appeared overnight and perished overnight. And should not I care about Nineveh, that great city, in which there are more than a hundred and twenty thousand persons who do not know their right hand from their left, and many beasts as well!

In many English translations, God's last quote is given in the form of a question in which "God spells out even more fully what His compassion implied, and Jonah is left with the question as to whether he is prepared yet to accept this knowledge for himself" (Magonet 91). But in the 1985 JPS translation, an exclamation point is used instead of a question mark: "...and many beasts as well!" Since biblical Hebrew does not contain punctuation equivalent to question marks or exclamation points, they are matters of interpretation. If God asks a question, it is certainly a rhetorical one, and its exclamatory nature is clear.

Another translation of the Hebrew verb "care about," חוס, which appears at lines 4:10 and 11, is "pity," which the 1917 JPS translation preserves in the speech of God: "Thou hast had pity on the gourd..." and "should not I have pity on Nineveh...." The plant is God's gift to Jonah, which is true of everything in the story. The prophet did not create it, earn it, or do anything to deserve it. Jonah has no right to claim ownership of the plant. It belongs to God, not to Jonah, and God may do with it as divine will dictates. By analogy, then, God may also exercise sovereign authority over Nineveh. If Jonah can feel so strongly about a single vegetable only because it provides him with relief from the sun, then how much more strongly must God, the Creator of all, feel about repentant human beings in Nineveh? Ironically, the verb חוס is used in two ways. Jonah pities a thing; God pities a people in crisis.

Furthermore, God implicitly tells Jonah that the prophet pities the plant only because he identifies with its transitory character. Jonah associates the gourd's impending destruction with his own and therefore laments (Goodhart 54). The plant is ephemeral; so too is Jonah's change of heart that comes in the belly of the fish. In fact, both ancient Israel and Nineveh will prove to be as transitory as the plant. Nineveh will destroy Jonah's northern kingdom of Israel, which will not achieve independent nation status again until 1948, and within a few hundred years of Jonah's prophecy, Nineveh will also be reduced to rubble, never to rise again. The plant's temporary quality is mirrored in the fate of both places.

God's primary concern is revealed to a sulking Jonah: to preserve life, both human and animal, rather than to destroy life. All creation is God's handiwork. The cattle are mentioned at 4:11 because they are innocent and ignorant and cannot be held responsible for their actions. Also, the text shows the lower animals to achieve a sort of solidarity with human beings, as every living thing is together in this predicament. God shows love and compassion for all 120,000 people plus other living creatures in Nineveh, and by analogy, throughout the world. The narrator, by allowing God to have the last word in the book of Jonah, "seeks to remove the blindness from a multitude of other eyes, equally restrictive in their conception of divine love" (Craigie 233). If Jonah (and the large portion of humanity he represents) is short on pity, God is not. Jonah pities one plant that is helpful to him, so surely God should show mercy toward many, many more living things. The natural human inclination to confine or restrict God's love to our own group is seen as an election theology that is too narrow in its focus. We are assured that we can leave the pitying to the Lord, who will decide when vegetables, animals, and humans deserve divine mercy. The rejoicing and the grieving are matters of divine consideration. God's compassion means that the Lord suffers with us, as the origin of the word suggests (*com* = with and *pati* = suffer) (Hampl 298). God is thus in primal union with all living things, and all of creation is bound together through God's love.

God emerges as the undisputed hero of the book of Jonah, and chapter 4 represents the climax of the story. The book is not meant to be a chronicle of factual data, but rather something much more glorious: a lesson on divine forgiveness and Jonah's explosive reaction to it. The text begins and ends with God's word, as befits the Creator of the universe. The Almighty's omnipotence and universal forgiveness are in opposition to humankind's free will and narrow-minded disobedience. The purpose of Jonah's misadventures is to teach the prophet, and through him to remind the Jewish people and the world, much more than the simple concept that God's heart is inclined to accept human repentance. Nor is its object only to proclaim a message as simple as the concept that God's love extends to non-Jews as well as Jews. The Israelite narrator forcefully reiterates throughout the book of Jonah the essential lesson that no one should begrudge or try to control God's love, mercy, and forgiveness to all the peoples of the earth. Jonah has always known this attribute of God, as 4:2 indicates, but it is difficult for the prophet to accept and embrace the notion gracefully and joyfully.

Yahweh pursues Jonah to the ends of the earth and drags him, nearly kicking in defiance and screaming for death, into a more universal view of love and acceptance, for God cares for all creatures great and small. In this respect, Jonah is a foil character to God. The greatness of God is elucidated against the backdrop of Jonah's imperfect understanding and hardness of heart. Nineveh is called "that great city" three times, but God is greater. The end of the book of Jonah contrasts the prophet's self-love and the deity's selfless devotion to all creation. God creates, controls, and cares for the natural world. No one and nothing can escape God's notice, and to evade forever the responsibility God wants us to assume is impossible. The Lord rescues those who are in trouble and cry out for help, and the delivered

ones respond with praise and thanksgiving. The Lord undergoes a change
of mind, overrides prophetic word for the sake of saving the repentant, and
refrains from punishing. Unlike Jonah, the Lord suffers at the thought of
losing any part of the human race.

As the Lord endeavors to teach Jonah the lessons of love and mercy,
many significant details emerge concerning their complex relationship. For
example, God makes direct appearances only to the prophet, regardless of
how recalcitrant he may be. These appearances trouble Jonah and cause him
anxiety. God's initial harshness, as reflected in unleashing the terrible forces
of nature to wreak havoc upon the world, are repeated in Jonah's callous reaction to outside peoples. When Jonah feels ill treated by God, the prophet
retaliates by showing coldness to others. Nevertheless, God eventually is
forgiving toward insiders and outsiders (Jonah and the pagans). Jonah's
understanding and appreciation of God's forgiveness are called into serious
question, yet the prophet demonstrates other admirable qualities, including
perseverance and resilience under pressure. He bounces back after adversity. God must have tender feelings for Jonah, continually demonstrated by
divine patience and restraint (Mather 287–88). Yet at the end of the story,
God's forgiveness of the Ninevites is clearly implied, but the story maintains
an open ending in at least four ways: (1) reflecting ancient Jewish belief in
the nothingness of Sheol rather than the everlasting reward of punishment in
heaven or hell, God does not comment on the immortal fate of the Ninevites;
(2) though suggesting that the Lord's forgiveness of the Ninevites is appropriate, God never directly says that Jonah should also pardon them; (3) while
showing possible differences between human and divine actions and attitudes, the Lord remains silent concerning future divine intentions *vis-à-vis*
Jonah; (4) demonstrating Jonah's initial reluctance to act magnanimously
toward the Ninevites, the text does not reveal whether God's exclamation
at 4:11 causes Jonah to change his mind.

We cannot be certain whether Jonah is convinced by God's noble, righteous argument concerning the sanctity of all life, but the inescapable fact
is that the narrator wants the Lord to have the last word. Maybe Jonah
understands God's conduct and maybe not; the Bible provides no record of
Jonah's reaction to the Lord's final pronouncement. Ultimately, convincing
Jonah is not nearly as important as convincing the rest of us of God's power
to forgive and redeem. The story offers no closure from Jonah's point of
view, but the prophet's attitudes are ultimately less important because they
have fewer short- and long-term consequences for the Ninevites than the
Lord's.

Dissatisfied with the author's open ending, editors over the centuries have sometimes closed it by adding a response from Jonah. Realizing that Jonah's life does not end at 4:11, some have speculated what the prophet would do with the remainder of his career. Though most scholars confine their exegesis to the text itself, others offer suggestions about what might have happened after the biblical narrative ends. More often than not, these additions reveal a Jonah consistent with 3:3, an obedient prophet who understands and obeys God's word. One thirteenth-century Jewish homily, attributed to Rav Shimon haDarshan of Frankfort, edits the text to add: "At that very moment, [Jonah] fell flat on his face saying, 'Direct your world according to the attribute of mercy, as is written, "Mercy and forgiveness belong to the Lord our God." ' " Contemporary children's Bibles, eager to impact positively on young minds, also tend to attach a moral tag to the end of the story: "And Jonah began, at last, to understand," or "And Jonah *learned* that men, and women, and little children, are all precious in the sight of the Lord, even though they know not God" (Person 151–52). Readers of these supplements would range from learned medieval rabbis to present-day children. To reach people at both ends of the audience spectrum, editors have emended the text so that a pious prophet vanquishes whatever anger, reluctance, stinginess, disobedience, or rebelliousness he previously demonstrated in favor of kindness and forgiveness. Jonah's dilemma is resolved in these cases.

Concerning Jonah's acceptance of God's message as presented in the text, the book has the ending given it by individual readers. We are left with a cliffhanger and must struggle to determine our own ending for the tale, to search our souls and see if we can view forgiveness as God does. This unconventional, open-ended conclusion begins to look highly appropriate. It is extremely compelling, for it draws readers into the paradox of the story and demands that we inspect our own potential responses to the prophet's dilemma. How big are our hearts? Down through the centuries, those of us who identify with Jonah's stiff-necked point of view regarding our enemies must feel like God's final exclamation is directed to us personally. When we eliminate the Jonah that lies within our hearts, then we can begin to grasp the meaning of God's forgiving grace. As the great fish spews Jonah from its innards, so we must try to expel the biases that lie deep within our hearts and souls. The field of psychology notes the "Zeigarnik Effect," wherein a completed task is more easily forgotten than an uncompleted one. To many readers, Jonah's mission seems only partially complete because his attitude at the end of the story is left unarticulated. Therefore, we feel a more profound psychological need to take up Jonah's unfulfilled work and finish it for him.

We need to become Jonah to ensure that his task is successfully concluded on earth (Lacocque and Lacocque *Complex,* 26).

The task of judging people "who do not know their right hand from their left" (4:11) is alluded to only four times in the Torah (Num 20:17, 22:26; Deut 2:27, 5:29), where it is used figuratively to demonstrate staying on the narrow path of righteousness, not turning to the right or left. The Ninevites are thus like children who have not yet learned the basics of correct behavior and do not know right from wrong. They are ignorant, and God does not hold them responsible for their prior lack of information, once they receive the divine word and accept it. They are rather like Oedipus when he has no idea that he has killed his father, or like Pharaoh (Gen 12:11–20) when he does not know that Sarai is Abram's wife, or like Uzzah (2 Sam 6:6–7) when he forgets or does not know that he is forbidden to touch the arc (Daube 37). Yet Oedipus, Pharaoh, and Uzzah all suffer serious punishment, even death. The Ninevites, on the other hand, deserve to be spared, not to die. Much of the Hebrew Scriptures reveals God's love for the chosen people, the insiders. The book of Jonah is one of the noteworthy extensions and shows divine tenderness toward unknowing outsiders as well. God loves the whole of creation and is capable of transcending cultural, ethnic, geo-political, and even religious boundaries among the nations, a trait that most humans lack. Jonah serves as a foil to God in these last lines so that the final lesson on human self-love verses divine universal love and forgiveness can be presented.

The dialogue between God and Jonah, which is the sole topic of chapter 4 and a contrast to the Lord's silence in other chapters, thus comes to an abrupt end. Arguably, God convinces the prophet and wins the dispute because Jonah is silent, and silence equals consent. Another way of interpreting Jonah's lack of retort is that he is dumbstruck by God's moral authority. What happens to the prophet after 4:11? We never hear of him again in the TANAKH. No matter. The dénouement of his personal story is irrelevant. He has served his purpose: to show us God's nature and prerogative to pardon anyone, including those like the Ninevites who know no better than their previous sinful ways. All humankind is a single family with a loving parent keeping watch over us.

The education of the prophet, and thus of the readers, is one of the book's central themes. Early in the story, Jonah learns that he cannot remain a fugitive from divine calling. Now, at the end of the tale, Jonah's response is not so important. Jonah is a perfect failure and an anti-hero. Nineveh is saved from punishment, against Jonah's will, which means that he fails to get his way. He fails in obtaining his wish to die. He possibly fails to understand God's final comments about the Ninevites. It is primarily the reader on whom God's final words land, the reader who is left to ponder their meaning, the reader who must decide what action to take next.

Jonah is the antithesis of what we expect a prophet to be. We anticipate that a prophet should be glad to receive a commission, but Jonah opposes God's plan to send him to Nineveh. A prophet, we imagine, will be obedient to God's calling, but Jonah is not. We expect a prophet to intervene on behalf of sinful people, but Jonah does as little as possible to save the Ninevites. The otherworldliness of a prophet's spiritual nature should, we think, cause him to show little concern for creature comforts, but Jonah is the opposite. Our image of a prophet is that he not be foolish or mean spirited, but Jonah is both. In chapter 4 God is faced with a renegade prophet and must utter final words that attempt to bring the refractory servant back into the fold. The book of Jonah is like two stories that have been combined: "the first is Jonah's story, the second is God's story *for* Jonah" (Hampl 296), and both of these stories are filled with God's compassion and forgiveness.

Over the generations many serious scholars have interpreted Jonah's distress anti-Semitically because Jonah is the prophet "*of, to, and for* Israel" (Dennison 33). *The Interpreter's Bible,* for example, calls it "anger that could not tolerate the thought of God having compassion upon the heathen" (6:891). Others chastise the entire Jewish population because of Jonah's response to God's forgiveness: "If the Jews had but listened to this appeal, they would have become the great missionaries of the world carrying the gospel of the one God to all the world until they had established the universal religion" (Bewer 424). Jonah's own words dispute this theory that Jonah despises outsiders. It is not that he hates foreigners, wants God only to love the chosen people, and flees to Tarshish because he hopes his enemies will be destroyed. Jonah simply holds onto the view, often expressed in the TANAKH, that God will harshly judge the nations.

The author of the book of Jonah embraces a broader view. Jonah is not really anti-Gentile. If he were, he would not be ready to sacrifice himself to save the sailors in chapter 1. Furthermore, he expresses no direct hostility toward the Ninevites. The anger Jonah feels is toward God. The author wants the Jews to fulfill the Isa 49:6 mandate and be a "light of the nations / That My salvation may reach the ends of the earth." To begrudge salvation to outsiders is anti-Jewish. The Jews are, in effect, ex-Ninevites, and the Ninevites are the new Jews (Goodhart 53). For the Jews to turn on the Ninevites is to turn on themselves, and the ancient Israelites used the book of Jonah to evaluate themselves and their theology. The prophets explain the Babylonian captivity as a punishment brought about not because the

Jews failed to minister to the Gentiles, but because they failed to remain faithful Jews.

Other anti-Semitic interpretations of the book of Jonah stem from the Jewish rejection of Jesus as the Son of God. In Matt 21:41 Jesus warns his listeners that on judgment day the Ninevites will rise up and condemn Israel, for the Ninevites wisely repent at the appropriate moment, but a stubborn Israel does not see that "something greater than Jonah is here."

Humankind's compassion for Jonah and the Jewish people has often been lacking. In general, commentaries composed by Jewish scholars condemn Jonah far less frequently than commentaries written by non-Jews, and non-Jewish scholars often fail to cite Jewish scholarship on the book of Jonah, while Jewish writers frequently quote Christian sources (Hoffer and Wright 148–50). However sincere and learned Bible commentators may be, exegeses are colored by the principles of their particular faith, and we often misunderstand the work we seek to explore. For Jews, Christians, and Muslims, traditionally held notions of what composes the true faith frame the meaning of the Bible. Unfortunately, the book of Jonah has been plagued by judgmental, anti-Semitic interpretations since the days of St. Augustine (354–430) and other Latin church fathers. Not only do church leaders display violent anti-Jewish vituperation; they are also likely to engender such hatred in their readers. Church fathers often held the notion that the exceptional sinfulness of Jonah spilled over onto the Jews of post-biblical times. For example, St. John Chrysostom (c. 347–407) wrote of Jonah's descendants: "It is because you killed Christ...that there is now no restoration, no mercy anymore and no defense. Long ago your audacity was directed against servants, against Moses, Isaiah and Jeremiah....But you have eclipsed everything in the past and through your madness against Christ, you have committed the ultimate transgression" (Holmgren 128).

Maliciously or naively, non-Jewish commentators have contended that Jonah is not grieved for the sake of his home country but because he, as a prophet of Israel, vindictively begrudges Gentiles their rightful place with God. St. Augustine explains that Jonah represents corrupt Israel, which resents the salvation of the nations. Even though St. Jerome (c. 342–420) disputes this malevolent viewpoint because it is inconsistent with Jesus' own words about Israel as a favored nation and about Jonah prefiguring Christ, the anti-Semitic view has persisted down through the ages. Some church leaders, notably Martin Luther, found in Jonah a convenient representative of a hated Jewish population. According to his view, the stiff-necked Jews consider God to be their private property and bitterly oppose the redemption of the Gentiles. What Jonah fears most, according to Luther, is that God's lovingkindness will be extended beyond the limits of an exclusive Jewish world (Goeser 210). Luther points out that Jonah is indignant and would rather die than share the love of God with Nineveh. Luther himself states: "Jonah's heart inclined to the view that the people of Nineveh were not deserving of God's grace and Word because they were not God's people, that is not Jews, or of the people of Israel" (19:44). One of Luther's underlying problems with Judaism is that it does not embrace the Pauline doctrine of justification by faith. The prophet Jonah may not trust the Ninevites to continue in worshipful actions, but Luther maintains that "the real and true God is He who is properly served not with works but with the true faith and with sincerity of heart, who gives and bestows mercy and benefactions entirely gratis and without our works and merits" (Luther 19:56). In Martin Luther's hermeneutics, it is just and fair that this prophet, a most grievous sinner who is worse than the idolatrous heathens whom he warns, is exposed and shamed in the book of Jonah.

One need not hearken back generations to find anti-Semitic interpretations of the book of Jonah. In a 1993 article entitled "The Sign of Jonah," James Dennison wrote: "Behold, O Israel, the supreme sign — an empty tomb and the streaming of Gentiles to the city of great David's greater son. . . . Let Jew and Gentile embrace the Son. For he has given us a sign . . ." (35). *The Interpreter's Bible* (6:888) claims that the book of Jonah shows God's rejection of the Jewish people in postexilic, and perhaps even preexilic, times because their nationalistic attitude is shown to be absurd and hateful to God. Not all criticisms of Jonah can be dismissed as anti-Semitism, but some examples of religious favoritism exist. Diction can suggest a God who is Christian. For example, Stephen L. Harris suggests that at the end of the tale, "There is no record that Jonah ever understands the meaning of Yahweh's catechism" (153). While "catechism" can designate any book of instruction, the term, not generally used in Judaism, is most often employed to mean a book containing the principles of Christianity. "Catechism" contains strong Christian connotations and seems to overlook the story's Jewish roots.

Perhaps the book's final lesson for the ages is that an anti-Semitic interpretation not only misses the point of the book of Jonah but also shows the arrogance and narrow-minded parochialism of biased commentators. In the minds of some non-Jewish commentators, precisely those "heathen" outsiders or Gentiles are compelled to revere God, as opposed to the spiteful hatefulness demonstrated by the Jewish prophet. In fact, the text itself does demonstrate that God's saving grace is so powerful that even those who have not previously worshiped the God of Israel must acknowledge the miraculous redemption offered, and nothing about Israel is specifically mentioned. The conflict between Israel and the Gentile world is advanced by exegetes who have their own axes to grind and see what is not necessarily there. They view Jonah (representing the entire people of Israel) despairing as he "contemplates others enjoying honey from the Jewish hive. This nationalistic prophet is running odiously true to type" (Allen 230). While the book of Jonah may point to sinful attitudes among ancient Israelites, these ideas can be found among people of every race and religion to the present day. Such shortcomings are real and serious, but hardly confined to the ancient Israelites.

German professors of the Enlightenment saw Jonah as the narrow-minded one and separated the prophet from the narrator of the story, whom they saw as a spokesman for God's universal love (Bickerman 25). Jonah favors loyalty to his people over duty to God and does not want to share God's divine mercy with the Gentiles, so the author of the book admonishes his intolerant countrymen and women. According to these scholars, Jonah relishes the mercy of God when it applies to the Jewish people but finds it unpalatable when applied to the rest of the world, especially Israel's enemies. They thought the purpose of the book was to protest the nationalism and exclusivity of the Jewish outlook. Jonah embodies Jewish hatred of Gentiles that the Jewish author wishes to ridicule (Eddy 248). This, too, misses the point as the writers focus on divine disapproval of Jonah, when the text itself does not reveal such wrath toward the prophet. Often the belittling, anti-Semitic lesson — rejected by Judaism — is driven hard: pitiless Jonah symbolizes benighted Judaism, while repentant Nineveh represents enlightened Christianity. Jonah typifies the pejorative view of Jews as stingy, heartless, vengeful, unforgiving, and wrongheaded, while Nineveh is seen to characterize the loving, compassionate, superior morality of Christians beloved to God.

The book of Jonah is a Jewish work, told and written by Jews to a Jewish audience and canonized in the Jewish Bible. With this in mind, the two false and simplistic stereotypes, Jewish elitism and Christian universalism, must be reconsidered. The gracious mercy of a benevolent deity is perhaps the most significant and beautiful of Judaism's teachings. To suggest that the Hebrew Scriptures deny the universal nature of God's love is to ignore Abraham's haggling on behalf of the residents of Sodom and Gomorrah, the eloquent acceptance of a Moabite woman in the book of Ruth, and Solomon's speech at the dedication of the temple in Jerusalem:

> Or if a foreigner who is not of Your people Israel comes from a distant land for the sake of Your name — for they shall hear about Your great name and Your mighty hand and Your outstretched arm — when he comes to pray toward this House, oh, hear in Your heavenly abode and grant all that the foreigner asks You for. Thus all the peoples of the earth will know Your name and revere You, as does Your people Israel; and they will recognize that your name is attached to this House that I have built. (1 Kgs 8:41–43)

There is much evidence in the Hebrew Scriptures that the ancient Israelites, those who were to become the forerunners of modern Judaism, have always professed a sincere and convincing conviction of God's universal warmth and compassion. In ancient Israel, writers feel free to expose wrongdoing and call for its removal. Nathan never hesitates to criticize King David's behavior, and the author of Jonah relates a tale of eternal human wrongdoing and divine forgiveness. Even the severest critics within Israel are not silenced, destroyed, forgotten, or modified. Their work is held up to the people as a model for right behavior, coming from the mouth of God. What kind of people engages in such self-examination? Not a group dedicated to destroying its enemies and denying them God's saving grace.

Furthermore, it is a profoundly Jewish activity to engage in self-examination, to recognize shortcomings, and not to subvert them. The Jewish narrator, realizing the presence of wrongs in Israelite society and zealots who hold a particular religious ethic, addresses them openly and passionately in the book of Jonah. Self-criticism is part of the religious tradition in Judaism, built into the religious calendar during the High Holy Days, so it is natural that the Jews devote entire books of the Bible to exploring their own shortcomings. Such rigorous self-examination should be applauded and admired, for in many communities, institutions, and nations dissent is viewed as a serious offense not to be tolerated.

Voicing doubt about God's fairness and equanimity is also not uncommon in the Hebrew Scriptures, so Jonah's conflict with the deity is quintessentially Jewish in nature. Not only do the Jews tolerate self-deprecating introspection, they sanctify it in the holiest of places. As the artist in the Lillian Hellman's memoir, the Jews see and then see again. Jewish leaders may have had doubts about canonizing the books of Proverbs, Job, Ecclesiastes, Ezekiel, and the Song of Songs, but the book of Jonah never seems to have been the object of controversy. It survives and is given a prominent place within the religion because it is an integral part of the Jewish soul. "The Jewish community preserved this author's caricatured, cartooned critique and held it as Holy Scripture! Extraordinary," says Holmgren (131). Perhaps the Jews did not anticipate how the book of Jonah would be used against them, falsely exploiting them as an example of an ugly, xenophobic people who care only about their own and not God's entire creation. Yet instead of ridding themselves of the book of Jonah or hiding it from the rest of humankind, they preserved it so that it could be presented to future generations of readers, Jewish and Gentile, to reveal the introspective nature of their hearts and the loving and forgiving nature of the God they introduced to the world.

CHAPTER 6

Jonah's Legacy

We recall our terrible past so that we can deal with it,
to forgive where forgiveness is necessary, without forgetting;
to ensure that never again will such inhumanity tear us apart.
— Nelson Mandela, Address

Forgiveness is only slightly less ancient than sin. Yet we are much less experienced in the craft of pardoning than we are in the practice of wrongdoing. There is a cycle of misconduct that diminishes everyone. Over and over again we commit transgressions by the shameful things we do and the righteous things we leave undone. Wounded, our instinct is to lash out, even though we have a desperate need both to give and receive forgiveness. Yet alongside the perpetual circle of wrongdoing there can also be a continuous cycle of forgiveness in which all the principal players engage — other people, ourselves, and God. In the wilderness of biblical days and the wasteland of modern life, God forgives us. Nevertheless, when we are injured, we cannot always fathom how to let go of the pain we feel. The sort of forgiveness extolled in self-help books and religious services, the kind that flows down to us from God and is presented by God to Jonah, seems difficult to emulate. The legacy of the story's final chapter is that we continue to struggle with the issue of forgiveness. Human and divine responses may of necessity differ.

According to Douglas Stuart (105–6) three kinds of temporal pardon appear in the book of Jonah. First is God's forgiveness of Jonah. Even though he may deserve death, Jonah is rescued by the big fish, which hardly constitutes blanket absolution of all Jonah's misdeeds, past and future. The rescue merely allows him a second chance to overcome a rebellious act. Second is God's forgiveness of the Ninevites. The great city's inhabitants, like Jonah himself, may have previously perpetrated deeds worthy of serious punishment, but God responds to the people's penitence and releases them from penalty. Again, deliverance is not necessarily for all time; it applies only to this single event. Third is Jonah's forgiveness of the Ninevites. Whether this occurs is open to debate. As we have seen, the text does not supply a definitive answer.

The prophet Jonah's story implies that forgiveness flows vertically from God to people, but the tale is silent on whether the prophet allows pardon to move horizontally among human beings who find its taste bitter. Feelings of hurt and hate might come more naturally than impulses toward mercy and compassion. Stubborn refusal to forgive allows people to hold others firmly in the bondage of uncompromising judgment. Deliberately withholding forgiveness can be a way of wielding power, perhaps even a way of trying to block others from receiving divine pardon. Sometimes we proffer only a perfunctory gesture that simulates forgiveness but is not the genuine article. Divine forgiveness is a gift freely given by a sovereign God, but human forgiveness appears indistinctly on our horizon, a goal the best in us strives to attain, despite footing that we, like Jonah, continually lose and regain. Ironically, when forgiveness is appropriate but we nonetheless withhold it as a means of punishing someone else, the tentacles of unforgiveness choke our own spirit too. We may become as sullen and dispirited as Jonah. On the other hand, we might wish to forgive but not know how. Surrounded by the debris of a broken existence, we do not know how or whether to cancel the debt owed to us, how to trade the ashes of anger for the beauty of life.

The process of forgiveness seems mysterious, nebulous, and elusive. Just as it challenged the prophet Jonah in days of old, it remains difficult for us to grasp today. No one in heaven or on earth can force us to forgive; we have to want to do it. If we can figure out how, we free ourselves of twisted emotions and actions involving disappointment, rage, spite, and vengeance. Nevertheless, at some times, forgiving seems inappropriate. So we look to God and to our religions for help, wondering if an unforgiving heart blocks us from receiving divine grace. Human forgiveness is not just a gift we magnanimously confer upon others; when bestowed in suitable ways, it can be a spiritual lift that provides multiple advantages for ourselves. In most cases where there is forgiveness, movement toward compassion and salvation also takes place. God expects us to engage in the same struggle that grips Jonah, to face fierce forgiveness skirmishes that we do not always win. During our lifetimes we will have to forgive many people, many times, but we may occasionally have good reason to withhold our forgiveness.

The field of psychology offers a paradigm for personal growth by suggesting five stages of initiation: separation, purification, symbolic death, new knowledge, and rebirth (Hedva 5). Jonah, representing us all, passes through these landmarks on his road to learning about forgiveness. He separates from God in chapter 1 by fleeing to Tarshish; he begins ritual purification by water when the sailors throw him overboard; he undergoes emblematic death in the darkness of the great fish's innards; he gains new knowledge, which he espouses via the poem in chapter 2 as he abandons old behavior and false identity so that he can carry out a mission for society's greater good; and he is reborn when he is spewed out again onto dry land. His rebirth brings him back into the service of God and allows him to fulfill his role of prophet in chapter 3. He gains emotional maturity and benefits a larger community by experiencing these five initiation stages. Yet Jonah's transformation is temporary, and he appears to suffer an ethical relapse in chapter 4. After gaining ground, he falters once again. Today influential psychologists and millions of ordinary people remain interested in these timeless rites of passage that signify Jonah's very old, very real predicament. As high-minded as platitudes on forgiveness might be, they remain difficult to live by, and perhaps Jonah's impulse not to forgive is sometimes fitting. He is, after all, a man and not a god.

The Inland Sunflower and the Island Prison

Jonah's dilemma has yielded an ambiguous legacy for today, for knowing how to employ forgiveness lessons in modern life is no less perplexing than in ancient times. Though an appalling number of atrocities is recorded through the millennia, two stunning contemporary examples stand out and exemplify Jonah's quandary about forgiveness. They are fascinating partly because while they both demonstrate atrocities, they show opposite answers about how to come to grips with pardoning the guilty. Enhancing the discussion of whether Jonah, representing Everyone, should forgive the Ninevites are two paradigms of forgiveness from two twentieth-century horrors, dissimilar in scope and intent: the Holocaust of Central Europe (1933–1945) and the apartheid system of South Africa (1948–1994). Holocaust survivor Simon Wiesenthal narrates his tale of denying forgiveness to an SS man who requests absolution for killing many Jews. Wiesenthal's report contrasts to the story of how former South African political prisoner Nelson Mandela, victim of a less radical incarnation of white elitism, manages to forgive his ex-oppressors. These two men come to opposite conclusions, yet perhaps they are both right. Their situations have things in common, as well as major differences. Wiesenthal does not feel he has the right to forgive a Nazi who murdered many people but not Wiesenthal himself. The SS man's victims are dead and cannot speak for themselves, so Wiesenthal believes he cannot put words into their mouths. Nelson Mandela, on the other hand, was placed in an inhumane prison, but it was not an extermination camp. He is still alive and can come face-to-face with his former jailors, who now seek reconciliation. Mandela forgives those who personally harmed him. In the context of the book of Jonah, however, we have an interesting situation. Since Jonah has suffered no harm from any Ninevite, his dilemma more closely parallels Wiesenthal's, yet who could deny the power and beauty of Mandela's dedication to forgiveness? If at the end of the Bible story (4:10–11), Jonah's answer to God's unanswered question is "no," the prophet resembles Wiesenthal and rabbinic tradition. If Jonah's response is "yes," he is comparable to Mandela. Both twentieth-century men are principled individuals of international renown; both have valid and reasonable stances. So whom should a Jonah of today follow? If the two options were not of similar ethical strength and validity, there would be no dilemma in this wounded world.

One of the most compelling treatments of this question of whether one ought to forgive those who have done wrong is found in Simon Wiesenthal's *The Sunflower: On the Possibilities and Limits of Forgiveness*. Known since the end of World War II for his efforts to identify Nazi war criminals and bring them to trial, Wiesenthal has long been tormented by one particular incident that occurred when he was a young man held captive by the Germans in a concentration camp. In *The Sunflower*, first published twenty-five years after the War, Wiesenthal relates this perplexing personal experience and ends by posing the question of whether he should have absolved one German officer who asked for forgiveness. Subsequent editions of the book contain an interfaith symposium on the subject with responses from forty-six well-known intellectuals — theologians, scholars, politicians, and writers — who give their views on Wiesenthal's moral dilemma. Today many people, especially Jews, are reluctant to compare anything in recorded annals to the Shoah (Holocaust). The wholesale slaughter of six million Jews, just because they were Jews, is different from any other tragic event in the dark history of humankind. It stands as a monolithic reminder of the evil impulse within people. Comparisons to other catastrophic atrocities, pogroms, and attempted genocides — and numerous examples are available just in the post–World War II era in Tibet, Cambodia, Rwanda, Bosnia, and elsewhere — still leave the Holocaust as a uniquely barbarous illustration of man's inhumanity to man. Though the technology of mass destruction has improved over the millennia, Simon Wiesenthal's situation has some basic points in common with the ancient dilemma presented in the Bible to Jonah the prophet. Both men are left with questions and doubts about whether and whom they can forgive. Though the enormity of Ninevite persecution of Jews may pale in comparison to the horrendous evil perpetuated by twentieth-century Nazis, the question remains: should we offer blanket forgiveness to those who have wronged our people? Are there limits to human forgiveness? Can we forgive a repentant criminal for crimes committed against someone other than ourselves?

Wiesenthal's tale is heart wrenching. He recalls debates he had while a prisoner, arguments with his fellow Jews about why God could allow them to suffer so terribly. As a young concentration camp inmate, Wiesenthal concluded that God must have been on leave: "Otherwise the present state of things wouldn't be possible. God must be away. And He has no deputy" (9). A poignant and sad moment occurs in the story when Wiesenthal recalls passing a German military cemetery one day as he was returning to camp from a work detail. All dead German soldiers had a sunflower planted on their graves, and Wiesenthal was envious. He believed his dead body would soon be thrown into a mass grave, heaped on top of other rotting corpses of slave laborers, with no marker and no one to remember the spot. Even in death, it seemed to Wiesenthal that the Germans retained their alleged superiority. They had sunflowers.

One day a German Red Cross nurse told Wiesenthal to follow her into a hospital, a building converted from the high school where Wiesenthal had, not too long before, received his diploma. Trained to be an obedient prisoner, he complied and was led in his rags to the private, antiseptically clean room of a dying German officer. Totally bandaged except for small openings for ears, nose, and mouth, and with little time to live, the officer wanted to confess his crimes to a Jew, be forgiven, and die in peace. Wiesenthal, who had ironically survived German "selections" before, was again selected as the Jew for the job. Without the power to refuse, Wiesenthal reluctantly listened as the young man in the hospital bed strained physically to tell his story. Wiesenthal thought about the sunflower that would soon be on the man's grave.

The German's name was Karl. He explained that he was twenty-one and a volunteer for Hitler's elite special forces, the SS. Karl's Catholic parents had hoped he would become a priest and seemed distressed when he joined the Hitler Youth. He was especially concerned that his mother never know the atrocities he had routinely committed during his military service, for she thought of her son as a kind and gentle boy. When the soldier recalled frolicking with his young school chums, Wiesenthal knew that few Jews would ever see parents or childhood friends again. Wiesenthal also began to wonder why a priest had not been called to hear the man's final confession,

why a Jew — condemned as a defenseless subhuman — was being forced
to listen to this story. Karl said he had never seen many Jews, except his
doctor, for whom his mother mourned after the trusted family physician
disappeared. All the soldier knew about Jews was what he was told over
loud speakers — that they were a demented race and the cause of all German
misfortunes.

In Dnepropetrovsk, Ukraine, Karl was involved in brutal fighting, including an assault on civilians. All the Jews of the town — about 150
unarmed men, women, and children — were rounded up and crammed into
a small three-story house. Cans of gasoline were dumped on the exterior,
and grenades were thrown through the windows of the building. The soldiers
clearly heard screams as the fire leapt from floor to floor. The SS man recalled
seeing a Jewish father with a baby in his arms, clothes aflame. The man with
the child jumped from a window, immediately followed by a woman. When
the three hit the ground, Karl stood ready to kill them and anyone else who
tried to escape the burning house. He shot the family. The SS man's description of the dead child made Wiesenthal immediately think of a young boy
named Eli, whom he had known in the Lemberg ghetto. For Wiesenthal, the
dead child *was* Eli. The soldier said that those people in the burning house
had died quickly and did not suffer as he himself had since then, though
they were more innocent than he. He said that his physical suffering was
terrible but that his pangs of conscience hurt him worse. Wiesenthal writes,
"Here was a dying man — a murderer who did not want to be a murderer
but who had been made into a murderer by a murderous ideology. He was
confessing his crime to a man who perhaps tomorrow must die at the hands
of these same murderers. In his confession there was true repentance" (53).
When the man asked for forgiveness, Wiesenthal silently rose and left the
room. Years after the macabre encounter, Wiesenthal visited the dead man's
mother and did not destroy her illusions about her "good boy" by telling her
what Karl had done during the war. *The Sunflower* concludes with Wiesenthal's probing questions about what Karl might have done if he had been put
on trial after the war, but the main question is far more personal. Wiesenthal asks whether his silence at the bedside of the dying man was right or
wrong. He asks us to consider what we would have done if we had been in
his situation.

In the remainder of the book, leading scholars attempt to answer the
question. Of the forty-six responses, thirty people write that they would not
have forgiven the SS soldier, that they would not expect Simon Wiesenthal to
do so, and that it is practically impossible to forgive Hitler's henchmen. Forgiveness trivializes the horror that the victims suffered and that the survivors

continue to endure. Some respondents point out that bitter resentment helps victims hold on to a sense of self-worth and resist future attacks. Eight respondents to Wiesenthal's question are ambiguous, and eight clearly say yes, they would forgive. Of the eight who unequivocally advocate forgiveness, all are non-Jews, including the Dalai Lama; Theodore Hesburgh, president emeritus of Notre Dame; and Dith Pran, victim of the Khmer Rouge whose biography is the basis for the film *The Killing Fields*. The Dalai Lama's words are especially poignant:

> I believe one should forgive the person or persons who have committed atrocities against oneself and mankind. But this does not necessarily mean one should forget about the atrocities committed. In fact, one should be aware and remember these experiences so that efforts can be made to check the reoccurrence of such atrocities in the future. (129)

Theodore Hesburgh declares that he would forgive "because God would forgive" (164). Confining his comments to human and not divine beings, Dith Pran maintains that he could not forgive Pol Pot and the dozen leaders of the Khmer Rouge, men roughly analogous to Hitler. Yet he can understand and therefore forgive the soldiers, ordinary men and boys who were uneducated and brainwashed into doing the actual killing. Though he will never be able to forget what they did, Pran can separate their actions from the "evil masterminds" of the slaughter (222).

Among the Jewish contributors who provide an ambiguous, "yes — but" response to Wiesenthal's question is Rabbi Harold Kushner, author of popular books such as *When Bad Things Happen to Good People*. Kushner acknowledges the standard Jewish theological position that Wiesenthal had neither the power nor the right to forgive the German soldier. He also points out that if the soldier had repented earlier instead of conveniently waiting until he was near death, he would have faced the menace of being in the same situation again and rejecting military orders.

In general, however, Rabbi Kushner recommends forgiveness because continued resentment causes too much harm to the victim. Kushner uses as an example a divorced mother who sought his advice. She could hardly pay her monthly bills, while her ex-spouse was living the high life with a new wife. The rabbi counseled the divorcée to forgive her former husband, lest his behavior turn her into a bitter woman. Continuing to resent the ex-husband only hurt her. She was held captive to his subjugation by her conscious or unconscious resentment of his new life. Forgiving him would free her from being a victim any longer. Applying this woman's situation to the Shoah is fraught with peril, and Rabbi Kushner certainly does not want to trivialize the Nazi years by comparing them to a domestic squabble. Yet the rabbi's response raises a possibility: Jews who forgive a specific, brutal Nazi act will always know that the crime is reprehensible and will continue to reject the ideology, but they may also finally be free of its domination.

The majority of people responding to Simon Wiesenthal's question say that if they had been in his position, they would not have forgiven the SS soldier. Albert Speer, Hitler's architect and minister of armaments who admitted his culpability at the Nuremberg trials, writes that he can never forgive himself, nor can anyone else remove his guilt. Auschwitz survivor Primo Levi (who later committed suicide) states that the genocide of European Jewry is unforgivable. The soldier's request for forgiveness "betrays his utter failure to understand the nature of his crime" (179). Catholic priest John Pawlikowski's judgment is that Wiesenthal was correct in not administering "cheap grace" to the dying soldier (212).

Jewish author Dennis Prager asserts that one of the greatest differences between Jews and Christians is their concepts of forgiveness. Conventional Jewish wisdom contends that moral debts are too personal to be transferable. In Judaism, as the High Holy Day liturgy affirms, a person who sins against another must ask the victim for forgiveness. Furthermore, there can be no time limit set on asking for forgiveness; sometimes years pass before a perpetrator is strong enough to seek pardon. Timeliness may be an issue, however, for if years have passed, the person who was wronged is arguably not identical to the person against whom the misdeed was originally committed. If a crime is committed in a person's childhood and the apology comes when the victim is an adult, the whole life may have been affected by the misdeed, and the victim is certainly not exactly the same person against whom the sin was perpetrated. Judaism also posits that even God does not automatically forgive a sinner for crimes committed against a human being. Prager maintains that while God may forgive a murderer, living people cannot. The only person empowered to forgive the killer is dead (217). In a sense all sin is an affront to God, so the Almighty has the power to forgive all iniquity, whereas human power is far more limited. *The Sunflower* contains an in-depth analysis of the pros and cons of forgiving crimes that are among the worst ever committed on the planet.

To what extent do human beings have authority to forgive? Scholars of different faiths (and no particular faith) often acknowledge that we have limited power over the matter. People have no right to forgive "except as it involves their own attitudes towards people who have wronged them. In other words, human forgiveness is a form of self-control, not control over anyone's destiny" (Stuart 104). Conversely, God — at least from the perspective of those who believe in a deity who intervenes in daily life and who determines the afterlife — holds sway over punishment on earth and after death. Given that divine authority to penalize far exceeds human jurisdiction, the consequences of God's decision are definitive on earth and final after death. In the book of Jonah God exercises power to pardon the temporal deeds of the Ninevites. Their eternal destiny is not discussed, but God's exoneration would be critical to their immortal character. By comparison, Jonah's ability to excuse has far less reaching significance during this life and certainly in the next. Whether Jonah exerts this more narrow ability to forgive remains unanswered; nonetheless, the consequences of Jonah's decision are more trivial than God's. At the end of the story (4:11) God implies that divine forgiveness should be extended to the Ninevites for their earthly deeds, but the Lord makes no mention as to whether Jonah should forgive the people. By analogy, then, even if Simon Wiesenthal cannot forgive the Nazi soldier, God retains the more authoritative prerogative to act according to divine discretion.

In the Hebrew Scriptures and the New Testament, perfect forgiveness belongs to God. Yet the nagging question remains: should Jonah forgive the Ninevites? Should Wiesenthal forgive the Nazi soldier? By analogy, should a sexually abused woman forgive the father who raped her when she was a child or the husband who beats her? On a smaller scale, should people forgive an egotistical employer who dominates them on the job? Forgiveness of such serious offenses is not always possible. In the context of grievous misdeeds, the prophet Jonah's ambivalent actions are understandable. Few people presume to advise Simon Wiesenthal that he has the power or the moral authority to forgive the Nazis. According to Jewish tradition, he is not empowered to forgive a sin not committed against himself personally. Since the SS man's victims are dead and not able to forgive him, his ultimate fate is in God's hands.

Also in the twentieth century, South Africa provides a sterling model of forgiveness, as attempts are made to compensate people who suffered from the injurious actions of others. South Africans have labored to dismantle the racist apartheid regime and establish a new, democratic government based on majority will, a country that belongs to all its citizens. The search for peace with themselves has been arduous; it led to the creation in 1995 of the Truth and Reconciliation Commission (TRC), chaired by Archbishop Desmond Tutu and Dr. Alex Boraine. In South Africa forgiveness has become a template for political and social justice. Instead of plunging into a bloody civil war, as many predicted in the early 1990s, the visionary TRC leadership has replaced models of revenge with models of forgiveness. Central to the program are confessions and apologies offered by apartheid officials and amnesty offered by a new government.

The Reparation and Rehabilitation Committee, part of the TRC, was given the responsibility of healing the wounds of apartheid by setting aside funds to help compensate victims for mental and physical pain endured during years of apartheid rule. Yet Nelson Mandela, the former political prisoner who later served a term as president of South Africa, reminded his nation that adequate payment could never be made:

> We are all fully aware that such [compensation] can only be symbolic rather than proportionate to the suffering and sacrifice. The best reparation for the suffering of victims and communities and the highest recognition of their efforts is the transformation of our society into one which makes a living reality of the human rights for which they struggled. (*Opening Address* 6)

In the 1990s the German and Swiss governments also started to send money to survivors of the Holocaust or their descendants, though little could be done to relieve the pain of the past. Then late in 1999, French Prime Minister Lionel Jospin announced that Jewish children whose parents were deported by the pro-Nazi Vichy regime would be given a pension. Such efforts at compensation may expedite forgiveness but cannot guarantee it.

The South African model suggests that the process of human forgiveness is not complete until the guilty party has realized the crime, confessed, repented, and made restitution to the victim. Yet God forgives the people of Nineveh when they fast and pray to seek forgiveness for their sins. No Ninevite asks Jonah's forgiveness for crimes committed against Israel, and no compensation is discussed in the Bible story. According to South Africa's paradigm, the Nazi soldier in *The Sunflower* is in a predicament. Since he is on his deathbed, he has no opportunity to make amends for murdering innocent people, nor is there any evidence that he would possess the fortitude to defy Germany's political tide of the 1940s if he were miraculously cured of his wounds and returned to active duty. Since his victims are dead, he cannot ask their forgiveness or make restitution to them personally. Simon Wiesenthal, had he wished to forgive the SS man, would lack the authority to do so. The situation is different from that of Nelson Mandela and other black South Africans who can seek reconciliation with those who actually harmed them personally. Yet for those on both sides of the apartheid government with the courage and creativity to apologize and forgive, self-redemption is available. South Africans are not just righting past wrongs; they are changing a collective consciousness and building a better future.

Forgiving does not equal forgetting. Former President Mandela admonished his people that they "should forgive but not forget" (7) the damage of apartheid, and he set the tone for his followers. Today travelers to South Africa can take a thirty-minute boat ride to Robben Island, the infamous penal colony where Nelson Mandela, Robert Sobukwe, Walter Sisulu, and other black political prisoners were incarcerated under inhuman conditions during the apartheid era. (Only one white man was ever jailed there during the apartheid years.) Past prisoners now conduct tours, and it is fascinating to hear them eloquently espouse their convictions regarding the need to forgive their former oppressors. Their talks to tourists are inspirational and unforgettable, and they serve as a model for the rest of the world to follow. They forgive the perpetrators of crimes against them, but they also remember the pain in their muscles from when they were forced to pound rocks into rubble at the island's quarry and the sadness in their hearts when they recall wasted years that can never be returned to them.

The danger in not forgetting, avoided by most former Robben Island inmates, is that remembering a horrific event can mutate into vengeance. Nevertheless, it would be inappropriate, burdensome, and even dishonorable to forget about serious harm done to us or those we love. Perhaps we should forget about small, petty indignities that routinely hurt our pride or annoy us. Yet memory of major assaults cannot be wiped out, nor should we attempt to suppress or erase from our minds the events of the past that leave us reeling with psychic or physical pain. Crimes against humanity— Native Americans, African Americans, and other specific groups— should not be expunged from our collective memory. It is also irresponsible to forget about crimes such as fraud, theft, mental and physical abuse, economic exploitation, or refusal to grant human rights (Thompson 17). We do not need to develop amnesia, repress facts, or deny reality in order to forgive wrongdoers. To do so would likely encourage repeat offenses. If everyone concerned maintains memory of the misdeed, future temptation to repeat it may be more effectively resisted. In fact, memory can be a legitimate part of the forgiving process if it is transformed into a "redemptive event" characterized by hope for a better future (Louw 394).

Nowhere has the two-way process of reconciliation been better demonstrated than in South Africa as the country struggles in a collective and protracted national effort to overcome the injustices and deep divisions caused by decades of apartheid. Realizing that the lesson to be learned from the experience of other nations is the need to deal constructively with the past so that it does not haunt the future, another of the Truth and Reconciliation Commission's purposes was to expose gross human rights violations occurring within a political context between 1960 and 1993; to investigate who was responsible for murder, abduction, torture, robbery, and other severe ill treatment of South Africans; and to hold public hearings giving victims an opportunity to tell their stories. Tens of thousands of South Africans demonstrated resilient spirit by gathering in public meeting halls across the country and telling about the inhumanities they had suffered. Oppressors were given an opportunity to disclose their role in inflicting those inhumanities, and amnesty was offered in some cases to perpetrators who confessed their crimes (*Truth: The Road to Reconciliation,* TRC pamphlet). Though the amnesty program was painful for many victims of terror, it was developed as a measure of peaceful transition to a fresh era of reconciliation. Many who suffered emotional scars from the loss of family members, disabilities, and personal horrors found the amnesty debate troubling or incomprehensible. Nelson Mandela therefore reminded his people that the process could produce a cathartic release of emotions and that there could be misery on both sides of the racial divide:

> We think of those apartheid sought to imprison in the jails of hate and fear; those it infused with a false doctrine of superiority to justify their inhumanity to others. But we think too of those it conscripted or encouraged into machines of destruction, exacting a heavy toll among them in life and limb, and in a warped disregard for life and the trauma that goes with it. (*Opening Address* 4)

The TRC, with its two-way communication between victim and victimizer, stands as a uniquely South African instrument implemented to help dismantle the cruel apartheid system and the measures that enforced it, thereby starting to remedy the injustices of past white minority domination of the black majority population. It represents a human miracle of collective effort to wrestle with the dilemma of forgiveness and to mend a portion of the wounded world. Nevertheless, Mandela warns that his country has only taken the first tenuous steps on the road to reconciliation: "When I walked out of prison, that was my mission, to liberate the oppressed and the oppressor both. Some say that has now been achieved [in South Africa]. But I know that is not the case . . .; we have merely achieved the freedom to be free, the right not to be oppressed" (*Long Walk* 617). If Simon Wiesenthal and other Nazi victims had had more opportunity for genuine dialogue with their oppressors, perhaps a willingness to forgive would prevail as it does in their South African counterparts. Under this rubric, forgiving would be part of the Jewish concept עולם תיקון (tikkun olam, repairing and transforming the world) and could help overcome obstacles faced by Jonah and his modern complements.

Jonah and Jewish Liturgy

Simon Wiesenthal and Nelson Mandela look to their religions to guide them in their ethical struggles. In religions throughout the world, prayers for forgiveness are included in liturgy year-round. Though many examples abound, one of the best comes during Judaism's ten Days of Awe, or High Holy Days, which form the most sacred and penitential time in the Jewish calendar and which include the story of Jonah. The High Holy Days begin with Rosh Hashanah (the religious new year) and end on Yom Kippur (the Day of Atonement), the most hallowed holiday in Judaism. The meaning of the Hebrew word "kippur" (כפר) is "to atone" and is rooted in a term meaning "to cover over" or "to purge." The name Yom Kippur thus implies a time when God covers over the blemishes of the people (Domeris 49). A day of ancient origin and enjoined in the Hebrew Scriptures at Lev 23:27–32, Yom Kippur is known as a Holy Day of most special rest, when the descendants of Jonah flock to their synagogues to fast and pray. It is a day of solemn assembly, called in the Reform Jewish prayer book, *Gates of Repentance,* "a cessation from work, a day of commemoration proclaimed by the sound of the Shofar [ram's horn]" (23). Jews are taught that it is the Day of Atonement "on which expiation is made on your behalf before the LORD your God" (Lev 23:28). Yom Kippur is the culmination of the Days of Awe, wherein Jews examine their behavior for the preceding year, pray to be forgiven of sin, and strive to be reconciled with both God and fellow human beings. The celebration of Yom Kippur leads to introspection, to cleansing the soul. On Yom Kippur the Jews uphold their rejection of original sin, through which people are "by nature hostile to God, slaves to Satan, and servants to sin" (*Book of Confessions* 11–12). In Jewish tradition people are fundamentally good. We may stumble off the right path, but we can choose to return. Yom Kippur stresses verbs like "purify," "wipe away," "cleanse," "purge," and "pardon" (Friedlander 7). What has been done cannot be undone, but ill effects can be removed.

Extra liturgy is added for the High Holy Days. The gateway celebration to the ten Days of Awe is Selihot, a service that takes place about one week prior to Rosh Hashanah. Selihot comes from the Hebrew word for pardon, סלח, the root meaning of which is "lightness" or "lifting up" (Emerson 82), suggesting that those who are forgiven are lighter because they have had a weight lifted from them. At the Selihot service congregants confess sins and repeat what have become known as the Thirteen Divine Attributes, characteristics of God originally proclaimed at the conclusion of the golden calf episode of Exod 34:6–7, the famous passage rephrased in the book of Jonah at 4:2: Jonah paraphrases the words of Moses and recalls that God's nature includes compassion, graciousness, and slowness to anger.

At many places in Scriptures, God specifically forgives the Israelite people, as in Mic 7:18–20:

> Who is a God like You,
> Forgiving iniquity
> And remitting transgression;
> Who has not maintained His wrath forever
> Against the remnant of His own people,
> Because He loves graciousness!
> He will take us back in love;
> He will cover up our iniquities,
> You will hurl all our sins
> Into the depths of the sea.
> You will keep faith with Jacob,
> Loyalty to Abraham,
> As You promised on oath to our fathers
> In days gone by.

These verses from Micah are read on the afternoon of the first day of Rosh Hashanah in a unique Tashlikh (Hebrew for "throw") service that arose during the Middle Ages. People gather near a river or other source of running water, recite prayers, and shake crumbs out of their pockets and into the water, symbolically casting off individual sins that are swept away by the current. The end of Yom Kippur replaces the particularistic sentiment of Micah with the universal message of Jonah. Jews remind themselves that God cares for all the people of the world, and in this way God is indeed loyal to the descendants of Abraham. Therefore, the essential message of Yom Kippur is contained not only in the passages of God's narrow forgiveness of Jews but also in the broader story of Jonah, the pagan sailors, and the Ninevites.

There is also special liturgy for the occasion of Yom Kippur. Influenced by biblical passages such as "And there was evening and there was morning, a first day" (Gen 1:5), traditional synagogue rituals begin and end at sundown. On Yom Kippur evening, Jews gather to worship; services then resume in the morning and run continuously until sundown. Excerpts from the Torah are read several times. During the morning of Yom Kippur, chapters from Leviticus are heard.

The sailors in the book of Jonah are indirectly connected to Yom Kippur early in the day's service because the mariners cast lots to determine that Jonah is the guilty party, the one responsible for the tempest at sea. This part of the Jonah plot is reminiscent of the lots used by Aaron, the brother of Moses and High Priest of the Israelites. Leviticus 16:8–10, the morning Torah portion, tells of Aaron's duty to take two goats and

> place lots upon the two goats, one marked for the LORD and the other marked for Azazel. Aaron shall bring forward the goat designated by lot for the LORD, which he is to offer as a sin offering; while the goat designated by lot for Azazel shall be left standing alive before the LORD, to make expiation with it and to send it off to the wilderness for Azazel.

In this manner the priest, human agent for the supernatural, chooses between the scapegoat and the goat designated for sacrificial service in the Tent of Meeting. Onto the scapegoat all the sins of the people are placed symbolically; then that goat is sent off into the wilderness to die, thus establishing a ritual for ridding the people of their sins. The other goat, the one on which the lot does not fall, is then used in a sacrifice to God. As the priest's lot falls upon the scapegoat, so the sailors' lot falls upon Jonah, indicating that the prophet will be designated to aid in human reparation of sin and subsequent salvation. Israel's responsibility to bring the holy message to the nations of the world is stressed annually at this special time during the Jewish religious calendar:

> And this shall be to you a law for all time: In the seventh month, on the tenth day of the month, you shall practice self-denial; and you shall do no manner of work, neither the citizen nor the alien who resides among you. For on this day atonement shall be made for you to cleanse you of all your sins; you shall be clean before the LORD. It shall be a sabbath of complete rest for you, and you shall practice self-denial; it is a law for all time. The priest who has been anointed and ordained to serve as priest in place of his father shall make expiation. He shall put on the linen vestments, the sacral

vestments. He shall purge the innermost Shrine; he shall purge the Tent of Meeting and the altar; and he shall make expiation for the priests and for all the people of the congregation.

This shall be to you a law for all time: to make atonement for the Israelites for all their sins once a year. (Lev 16:29–34)

Here, the actions of a single leader are described as he assumes responsibility for the entire Israelite community by performing the ritual and proclaiming forgiveness of the people.

By the end of Yom Kippur, in the late afternoon, focus shifts to the Haftarah concerning Jonah. ("Haftarah" is a Hebrew term meaning "conclusion" and applied to a selection from the prophetic books of the Bible, read in the synagogue immediately following the Torah on Shabbat and festivals.) The Haftarah is generally related thematically to the Torah portion or is especially appropriate for the holiday being celebrated. Isaiah 57:14– 58:14 is the morning Haftarah selection, for it deals with proper fasting. Even though repentance and forgiveness are not the sole theme of the book of Jonah, its designation as the afternoon Haftarah illustrates how strongly it depicts the message that people can repent and modify their behavior. On the afternoon of Yom Kippur, as congregants are becoming uncomfortable from fasting and anxious for the long services to end, the book of Jonah is read to remind everyone of the prophet's discomfort at the notion of following the will of God and forgiving the Ninevites.

In synagogue tradition, the book of Jonah is considered a peak of moral instruction. Far more than a story about a giant fish, it brings home some of the most important teachings of Judaism: the God of Israel belongs to anyone who seeks the deity; all human beings, regardless of nationality, are children of God; God is merciful and forgiving, longing for people to turn away from evil; everyone is capable of abandoning evil and yielding to good; all humanity has the responsibility to lead a moral life (Millgram 258). The book of Jonah tells about the repentance of an entire city — a Gentile city — and God's revoking of the prophecy to destroy the place. The Ninevites do not sin against Jonah personally or ask his forgiveness. The reading of the Jonah story on Yom Kippur indicates a point in the liturgy where sentiment has moved from the specific, as in the morning Torah portion of Lev 16, to the general. Both collective and personal responsibilities are therefore stressed on Yom Kippur. With the book of Jonah the biblical readings end, acknowledging that salvation is available to all who pursue it, regardless of their upbringing or background. One lesson of Jonah is that the will of

God may change. Even though punishment has been prescribed, it may be canceled. Inexorable fate does not exist. Everyone gets a second chance to divert, abort, or vanquish evil. Yom Kippur reminds Jews that it is they, through Jonah, who bring this message to the Gentiles. Without ceasing to be a Hebrew or forsaking his own people, Jonah teaches this lesson of universal forgiveness to the world.

The power of the story of Nineveh's repentance impressed ancient religious authorities so much that they selected the brief book of Jonah as the central reading for Yom Kippur afternoon. Called upon to deliver a message of doom to his enemies, Jonah at first refuses and then is forced to fulfill God's plan. On the holiest day of the year, Jews are reminded that even their worst enemies are beloved to God. Rabbi Joseph Telushkin points out how tolerant the Jewish narrative is of other religions, though there is something slightly ironic about the rabbi's comment, given his tone of disdain: "If the book of Jonah had appeared in the New Testament or the Koran, the undoubted proof of the Ninevites' repentance would have been their conversion to Christianity or Islam. The Hebrew Bible makes a considerably more restrained appeal to the non-Jewish world: just that people refrain from evil behavior and do good" (Telushkin 99). Actually, the story of Jonah does appear in the Koran and in Christian liturgy. It is placed in the liturgical calendar of the Greek Orthodox Church and in the Episcopal and Common Eucharistic lectionaries. But Jonah's story is on center stage in Judaism's most sacred celebration.

The Yom Kippur liturgy focuses Jewish attention on the universal concerns of God, a theme repeated through to the next eight-day holiday of Sukkot, when Jews "plead for humanity as a whole, in all its political diversity" (Trepp 129). Seventy bulls were, in biblical times, sacrificed in expiation of the evil in the world's "seventy nations." On the first day of Sukkot, thirteen bulls were sacrificed; twelve on the second day; eleven on the third; and on down through the seventh day until the total was seventy (Num 29:12–32). Thus from Yom Kippur through to Sukkot, Jews acknowledge responsibility for influencing the conduct of the outside world. Ancient legal practices of ritual scapegoating and animal slaughter for sacrifice support this conclusion.

Another connection that the book of Jonah has to the Days of Awe is rather subtle. As already suggested, a leitmotif from the liturgy of Selihot through the High Holy Days is the recitation of God's thirteen attributes, suggested in the Torah at Exod 34:6–7 and Num 14:18, then reinterpreted in Jonah 4:2. The interesting thing about the Torah portions is that while they do state that God pardons sin, they do not promise that no one will be held accountable as the result of that sin. The Exodus version states, "yet He does not remit all punishment, but visits the iniquity of parents upon children. . . . " Guilt is not canceled out; sooner or later there will be a price to pay, as the Ninevites discovered when their city was eventually destroyed. The full picture of God is a balanced one, blending justice and mercy, and this view of God is consistent with the picture of the deity in the book of Jonah. Yet during the Days of Awe, the forgiveness of God is stressed.

Considering the facts of world history and Jewish suffering at the hands of the Gentile nations, from ancient times to the present day, the deliberate decision to include the story of Jonah in the Yom Kippur liturgy is extraordinary. On the holiest day of the year, Jews allow the Ninevites to become a model of repentance for the Jewish community to emulate. The Jewish people listen to the voice of God, even when — perhaps especially when — the divine message stings. As God nudges human beings to change our ways and follow a more righteous path in the new year, Jews are forced to examine their prejudices, mixed motives, and childish behaviors. Then, as God forgives the characters in the Jonah story, perhaps humans can begin to forgive themselves and others.

An analysis of the book of Jonah begs the question of whether the prophet and his deity should forgive the Ninevites. The Jewish concept of forgiveness, as reaffirmed during the Days of Awe, is not simple and not identical to ideas of forgiveness found in other religions. *Gates of Repentance* states, "For transgressions against God, the Day of Atonement atones; but for transgressions of one human being against another, the Day of Atonement does not atone until they have made peace with one another" (251). In times past, the Ninevites may have trespassed against Jonah's people, but those inhabiting the city when the prophet arrives have never personally sinned against Jonah. Nor do they ask Jonah for his forgiveness. These two factors make it difficult for us to expect Jonah to forgive the Ninevites. According to Jewish religious and ethical customs, Jonah is in an awkward position when it comes to forgiving them.

The prophet does not say that he forgives the Ninevites for the sins they have committed against the Jewish people and God. The open-ended conclusion of chapter 4 of the book of Jonah leaves significant doubt in the reader's mind as to whether Jonah even agrees with God's decision to forgive the people. In order to be viewed as a caring, compassionate, loving human being, does Jonah need to forgive those whom he believes have transgressed? By the same token, can the rest of us hate the sin but not the sinner?

Other Biblical Models of Forgiveness

Forgiveness permits healing in our own lives, restoration with the community, and renewed kinship to God (Risher 9). Sometimes, however, a deity who invokes strict commandments and doles out harsh punishment is easier to understand than the merciful and forgiving God. To imitate the forgiving side of God's nature, we need spiritual guidance. In an effort to understand and implement the process of forgiveness, we turn to contemporary examples of the forgiveness dilemma and to organized religion to point the way. Biblical works such as the book of Jonah have also traditionally played a significant role in helping us understand forgiveness, for "only when the proponent of strict justice realizes his own humanity can he understand the fundamental dependence of mortals on human and divine mercy" (Simon xii).

Against the background of forgiving the perpetrators of the Shoah and apartheid, how can forgiveness in the book of Jonah be applied to our lives? Many passages in the Hebrew Scriptures discuss the issue, and we can also look to them for guidance before passing judgment on the prophet Jonah. The story of Jonah does not define forgiveness, but the prophet, who represents humankind throughout the ages, seems unable or unwilling to grant a blanket pardon to those who offend him. This stance suggests something deeply embedded in human nature that does not allow wounded human beings to shrug off transgressions committed against them. Modern analyses such as *The Sunflower* and biblically based Yom Kippur liturgy explore the issue of forgiveness, but what other Bible passages deal with the subject? In order to heal ourselves and the tragically broken world we inhabit, further biblical insights into forgiveness should be examined.

In the Hebrew Scriptures God, the Holy One, is the source and model of forgiveness. God's nature is to forgive, a fact that produces harmonious life:

> I wipe away your sins like a cloud,
> Your transgressions like mist —
> Come back to Me, for I redeem you.
> (Isa 44:22)

The deity initiates forgiveness of the penitent and absolves whole societies as well as individuals (Weaver 152). God bestows pardon; it is what the Lord gives and people receive. A fundamental characteristic of God is the ability and willingness to forgive, as Exod 34:6–7, Num 14:17–18, Isa 55:7, Ps 86:5, Dan 9:9, Neh 9:17, and numerous other Scriptures eloquently demonstrate. Therefore, people of all nations appeal to and rely upon God's forgiving nature and find comfort in Yahweh's mercy. The Lord forgives sin from one end of the world to the other and displays love that suspends the strictest concepts of justice (Gibbs 324). God's love is pure and offers to us a gift that human beings cannot always give. Though we all have the capacity to forgive, we do not always exercise it. The Bible often emphasizes the difference between the scope of divine and human nature: God's forgiveness is perfect; human forgiveness is not.

The earliest stories of the Bible contain tales of almost unimaginable betrayal and barbarism. Adam and Eve must learn to forgive their elder son, Cain, for murdering their younger son, Abel. Isaac must strive to reconcile with a father who nearly sacrifices him. Years after Esau is swindled out of his birthright, he welcomes Jacob back home, and Joseph absolves his brothers for selling him into slavery. Moses, a murderer himself, must pardon his brother and sister for fomenting rebellion against him. Forgiving such horrendous deeds necessitates calling forth the strongest love contained within the human soul. These biblical characters teach us not to delude ourselves that we can heal our suffering without forgiving those who sin against us.

One advantage to suffering is that it may bring believers in closer communion with God. In the degree and method that we forgive others, so we may be forgiven (Wang 64), though life offers no guarantees on the matter. There is much comfort in the notion that God also suffers and will bless those who are in distress. Since the day when Cain murdered Abel, God seems to have suffered because of human misbehavior. God says, "Hark, your brother's blood cried out *to Me* from the ground!" (Gen 4:10, author emphasis). In biblical texts God rejoices when we do what is right and feels sorrow when we do wrong. When we experience the inhumanity of others, we hope that God, who has experienced similar sadness and pain, understands our plight. If God had not also been hurt by human misconduct, there would be no reason for divine forgiveness. In fact, one optimistic view is that when the Lord pardons, "God determines to absorb into his own being the consequences of human sin and thus exhaust its virulence" (Jensen 154). Perhaps we are at one with God when misery causes us to forgive those whose trespasses seem inexcusable. Those who forgive suffer twice before relief occurs — first when the effects of the harmful act are originally felt and second when experiencing the internal, psychological consequences of terminating the debt owed. The allegorical story of spousal fidelity in the first three chapters of Hosea teaches that if God's forgiving love prevails over betrayal, our own love should strive to be as noble. For Christians who recall the agony of Jesus on the cross, this concept is especially vivid. In the Hebrew Scriptures, God forgives what seems unforgivable. To emulate God is a difficult but worthy goal. The Jonah in all of us knows how painful it is to forgive and how frequently we fall short of the goal. Jonah's dilemma, his reluctance to forgive, lies deep within the collective human consciousness.

The fascinating aspect about biblical stories is that God dares to be the deity who sides with Cain and his descendants (Olson 13). The Almighty refuses to allow anyone to kill Cain, whose punishment includes whatever guilt pangs the murderer himself feels. God reunites Esau and Jacob as well as Joseph and his brothers, allowing reconciliation to take place. And instead of punishing Moses for slaying an Egyptian, God selects Moses to confront Pharaoh and lead the children of Israel out of bondage. This is no ordinary God. This is the one who dares to forgive and encourages people to follow the divine example, though they cannot always follow through. Regardless of calamities past and present, starting with the characters in Genesis and going to the present day, God stands ready to take the only action that has a chance of breaking the cycle of violence. God forgives.

Early biblical stories about God's forgiveness relate it to the divine covenant with humanity. After the floods experienced by Noah, God declares, "I will maintain My covenant with you: never again shall all flesh be cut off by the waters of a flood" (Gen 11:9). The Hebrew patriarchs carry the promise of the covenant to new generations that know God's lovingkindness, and in the days of Moses, God repeatedly forgives the people. The prophet Amos relates a vision in which God mandates that a plague of locusts destroy crops, trigger famine, and cause the death of thousands. Amos intercedes and God stands by the covenant people: " 'Oh Lord God, pray forgive. How will Jacob survive? He is so small.' The Lord relented concerning this. 'It shall not come to pass,' said the Lord" (7:2–3). After the exile, God reaffirms the covenant with the remnant of the chosen people, and again forgiveness exists within the context of covenant (Emerson 84). The prophet Isaiah, speaking to the people of Judah, proclaims that those who remain alive after the Babylonian captivity are in a covenantal relationship to God:

> Had not the Lord of Hosts
> Left us some survivors,
> We should be like Sodom,
> Another Gomorrah. (1:9)

In these instances, despite the people's infidelity, God's constancy is sure. Forgiveness is eternal, so that the people are not destroyed from the earth.

In the TANAKH, Abraham, Moses, Amos, Daniel, and tribal priests intervene and ask God to forgive whole groups of people, especially Israelites. Yet individuals also ask forgiveness for their own personal misdeeds. After taking a census of the people, always a dangerous undertaking since God promised Abraham that the Israelites would be too numerous to count, King David begs God to "remit the guilt of Your servant, for I acted foolishly" (2 Sam 24:10). Sometimes God promises to forgive in the future, in eschatological time when perfection can theoretically be reached: "when My people, who bear My name, humble themselves, pray, and seek My favor and turn from their evil ways, I will hear in My heavenly abode and forgive their sins and heal their land" (2 Chr 7:8).

Most Bible passages involving God's forgiveness also show people doing their part by humbling themselves, admitting guilt, and asking to be released from blame and penalty. Though God embodies forgiveness, sincere human participation is usually required in the process. Forgiveness is not a one-sided, unilateral undertaking in which God alone participates. Though God always remains free to act according to divine will, forgiveness usually necessitates a kind of human partnership with God, in which the people and the deity interact, engaging in mutual responsibilities. Job repents (42:6) not because he acknowledges previous sin but because he has come to a new understanding of God. Both an omniscient narrator and the Lord indicate that Job is "blameless and upright" (1:1, 1:8, 2:3) at the beginning of the story, though at the end he confesses enmity concerning recent woes: "I spoke without understanding / Of things beyond me, which I did not know" (42:3). His character is unique in the Hebrew Bible, for he has no lifetime of indiscretions to confess.

Aside from a slight departure in the story of Job, the Hebrew Scriptures unambiguously require human beings to confess and repent of past misdeeds before divine forgiveness occurs. The ultimate fate of people who do not believe in God or refuse to seek forgiveness is left to divine mercy. Reducing forgiveness to a prescription is dangerous, because God can alter the formula at any time, and for human beings to attempt to dictate what divine behavior can and cannot be is foolish. Yet confession is a major factor in the process. Avowing a fault, crime, or weakness can be private and confidential or public and communal. Humbling ourselves and revealing our guilt to a fellow human being is more difficult than acknowledging our sins quietly to God. The deity within us is unseen, but our neighbor is outside ourselves and entirely visible, complicating our disclosure. Confession presupposes people's understanding that they have transgressed; it does not take into consideration the situation of people who do not believe they need forgiveness or do not care whether they receive it. The Torah (Num 15:22–28) outlines a ritual offering for sins unwittingly committed, as it is even necessary to confess to unintentional transgressions that people do not realize they have committed. Confession of known misconduct links the perpetrator, the victim, and God by binding "our ability to tell the truth about ourselves... to God's forgiveness and the promise of community" (Jones "Craft," 357). Harming others alienates us from our true selves, from others, and from God. Confession attenuates guilt, and "the antidote to suffering the consequences of sin and guilt is to make confession and to hear the gracious words of forgiveness" (Albers 348). The story of Jonah and the Ninevites serves as an excellent case in point, for the behavior of the Ninevites — their general confession of sin as they fast, don sackcloth, and "cry mightily to God" (Jonah 3:8) — is a crucial ingredient in God's renouncing the punishment.

Other biblical examples are available as well. Leviticus 5:5 demands that when a guilty person recognizes culpability, "he shall confess that wherein he has sinned." In the Torah a sacrifice is then brought, but confession must precede the religious rite if atonement is to occur. After building the first temple in Jerusalem, King Solomon asks God to "hear the supplications which Your servant and Your people Israel offer toward this place, give heed in Your heavenly abode — give heed and pardon" (1 Kgs 18:30). Confession is thus linked to repentance, part of the ritual that survives in contemporary daily and weekly religious services. In addition, the TANAKH also warns that where there is no repentance, there is no forgiveness. The prophets constantly harangue the people to avow their sins and receive God's mercy. The beautiful poetry of Lam 3:42 details what happens when the people do not examine and turn from their evil ways: "We have transgressed and rebelled, / And You have not forgiven." The unrepentant experience dire consequences. Naming and confessing the error and then acknowledging guilt are prerequisites for (though not guarantees of) God's forgiveness, for pardon is a commodity not administered lightly.

If the first step is the guilty party's confession, the second step is reaching out to the victim, apologizing, and offering appropriate restitution, if possible, for the wrong committed. The Torah demands that a penalty of 20 percent be paid: "When a man or woman commits any wrong toward a fellow man, thus breaking faith with the LORD, and that person realizes his guilt, he shall confess the wrong that he has done. He shall make restitution in the principal amount and add one-fifth to it, giving it to him whom he has wronged" (Num 5:6–7). In biblical times, penitents were also required to go to the Tent of Meeting and make a ritual sacrifice. The priest then became involved in the process, intervening on behalf of the sinners and asking God to forgive: "Thus the priest shall make expiation for them, and they shall be forgiven" (Lev 4:20). Furthermore, the Philistines realize that they must include a guilt offering when they return the captured Ark of the Covenant to Israelite land: "Take the Ark of the LORD and place it on the cart; and put next to it in a chest the gold objects you are paying Him as indemnity" (1 Sam 6:8). In some extreme cases, such as murder, compensating either human victims or God for the crime committed is impossible. But when recompense is possible, it is required.

In the Bible, "the focus on forgiveness as human initiative appears almost exclusively within the writings of the New Testament" (Weaver 161). The belief that through Christ's death all sins are forgiven accounts for distinctions in how Jews and Christians view forgiveness. On the cross Jesus asks that his murderers be forgiven, yet he is presented as being God *and* man, so the Jewish concept of God's involvement in the forgiveness process is not necessarily violated by Jesus' pleadings, "Father, forgive them; for they do not know what they are doing" (Luke 23:34). Yet Christian doctrine also involves confession in the church as an essential ingredient in the process. In no less degree than is found in the Torah, in the New Testament "the task of forgiveness does not belong—in purely individualistic fashion—strictly to the one who has been wronged" (Weaver 164). Some Christian scholars worry that the concept of blanket forgiveness through Christ's death on the cross offers a hope for "cheap grace" to those who deliberately misunderstand the complexities of Christian theology. Because Christ has forgiven humankind, people are empowered and encouraged to forgive one another. By imitating Christ and forgiving those who do not ask for forgiveness, we become part of a circular process involving the divine and the human, collaborating with God to heal the broken world around us.

Penalizing wrongdoers remains a way of mending what is broken, and forgiving does not automatically mean that punishment will be abrogated. Though God decides not to punish the Ninevites, in other Bible stories God exacts harsh penalty, despite the penitent's confession. Much of the TANAKH interprets natural calamity—flood, drought, locusts—as God's punishment of sin. The tendency exists to associate forgiveness with remittance of the punishment, but this is not always the case. For example, when Achan violates divine injunction and steals the spoils of war after a battle, he confesses his wrongdoing to Joshua, who declares, " 'The LORD will bring calamity upon you this day.' And all Israel pelted him with stones.... Then the anger of the LORD subsided" (Josh 7:25–26). God's wrath is perfect love's response to a wrongdoer's need for castigation.

Sometimes the Bible asserts that forgiveness has already taken place, though punishment is still to come. Returning to the example of King David, he confesses his adultery with Bathsheba to the prophet Nathan: "David said to Nathan, 'I stand guilty before the LORD!' And Nathan replied to David, 'The LORD has remitted your sin; you shall not die. However, since you have spurned the enemies of the LORD by this deed, even the child about to be born to you shall die'" (2 Sam 12:13–14). Forgiveness and punishment are two separate issues.

The passage in 2 Sam 12 illustrates an aspect of divine forgiveness that is sometimes overlooked by those who seek it. God is willing to pardon trespasses, but that does not mean there will be no punishment for the guilty. For example, in Num 14:20 when Moses asks God to forgive the people after the golden calf incident, the Almighty responds, "I pardon, as you have asked." Yet the next sentences outline the penalty that must follow the apostasy: those who came out of bondage in Egypt, saw God's miracles, and still disobeyed will not be allowed to enter the promised land. Pardon does not equal suspension of punishment. Furthermore, Exod 34:7 indicates that God "does not remit all punishment." An individual must confess and be sorry for offenses, but a contrite heart does not guarantee that punitive measures will not be administered. This condition makes the case of the Ninevites even more interesting, and the story of the prescribed punishment being lifted from them therefore seems to contradict the notion of forgiveness as other Bible passages present it. The all-powerful deity is free to change things at any time and behave according to divine wishes. Human beings may not comprehend the overall plan. No wonder Jonah seems confused.

On the surface, Bible stories do not always make an obvious connection between forgiveness and the withholding of punishment, but a closer reading reveals the union. The punishment serves to warn, to unite, and to save the entire community. Punishment of individuals makes broader punishment — total annihilation of the people — unnecessary. Returning to Num 14:20–22, where the famous attributes of God in Exodus are revisited, God forgives the people and in the same breath pronounces the punishment: those who came out of Egypt will never see the promised land. Their sin is not casual or inadvertent; the Israelites have deliberately spurned their Lord (14:11). Even after the people's eventual repentance, their sentence is not rescinded. Nor does punishment mean that God has not already forgiven the people, even before they pay the price for disobedience. The essential nature of Yahweh's forgiveness in Numbers is that the Israelites are not destroyed, their community is not eliminated, and their covenant with God is not nullified, despite their apostasy (Sakenfeld 326). Furthermore, the theology behind the book of Lamentations and the prophetic books is that God punishes the people for their transgressions by forcing them into exile. In these stories, God is relentlessly faithful to the divine commitment to rebuild the nation after punishing the sinful. Forgiveness is understood as the postexilic ingathering of the surviving remnant, an assembly that is made possible by the previous punishment. The connection among the Jonah, Achan, promised land, and other stories is that in all of them, God remits the punishment of total destruction of a people. The Ninevites (representing outsiders previously unacquainted with God's majesty) and the Israelites (representing insiders) are preserved as groups.

In a similar manner, Yahweh's parental love for Israel is expressed in Hos 11:1:

> I fell in love with Israel
> When he was still a child;
> And I have called [him] My son
> Ever since Egypt.

This passage can be seen as expressing divine love for all Israel, the entire world of believers. God, the ultimate righteous parent, experiences the same need as human parents to punish our faults. As a loving protector and guardian, God needs both to forgive sin and also to implement deserved punishment. Consequently, "we need to have no fear that God, whose responsibility for the moral and spiritual welfare of created persons is far greater than that of any earthly father, might fail to discharge one of his obligations as the Creator" (Talbott 165). Condemnation is neither God's first nor last word; love and forgiveness are ubiquitous. The world was created in a love that overcomes human errors, for God does "not bear a grudge for all time" (Jer 3:12). Both human and divine punishments do not imply a lack of forgiveness. Those who believe that forgiveness precludes punishment misunderstand God's prerogative to impose penalty when it is needed. Instead of viewing God as torn between the need to punish and the need to forgive, readers see a deity who may choose to execute perfect justice, which includes imposing an appropriate consequence and granting forgiveness. To consider Yahweh's justice to be devoid of either element is simplistic, for punishment and mercy are equal components of God's lovingkindness. God grants forgiveness not because we deserve it, but because it is part of a loving parent's character. To fail to forgive would mean that God would fail to be true to the divine nature. Therefore, God forgives.

The Secular World: What Forgiveness Is and Is Not

Perhaps a more contemporary definition of forgiveness, one that builds upon but departs from biblical sources and religious tradition, is necessary. Wrongdoing separates us from God and each other; forgiveness brings us back together. Theological forgiveness and psychological forgiveness are not identical (Bustanoby 98). In fact, Jacob Loewen has identified four kinds of forgiveness: divine, religious, social, and self (153). A close connection exists among these different types, and all may be necessary for one to feel fully forgiven.

The field of psychology presents many definitions of forgiveness, a term that is never fully explained in the Bible. People are sometimes unable to forgive because they do not know what forgiveness is. Today human forgiveness is called "a voluntary foreswearing of negative affect and judgment by an injured party directed at someone who has inflicted a significant, deep, and unjust hurt; this process also involves viewing the wrongdoer with love and compassion" (Gassin and Enright 38–39). Though rather stilted in its language, this definition is clear: forgiveness occurs when injured people voluntarily shed the harmful effects of wrongs done to them by others and do not exact all justice that is due. Human beings usually begin with a conscious decision to forgive those who have wounded us, a cognitive act followed by an often lengthy and difficult spiritual process (Beck 272).

Though forgiving and pardoning are used as synonymous terms throughout this book, they are not technically the same thing. In modern society "pardon" is a legal rather than a personal term. A governor can pardon a convicted murderer, for example, although the victim's family may not be able to forgive the killer. By the same token, personal forgiveness may take place when official pardon is denied (Guelzo 44).

Forgiveness is love as it is practiced among people who do not behave perfectly. When we forgive we consciously release from our judgment the person who has hurt us. However fair and justified our anger may be, we leave it behind. We in the great family of humanity need to forgive and be forgiven every day. When we forgive those who have damaged us personally, we imitate God (or act on the divine within us) and thus participate in the mystery of divine love. We release ourselves from the corrosive burden of hostility. The ability to forgive puts us on secure ground in our own relationship with the Lord.

Forgiving means overcoming resentment and can therefore be understood as a change in outlook rather than a change in behavior. Shedding resentment is certainly not easy; "actually to forgive means to exhaust in one's own being the consequences one has suffered so that those consequences will not cause further damage" that is psychological, social, or even financial (Jensen 154). Strong emotions, such as anger, are part of resentment. To forgive someone is to stop being angry, to undergo an emotional change so that future hostile actions, such as paybacks and recriminations, are forsworn. Forgiveness eliminates resentment and makes a restored relationship possible, at least in theory (Gladson 126). When people manage to say, "I forgive you," that statement does not reveal how the injured people have managed to stop feeling resentment. The process may be mysterious, but the statement does imply that the forgivers have learned a lesson: continued resentment causes them too much hardship (Calhoun 77).

Whether the damage is physical, emotional, or both does not matter. When we forgive, we willingly pardon and demand no restitution in return. Forgiving is an internal process as much as an external one. In our hearts we stop holding on to the hurt that others inflicted on us. We discard the resentment we feel at being harmed (Guelzo 43). This view of forgiveness does not depend upon the repentance of the offender, which will often be absent. We choose to get close to the God within us rather than to get even with the people around us. Consciously we can make the difficult decision not to let our past dominate our future. Instead of demanding a strict accounting for the debt against us, which may be impossible for the debtor to repay, "forgiving is love's revolution against life's unfairness" (Wahking 198). Victims can find meaning and even purpose in their suffering if they engage in the healing process of forgiveness. In short, they can free themselves, not from the memories or the reality of what has happened, but from the ongoing dominance the oppressor has over them. If forgiveness does not occur, the victim will never be emancipated, the oppressor will continue to win the power struggle, and the victim will remain inwardly divided. The oppressor's boot is still at the throat of the one who shrinks from letting go of a grudge. If we want God to forgive us of our transgressions, we need to remember that the same pardon is available to all God's creatures.

Forgiving is a time-consuming process — so difficult, in fact, that people often do not make the attempt or fail in the effort. Pain, humiliation, alienation, sorrow, and rage may overwhelm us. Sometimes it is even hard to admit that we have been hurt, lest we leave ourselves vulnerable to future pain. In this way our wounded psyche is like a person inside a limousine with tinted windows. He can see out, but no one can see in. Only with the passage of time can we gradually begin to roll down the window, so to speak, and let others see the pain, resentment, hostility, or mistrust hidden inside. The angrier we feel, the less likely we are to forgive a failure in others, even though we sometimes tolerate that same weakness in ourselves. When this happens, we lose touch with our authentic selves.

Ironically, the arduous first step in forgiving may be full awareness that a wrong has been done to us. Though most misdeeds are immediately obvious, cases involving childhood abuse or adult subterfuge may not surface for many years. Only after we sense the debt that has been incurred against us can we start the premeditated act of canceling that debt. As Nelson Mandela has made clear, forgiving does not mean saying that what was done to us is all right or that the past can be undone. Understanding someone's shortcomings is not the same as excusing them, for to excuse implies that the perpetrators had no choice and thus removes them from personal responsibility for the offense. We must not legitimize abuse by convincing ourselves that we deserve someone else's hateful behavior toward us. Rather than legitimizing past offenses, forgiving heals the past's brokenness and allows us to focus on the future.

Whether or not we know we have been wronged, confession by the guilty has always been recognized as essential in extrabiblical writings. A prime example is one of the earliest and most famous of the morality plays, the anonymously authored *Everyman* (c. 1495). The hero, Everyman, is summoned by Death and told to prepare an accounting of his life on earth. Everyman attempts to convince his companions — personified as temporal concerns including Fellowship, Worldly Goods, and Beauty — to follow him on the arduous journey to immortal life. All earthly friends desert the hero except Good Deeds, who is so small and weak that Confession is necessary to bolster Good Deeds's strength. Without Confession, salvation is unattainable, so Everyman asks for forgiveness:

> O blessyd God-heed, electe and hye deuyne,
> Forgyue me my greuous offence!
> Here I crye the mercy in this presence.
> O ghostly treasure, O raunsomer and redemer,
> Of all the worlde hope and conduyter,
> Myrrour of ioye, foundatour of mercy,
> Whiche enlumyneth heuen and erth therby,
> Here my clamorous complaynt, though it late be,
> Receyue my prayers vnworthy in this heuy lyfe!
> Though I be a sinner moost abhomynable,
> Yet let my name be wryten in Moyses table. (22)

Thus, one of the oldest secular treatises on forgiveness compels humankind to confess to God.

Privately admitting faults to the Lord may be simpler and less embarrassing than personally confessing to the person we have hurt. Yet even when such an admission occurs, forgiving and reconciling are still not identical. Forgiveness can be unilateral, but reconciliation is a two-way street. It involves deliberate mutuality. For many, the ultimate goal is to reestablish good relations, but when chaos is created in our lives, reconciliation with the one who is responsible for wreaking the havoc may be impossible. Reconciliation may feel to the victim like another blow from the club. For personal reconciliation to happen, all the injured must be involved in the process — those sinned against and sinning. From this perspective, confession and forgiveness are antecedents to reconciliation (Koontz 189). Repentance in word and deed may create a bridge that allows reconciliation to occur. When we forgive people who hurt us, we do not have to become their best friend, though forgiveness may eventually open a door to more amicable relations. The disruption that wrongdoing causes sometimes may result from the action of just one person, but reconciliation requires the good will of all concerned. When one or more of the individuals involved in the situation cannot or will not cooperate, reconciliation fails.

Whether or not reconciliation takes place, punishment is generally necessary. In the Bible the process of divine forgiveness includes punishment that stops short of annihilating an entire nation, but the deity exacts appropriate disciplinary action when it is needed. Modern judicial systems do the same thing. Though prison terms and other punishments have had limited success in deterring crime, protecting innocent citizens, or rehabilitating criminals, penalty does serve the cause of justice. An apology from the guilty person may hasten societal forgiveness but will not eliminate the need for court-ordered punishment. In our personal relationships, we may also need to punish even when we want to forgive, for penalty is often the best way to communicate our opposition to wrong behavior. All parents know that they must sometimes impose punitive measures on wayward children in an effort to teach lessons and bring their progeny back to right behavior. Parental punishment should be redemptive, not vindictive. Its purpose is not to inflict pain but to restore balance and order. It is an expression of ongoing love.

Punishment has specific advantages for the offender and for society. If wrongdoing results in a moral debt that is owed to the victim, then penalty has an important role to play in eliminating that debt. Serving jail time, for instance, endeavors (but sometimes fails) to cancel the debt to all concerned — the individual and society as a whole. Paying off the debt is efficacious; some benefits are immediate and obvious, while others are subtle and delayed. Punishment is a natural consequence of the harmful act, though some guilty people never pay the price for their misdeeds. Deceitful politicians are reelected; drug dealers elude the police; murderers die naturally of old age. In an ideal world, all the guilty and only the guilty would be punished. We do not live in a perfect world, however, so people of faith often look to the absoluteness of divine justice to make things come out right. Meanwhile, victims try to console themselves with the conviction that punishment is a necessary part of the forgiveness process.

Bestowing forgiveness does not necessarily mean that the perpetrator deserves to be forgiven. Entitlement questions are difficult to resolve. We may not know whether a person is truly worthy of forgiveness; only God can know all. It would be irrational not to forgive those who deserve it, but worthiness is not always the deciding factor. Judging another's merit is so daunting a task that we may shy away from it. Forgiving only when it is warranted is a minimalist approach to forgiveness. Those who have the spiritual fortitude may choose to forgive the unrepentant and unpunished. Yet if we require that forgiveness be deserved before we grant it, we rightfully demand that wrongdoers engage in reflection, make moral sense of their egregious actions, repent, and reform. Should they refuse, they "will have confirmed their diminished personhood" (Calhoun 92). Martin Luther, for whom Christ was the embodiment of forgiveness, also agrees that forgiveness is most appropriate for those who have truly reformed:

> He who sincerely desires the forgiveness of sins must at least have the resolve not to incur guilt any more, that is, to abstain from sins, to reform himself and become more pious. For to continue in sins and not to want to abstain from them but nonetheless to pray for forgiveness of sins, is mocking our Lord God. (Plass 520)

Danger exists in granting "cheap grace" to those who do not confess, repent, and change their ways and in overlooking both an individual's minor infractions and society's grossly unjust events such as the Holocaust or apartheid. Therefore, because of its obvious drawbacks, granting unmerited forgiveness is more a gift we give to ourselves than to the one who has hurt us. It offers consolation to the victim without requiring change of the wrongdoer, and it also allows the victim to live in fidelity to God's perfect sovereignty.

At times, like Jonah, we are ambivalent about forgiving others. But another equally thorny situation also arises in our lives when we refuse to forgive ourselves, which may occur partly because we do not own up to our failings. To forgive ourselves we have to admit failures and give up the illusion of our own rightness and blamelessness. The constant struggle "of self-forgiveness does not end as long as love is alive, for to be alive is to be fallible, to provide material for forgiveness" (Halling 112). As long as we live with unacknowledged and unexpiated guilt, we will have trouble accepting ourselves and will be forced to live with the consequences of self-deception, if not self-hate. As soon as we accept our guilt, we open ourselves to the possibility of forgiveness and self-acceptance. When the damage to our psyches has been especially egregious, we sometimes blame God for allowing harm to come to us. Forgiving God can be as arduous a task as forgiving ourselves or our fellow human beings.

For those who suffer, forgiveness has many advantages. Laying down the burden of wrath can be a relief that contributes to the victim's emotional adjustment. Forgiving gives us the freedom to move on with our lives. As we retreat further from mercy and deeper into obstinacy, we give up the ability to reach out to other people. Forgiveness educates us and moves us from spiritual death to spiritual life. Aggrieved people can learn from the ill treatment they have experienced — learn how not to hurt others in the same way and learn how to avoid being hurt again in the future.

Despite the difficulty in bringing ourselves to pardon, we have an opportunity to grow spiritually when we engage in the process of forgiveness. Our humanity develops as we open our hearts to those who do not ask for and perhaps do not even want our forgiveness. When we show compassion and forgive them, we may help ourselves more than we help those who have caused us anguish. In fact, "healing comes as we see ourselves in those who hurt us" (Meek and McMinn 53) and as we recognize our own imperfections in the faces of our tormenters. Forgiveness is a therapeutic tool that helps us end our isolation, anxiety, depression, anger, and fragmented spirit. Without God's forgiveness, human beings would remain in a broken state, and without forgiving our fellow human beings, we remain locked in a metaphorical prison. Originally the prison is not of our own making, but when we refuse to forgive those who have hurt us, we lock ourselves in a dark and cold dungeon that we help to perpetuate. Our own stories are as open-ended as the book of Jonah wherein God forgives the Ninevites but stops short of saying that Jonah should do the same. Will we or will we not forgive those who hurt us?

How can we break out of our prison? Some of us never can. When we learn from the book of Jonah that all humanity is beloved of God, escape from confinement becomes more possible, however. God knows us as the beloved before we experience the warmth of family, friends, or spouses. God forgives us, even when others cannot. Because we are God's beloved, forgiveness is ours for the asking. The Lord, the One of perfect love, can forgive even the most heinous sins. In an increasingly complicated world where political domination, corporate greed, personal indiscretion, and private abuse take control of many lives, "beloved" may be the single word that lifts us up. It is an old-fashioned word. The 1985 JPS Bible discards it in translating many lines where God's love for human beings is found, but the 1917 version uses the term. As the prophet Daniel confesses his sin, Gabriel comes in a vision and says, "At the beginning of thy supplications a word went forth, and I am come to declare it; for thou art greatly beloved" (Dan 9:22). Beloved is the name by which God knows us, but "our driven lives, surrounded by so many loud, demanding voices, make it difficult to hear the small voice that reminds us of our real name" (Nouwen 12). Our lives include a perpetual effort to recover from lacerations and wounds inflicted upon us. We are embroiled in a continual dilemma over how to forgive God, ourselves, and others. Much of history can be seen as a struggle to give and receive forgiveness. The complex characters and situations in the book of Jonah point the way. By understanding that the recalcitrant prophet, the ignorant sailors, and the repentant Ninevites are all beloved to God, we can begin to reach for forgiveness in our wounded world.

Works Cited

Albers, Robert H. "The Shame Factor: Theological and Pastoral Reflections Relating to Forgiveness." *Word and World* 16 (Summer 1996): 347–53.

'Ali, 'Abdullah Yusuf. *The Meaning of the Holy Qur'an*. Brentwood, Md.: Amana, 1994.

Allen, Leslie C. *The New International Commentary on the Old Testament: Joel, Obadiah, Jonah, and Micah*. Grand Rapids: Wm. B. Eerdmans, 1976.

Angel, Hayyim. "The Book of Jonah: A Call to Personal Responsibility." *Tradition* 30 (1995): 56–67.

The Apocrypha or Non-Canonical Books of the Bible. The King James Version. Ed. Manuel Komroff. New York: Tudor, 1936.

Band, Arnold. "Swallowing Jonah: The Eclipse of Parody." *Prooftexts* 10 (1990): 177–95.

Beck, James R. "When to Forgive." *Journal of Psychology and Christianity* 14 (Fall 1995): 269–73.

Bewer, Julius. *The Literature of the Old Testament*. Ed. Emil G. Kraeling. Rev. 3d ed. New York: Columbia University Press, 1962.

Bialik, Hayim Nahman, and Yehoshua Hana Ravnitzky, eds. *The Book of Legends: Legends from the Talmud and Midrash*. Trans. William G. Braude. New York: Schocken Books, 1992.

Bickerman, Elias. *Four Strange Books of the Bible*. New York: Schocken Books, 1967.

Blake, William. *Poems from MSS*. Untitled poem, stanza 14.

Bolin, Thomas M. *Freedom beyond Forgiveness: The Book of Jonah Re-Examined*. Sheffield, England: Sheffield Academic Press, 1997. [*Journal for the Study of the Old Testament*, Supplement Series, 236]

Book of Confessions. Part I of *The Constitution of the Presbyterian Church (U.S.A.)*. Louisville: Office of the General Assembly, 1999.

Brown, Dale W. "The Sign of Jonah." *Sojourners* 13, no. 6 (June–July 1984): 20–22.

Bryan, William Jennings. Reprinted in the transcript of the Scopes Trial. <www.uncc .edu/jmarks/darrow.html>.

Budde, Karl. "Jonah, Book of." *The Jewish Encyclopedia*. 12 vols. London: Funk and Wagnalls, 1904. 7:227–30.

Bustanoby, Andre. "How Do You Forgive the Unrepentant?" *Leadership* 12 (Fall 1991): 98–102.

Butterworth, G. M. "You Pity the Plant: A Misunderstanding." *Indian Journal of Theology* 27 (1978): 32–34.

Calhoun, Cheshire. "Changing One's Heart." *Ethics* 103 (1992): 76–96.

Campbell, Joseph. *The Hero with a Thousand Faces.* 2d ed. Princeton: Princeton University Press, 1968.

————. *The Power of Myth.* Ed. Betty Sue Flowers. New York: Doubleday, 1988.

Canham, Elizabeth J. "Of Whales and Wisdom." *Weavings* 9 (1994): 14–22.

Chow, Simon. "The Sign of Jonah Reconsidered: Matthew 12:38–42 and Luke 11:29–32." *Theology and Life* 15 (1993): 53–60.

Cohen, A., ed. *The Twelve Prophets: Hebrew Text, English Translation and Commentary.* Bournemouth, Hants: Soncino Press, 1948.

Cohen, Abraham D. "The Tragedy of Jonah." *Judaism* 21 (Spring 1972): 164–75.

Collins, Clifford John. "From Literary Analysis to Theological Exposition: The Book of Jonah." *Journal of Translation and Textlinguistics* 7, no. 1 (1995): 28–44.

Cooper, Alan. "In Praise of Divine Caprice: The Significance of the Book of Jonah." In *Among the Prophets: Language, Image and Structure in the Prophetic Writings,* ed. Philip R. Davies and David J. A. Clines. Sheffield, England: Sheffield Academic Press, 1933, 143–63.

Corey, Michael A. *Job, Jonah, and the Unconscious.* Lanham, Md.: University Press of America, 1995.

Craig, Kenneth M., Jr. *A Poetics of Jonah: Art in the Service of Ideology.* Columbia: University of South Carolina Press, 1993.

Craigie, Peter C. *Hosea, Joel, Amos, Obadiah, and Jonah.* Vol. 1. In *Twelve Prophets.* 2 vols. Philadelphia: Westminster Press, 1984–85.

Crenshaw, James L. "Jonah, The Book of." *The Oxford Companion to the Bible.* Ed. Bruce M. Metzger and Michael D. Coogan. New York: Oxford University Press, 1993.

Crouch, Walter B. "To Question an End, to End a Question: Opening the Closure of the Book of Jonah." *Journal for the Study of the Old Testament* 62 (1994): 101–12.

Daube, David. "Jonah: A Reminiscence." *Journal of Jewish Studies* 35 (1984): 36–43.

Dennison, James T., Jr. "The Sign of Jonah." *Keurx* 8 (December 1993): 31–35.

Domeris, W. R. "Biblical Perspectives on Forgiveness." *Journal of Theology for Southern Africa* 54 (March 1986): 48–50.

Dorsey, David A. "Can These Bones Live? Investigating Literary Structure in the Bible." *Evangelical Journal* 9 (September 1991): 11–25.

Dozeman, Thomas B. "Inner-Biblical Interpretation of Yahweh's Gracious and Compassionate Character." *Journal of Biblical Literature* 108 (Summer 1989): 207–23.

Dyck, Elmer. "Jonah Among the Prophets: A Study in Canonical Context." *Journal of the Evangelical Society* 33 (March 1990): 63–76.

Eddy, G. T. "The Threshold of the Gospel." *Expository Times* 107 (May 1996): 247–48.

Elata-Alster, Gerda, and Rachel Salmon. "The Deconstruction of Genre in the Book of Jonah: Towards a Theological Discourse." *Journal of Literature and Theology* 3 (March 1989): 40–60.

Emerson, James G., Jr. *The Dynamics of Forgiveness.* Philadelphia: Westminster Press, 1964.

Emmerson, Grace I. "Another Look at the Book of Jonah." *Expository Times* 88 (December 1976): 86–88.

Ephros, Abraham Z. "The Book of Jonah as Allegory." *Jewish Bible Quarterly* 28 (July–September 1999): 141–51.

Everyman. Ed. A. C. Cawley. Manchester: Manchester University Press, 1961.

Ferguson, Paul. "Who Was the 'King of Nineveh' in Jonah 3:6?" *Tyndale Bulletin* 47 (1996): 301–14.

Fineman, Howard. " 'I Have Sinned': Will America Forgive the President?" *Newsweek* September 21, 1998: 26–36.

Fingert, Hyman. "The Psychoanalytic Study of the Minor Prophet Jonah." *Psychoanalytic Review* 41 (1954): 55–65.

Fretheim, Terrence E. "Jonah and Theodicy." *Zietschrift für die alttestamentliche Wissenschaft* 90, no. 2 (1978): 227–37.

———. "The Repentance of God: A Key to Evaluating Old Testament God-Talk." *Horizons in Biblical Theology* 10, no. 1 (1988): 47–70.

Friedlander, Albert H. "Judaism and the Concept of Forgiving." *Christian Jewish Relations* 19 (March 1986): 6–13.

Gabel, John B., Charles B. Wheeler, and Anthony D. York. *The Bible as Literature: An Introduction.* 3d ed. New York: Oxford University Press, 1996.

Gassin, Elizabeth A., and Robert D. Enright. "The Will to Meaning in the Process of Forgiveness." *Journal of Psychology and Christianity* 14 (Spring 1995): 38–49.

Gates of Repentance: The New Union Prayerbook for the Days of Awe. Ed. Chaim Stern. New York: Central Conference of American Rabbis, 1978.

Gershwin, George. "It Ain't Necessarily So." *Porgy and Bess.*

Gibbs, Robert. "Fear of Forgiveness: Kant and the Paradox of Mercy." *Philosophy and Theology* 3 (Summer 1989): 323–34.

Ginsberg, H. L. Introduction. *The Five Megilloth and Jonah.* Philadelphia: Jewish Publication Society, 1969.

Gladson, Jerry A. "Higher Than the Heavens: Forgiveness in the Old Testament." *Journal of Psychology and Christianity* 11 (Summer 1992): 125–35.

Goeser, Robert J. "From Exegesis to Proclamation." *Historical Magazine of the Protestant Episcopal Church* 53 (September 1984): 209–20.

Goodhart, Sandor. "Prophecy, Sacrifice and Repentance in the Story of Jonah." *Semeia* 33 (1985): 43–63.

Guelzo, Allen C. "Fear of Forgiving." *Christianity Today* 37 (February 8, 1993): 42–45.

Gunn, David M., and Danna Nolan Fewell. *Narrative in the Hebrew Bible.* Oxford: Oxford University Press, 1993.

Halling, Steen. "Embracing Human Fallibility: On Forgiving Oneself and Forgiving Others." *Journal of Religion and Health* 33 (Summer 1994): 107–13.

Hamel, Gildas. "Taking the Argo to Nineveh: Jonah and Jason in a Mediterranean Context." *Judaism* 44 (Summer 1995): 341–61.

Hamilton, Edith. *Mythology.* New York: Mentor Books, 1961.

Hampl, Patricia. "In the Belly of the Whale." In *Out of the Garden,* ed. Christina Büchmann and Celina Spiegel. New York: Fawcett Columbine, 1994, 289–300.

Harris, Stephen L. *Understanding the Bible.* 3d ed. London: Mayfield Press, 1992.

Hauser, Alan Jon. "Jonah: In Pursuit of the Dove." *Journal of Biblical Literature* 104 (May 1985): 21–37.

Havazelet, Meir. "Jonah and the Prophetic Experience." *Tradition* 10 (1969): 29–32.

Hedva, Beth. *Betrayal, Trust, and Forgiveness: A Guide to Emotional Healing and Self-Renewal.* Rev. ed. Berkeley: Celestialarts, 2001.

Hellman, Lillian. *Three: An Unfinished Woman, Pentimento, Scoundrel Time.* Boston: Little, Brown, 1979.

Hirsch, Emil G. "Jonah." *The Jewish Encyclopedia.* 12 vols. London: Funk and Wagnalls, 1904, 7:225–30.

Hoffer, Victoria, and Rebecca Abts Wright. "A Jewish and Christian Reading of Jonah: How (Dis-)Similar." *Sewanee Theological Review* 37 (1994): 144–50.

Holmgren, Fredrick C. "Israel, the Prophets, and the Book of Jonah." *Currents in Theology and Mission* 21 (1994): 127–32.

The Holy Scriptures. Philadelphia: Jewish Publication Society, 1917.

Horace: The Complete Works. Ed. Charles E. Bennett and John C. Rolfe. Rev. ed. Boston: Allyn and Bacon, 1958, 385–87.

Hunt, Terence. "Clinton Touched by Forgiveness." *Albuquerque Journal,* September 29, 1999, A1.

Huxley, Aldous. "Jonah." In *Collected Poetry of Aldous Huxley.* Ed. Donald Watt. New York: Harper & Row, 1971.

The Interpreter's Bible. Ed. George Arthur Buttrick. 12 vols. New York: Abingdon, 1951–57, 6:871–94.

Jensen, Paul. "Forgiveness and Atonement." *Scottish Journal of Theology* 46 (1993): 141–59.

Johnson, Susan B. W. "Love's Double Victory." *Christian Century* 114 (January 15, 1997): 47.

Jones, L. Gregory. "The Craft of Forgiveness." *Theology Today* 50 (1993): 345–57.

———. *Embodying Forgiveness.* Grand Rapids: William B. Eerdmans Publishing, 1995.

Josephus, Flavius. *The Antiquities of the Jews: The Works of Josephus.* Trans. W. Whiston. Peabody, Mass.: Hendrickson Publishers, 1987, 27–542.

Jung, C[arl] G[ustav]. *Symbols of Transformation: An Analysis of the Prelude to a Case of Schizophrenia.* Collected Works of C. G. Jung 5. Trans. R. F. C. Hull. New York: Pantheon, 1956.

Kahn, Paul. "An Analysis of the Book of Jonah." *Judaism* 43 (1994): 87–100.

Kierkegaard, Søren. *The Sickness unto Death: A Christian Psychological Exposition for Upbuilding and Awakening.* Trans. Howard V. Hong and Edna H. Hong. Princeton: Princeton University Press, 1980.

Kinder, F. D. "The Distribution of Divine Names in Jonah." *Tyndale Bulletin* 21 (1970): 126–28.

Klein, Ralph W. "Israel/Today's Believers and the Nations: Three Test Cases." *Currents in Theology and Mission* 24 (June 1997): 232–37.

Koontz, Gayle Gereber. "As We Forgive Others: Christian Forgiveness and Feminist Pain." *Mennonite Quarterly Review* 68 (April 1994): 170–93.

Lacocque, André, and Pierre-Emmanuel Lacocque. *The Jonah Complex.* Atlanta: John Knox Press, 1981.

———. "The Jonah Complex Revisited." *Chicago Theological Seminary Register* 72, no. 1 (Winter 1982): 13–21.

———. *Jonah: A Psycho-Religious Approach to the Prophet.* Columbia: University of South Carolina Press, 1990.

Lacocque, Pierre E. "Fear of Engulfment and the Problem of Identity." *Journal of Religion and Health* 23 (Fall 1984): 218–28.

Landes, George M. "The Kerygma of the Book of Jonah: The Contextual Interpretation of the Jonah Psalm." *Interpretation* 21 (January 1967): 3–31.

Lawrence, Paul J. N. "Assyrian Nobles and the Book of Jonah." *Tyndale Bulletin* 37 (1986): 121–32.

Lewis, Chaim. "Jonah — A Parable for Our Time." *Judaism* 21 (Spring 1972): 159–63.

Lillegard, David. "Narrative and Paradox in Jonah." *Keurx* 8 (December 1993): 19–30.

Limburg, James. *Jonah: A Commentary.* The Old Testament Library. Louisville: Westminster/John Knox Press, 1993.

Loewen, Jacob A. "Four Kinds of Forgiveness." *Practical Anthropology* 17 (July–August 1970): 153–68.

Louw, D. J. "Guilt and Change — The Healing Power of Forgiveness." *Scriptura* 59 (1966): 383–95.

Lubeck, R. J. "Prophetic Sabotage: A Look at Jonah 3:2–4." *Trinity Journal* 9 (1988): 37–46.

Luther, Martin. *Works.* Ed. Jaroslav Jan Pelikan et al. 1955–1986. 55 vols. Vol. 19. St. Louis: Concordia, 1959.

Magonet, Jonathan. *Form and Meaning: Studies in Literary Techniques in the Book of Jonah.* Bern, Switzerland: Herbert Lang, 1976.

Maimonides, Moses. *The Guide of the Perplexed.* Chicago: University of Chicago Press, 1963.

Mandela, Nelson. *Long Walk to Freedom*. Randburg, South Africa: Macdonald Purnell, 1994.

———. "Opening Address by President Nelson Mandela in the Special Debate on the Report of the Truth and Reconciliation Commission." South Africa, February 25, 1999.

Marcus, David. *From Balaam to Jonah: Anti-Prophetic Satire in the Hebrew Bible*. Atlanta: Scholars Press, 1995.

Maslow, Abraham. "Neurosis as a Failure of Personal Growth." *Humanities* 3 (1967): 165–66.

———. *Toward a Psychology of Being*. Princeton: Van Nostrand, 1962.

Mather, Judson. "The Comic Art of the Book of Jonah." *Soundings* 65 (1982): 280–91.

Meek, Katheryn Rhoads, and Mark R. McMinn. "Forgiveness: More Than a Therapeutic Technique." *Journal of Psychology and Christianity* 16 (1997): 51–61.

Melville, Herman. *Moby Dick; or, the Whale*. 1851. Norwalk, Conn.: Easton Press, 1977.

Miles, John A. "Laughing at the Bible: Jonah as Parody." *The Jewish Quarterly Review* 65 (January 1975): 168–81.

Millgram, Abraham. *Jewish Worship*. 2d ed. Philadelphia: Jewish Publication Society, 1975.

The Mishnah. Trans. Herbert Danby. London: Oxford University Press, 1933.

More, Joseph. "The Prophet Jonah: The Story of an Intrapsychic Process." *American Imago* 27 (1970): 3–11.

Nouwen, Henri J. M. "Forgiveness: The Name of Love in a Wounded World." *Weavings* 7 (1992): 6–15.

Olson, Mark. "The God Who Dared." *Other Side* 26 (May–June 1990): 11–15.

Payne, David F. "Jonah from the Perspective of its Audience." *Journal for the Study of the Old Testament* 13 (1979): 3–12.

Perkins, Larry. "The Septuagint of Jonah: Aspects of Literary Analysis Applied to Biblical Translation." *Bulletin of the International Organization for Septuagint and Cognate Studies* 20 (1987): 43–53.

Person, Raymond F., Jr. *In Conversation with Jonah: Conversation Analysis, Literary Criticism, and the Book of Jonah*. Sheffield, England: Sheffield Academic Press, 1966. [*Journal for the Study of the Old Testament*, Supplement Series, 220]

Pirkê de Rabbi Eliezer. Trans. Gerald Friedlander. London: Kegan Paul, Trench, Trubner, 1916.

Plass, Ewald M., ed. *What Luther Says: A Practical In-Home Anthology for the Active Christian*. St. Louis: Concordia, 1994.

Pope, Alexander. "An Essay on Criticism." *Eighteenth-Century English Literature*. Ed. Geoffrey Tillotson, Paul Fussell Jr., and Marshall Waingrow. New York: Harcourt, Brace & World, 1969, 635–51.

Ratner, Robert J. "Jonah, the Runaway Servant." *Maarav* 5–6 (Spring 1990): 281–305.

Risher, Dee Dee. "The Way to God." *The Other Side* 31 (1995): 8–11.

Roffey, John W. "God's Truth, Jonah's Fish: Structure and Existence in the Book of Jonah." *Australian Biblical Review* 36 (1988): 1–18.

Rogerson, J. W. "Mercy of God." *The Oxford Companion to the Bible*. Ed. Bruce M. Metzger and Michael D. Coogan. New York: Oxford University Press, 1993.

Sakenfeld, Katharine D. "The Problem of Divine Forgiveness in Numbers 14." *Catholic Biblical Quarterly* 37 (July 1975): 317–30.

Salters, R. B. *Jonah and Lamentations*. Sheffield, England: Sheffield Academic Press, 1994.

Sasson, Jack M. *Jonah: A New Translation with Introduction, Commentary, and Interpretation*. Anchor Bible. New York: Doubleday, 1990.

Schochet, Elijah Judah. *Animal Life in Jewish Tradition: Attitudes and Relationships*. New York: KTAV, 1984.

The Septuagint with Apocrypha: Greek and English. Ed. Lancelot C. L. Brenton. [1851] Peabody, Mass.: Hendrickson Publishers, 1986.

Sherwood, Yvonne. *A Biblical Text and Its Afterlives: The Survival of Jonah in Western Culture*. Cambridge: Cambridge University Press, 2000.

Simon, Uriel. *The Jewish Publication Society Bible Commentary: Jonah*. Trans. Lenn J. Schramm. Philadelphia: Jewish Publication Society, 1999.

Simpson, William. *The Jonah Legend: A Suggestion of Interpretation*. London: Grant Richards, 1899.

Sponheim, Paul R. "Is Forgiveness Enough? A Kierkegaardian Response." *Word and World* 16 (Summer 1996): 320–27.

Stuart, Douglas. *Word Biblical Themes: Hosea–Jonah*. Dallas: Word Publishing, 1989.

Swetnam, James. "Some Signs of Jonah." *Biblica* 68, no. 1 (1987): 74–79.

Talbott, Thomas. "Punishment, Forgiveness, and Divine Justice." *Religious Studies* 29 (June 1993): 151–68.

Talmud, The Babylonian. Ed. I. Epstein. 17 vols. London: Soncino Press, 1938.

TANAKH: The Holy Scriptures, The New Jewish Publication Society Translation According to the Traditional Hebrew Text. Philadelphia: Jewish Publication Society, 1985.

Telushkin, Joseph. *Jewish Literacy*. New York: Wm. Morrow, 1991.

Thompson, Marjorie J. "Moving Toward Forgiveness." *Weavings* 7 (March–April 1992): 16–26.

Tigay, Jeffrey H. "The Book of Jonah and the Days of Awe." *Conservative Judaism* 38 (Winter 1985–86): 67–76.

Trepp, Leo. *The Complete Book of Jewish Observance*. New York: Behrman House, 1980.

Trible, Phyllis L. *Studies in the Book of Jonah*. Diss. (Columbia University, 1963). Ann Arbor: University Microfilms, 1967.

Truth: The Road to Reconciliation. Cape Town: South Africa: Truth and Reconciliation Commission, 1996.

Wahking, Harold. "Spiritual Growth Through Grace and Forgiveness." *Journal of Psychology and Christianity* 11 (Spring 1992): 198–206.

Walton, John. *Jonah: Bible Study Commentary.* Grand Rapids: Zondervan, 1982.

Wang, Richard. "Forgiveness and Reconciliation." Trans. Peter Barry. *Tripod* 52 (1989): 60–66.

Warshaw, Thayer S. "The Book of Jonah." In *Literary Interpretations of Biblical Narratives,* ed. Kenneth R. R. Louis Gros. Nashville: Abingdon, 1974, 191–207.

Watts, James W. "Song and the Ancient Reader." *Perspectives in Religious Studies* 22 (Summer 1995): 135–47.

Weaver, Dorothy Jean. "On Imitating God and Outwitting Satan: Biblical Perspectives on Forgiveness and the Community of Faith." *Mennonite Quarterly Review* 68 (April 1994): 151–69.

Wendland, Ernst R. "Text Analysis and the Genre of Jonah (Part 1)." *Journal of the Evangelical Theological Society* 39 (June 1996): 191–206.

West, Mona. "Irony in the Book of Jonah: Audience Identification with the Hero." *Perspectives in Religious Studies* 11 (1984): 233–42.

Wiesel, Elie. *Five Biblical Portraits.* Notre Dame: University of Notre Dame Press, 1981.

Wiesenthal, Simon. *The Sunflower: On the Possibilities and Limits of Forgiveness.* Symposium Ed. Harry James Cargas and Bonny V. Fetterman. Rev. ed. New York: Schocken Books, 1997.

Willis, John T. "The 'Repentance' of God in the Books of Samuel, Jeremiah, and Jonah." *Horizons in Biblical Theology* 16 (December 1994): 156–75.

Wineman, Aryeh. "The Zohar on Jonah: Radical Retelling or Tradition?" *Hebrew Studies* 31 (1990): 57–69.

Wiseman, Donald J. "Jonah's Nineveh." *Tyndale Bulletin* 30 (1979): 29–51.

Wohlgelernter, Devora K. "Death Wish in the Bible." *Tradition* 19 (Summer 1981): 131–40.

Wolff, Hans Walter. *Obadiah and Jonah: A Commentary.* Trans. Margaret Kohl. Minneapolis: Augsburg Publishing House, 1977.

Woodard, Branson L. "Death in Life: The Book of Jonah and Biblical Tragedy." *Grace Theological Journal* 11 (1991): 3–16.

Zimmermann, Frank. "Problems and Solutions in the Book of Jonah." *Judaism* 40 (1991): 580–89.

Zlotowitz, Meir. *The Twelve Prophets: Yonah.* New York: Mesorah Publications, 1978.

Zohar. Trans. M. Simon and P. Levertoff. 5 vols. London: Soncino Press, 1984.

Index

Aaron, 148
Abel, 14, 106, 153
Abraham, 12, 14, 40, 49, 103, 109,
    131, 155
Abravanel, 18–19
Achan, 157, 159
Adam, 38, 153
Akiva, Joseph ben, 115
Alexandretta. *See* Turkey
Allah, 12, 74, 80
Amittai, 15, 18, 32, 37, 71
Amos, 17, 24, 32, 59, 73, 88, 99,
    154
angel, 14, 45, 49
Apartheid, ix, 1–2, 142–46
Aphrodite, 55
Apocrypha, 14, 24, 90, 105
Arion, 64
Ark of the Covenant, 10, 106, 157
Astarte, 45
Augustine, Saint, 129
Azazel, 148

Baal, 45
Babylon, 21, 25, 33, 45, 47, 56, 59,
    65, 78, 82–83
Babylonian captivity, 12, 21, 25–26,
    31, 56, 59, 79, 128, 154
Bathsheba, 98, 100, 158
Batman, 10
Beer-sheba, 109, 115, 117
Behemoth, 84
Book of the Dead, 65

Boraine, Alex, 142
Bryan, William Jennings, 19

Cain, 38, 106–7, 113, 153–54
Calvin, John, 76
Campbell, Joseph, 61–62
Cassandra, 88
Christ. *See* Jesus
Chrysostom, Saint John, 129
Clemens, Samuel L. *See* Twain, Mark
Clinton, William Jefferson, 2
Collodi, Carlo, *Pinocchio,* 65
Conrad, Joseph, *Heart of Darkness,*
    11
Cyrus, 25

Dagon, 54
Dalai Lama, 140
Damascus. *See* Syria
Darrow, Clarence, 19
David, 9, 55, 98, 100, 106–7, 118–19,
    132, 155, 158
Days of Awe. *See* High Holy Days
Dead Sea Scrolls, 67
Deborah, 67
Defoe, Daniel, *Robinson Crusoe,* 64
Diaspora, 39
Disney, Walt, 65

Eastwood, Clint, *Unforgiven,* 97
Ecclesiasticus, 34
Eden, 14, 38, 103, 113, 117–18, 120
Edom, 17

ego, 33–34, 45, 47, 53, 119
Elijah, 13, 16, 20, 22, 40, 44, 111, 115, 117
Elisha, 16, 20
Ephraim, 36, 56, 100
Esau, 153, 154
Esther, 52
Eve, 38, 153
Everyman, 9, 162
Ezekiel, 26, 42–43, 60, 101, 109, 132
Ezra, 52–53

false prophet, 38, 91–92, 101, 113
Freud, Sigmund, 40, 119

Gabriel, 166
Gates of Repentance, 2, 146, 151
Gershwin, George, *Porgy and Bess*, 57
Gilgamesh, 75
God, names for, 120–21
Golden Fleece, 10, 11, 63, 117
gospel, 9, 57, 89, 92–93, 128
"grace formula," 108
Grimm Brothers, "Little Red Riding Hood," 65

haDarshan, Shimon, 126
Hades, 63
Haftarah, 149
Hagar, 38, 109
Haggai, 7
Hera, 63
Herodotus, 25, 46, 86, 96
Hesburgh, Theodore, 140
Hesione, 63
Hezekiah, King, 36, 95
High Holy Days, ix, 2, 132, 146–52
Hitler, Adolf, 138–41
Holocaust, ix, 1–2, 14, 53, 83, 136–143

Holy Grail, 11
Horace, 85
Horeb, Mount, 40, 115
Hosea, 16, 36, 104, 153

Ibn Ezra, 20, 69, 76, 118
Iraq, Mosul, 18, 84
Isaac, 12, 40, 103, 153
Isaiah, 16, 31, 40, 47, 104, 129, 149, 154
Ishmael, 12
Ishtar, 45

Jacob, 12, 147, 153, 154
Jehu, 16
Jeremiah, 16, 22, 40, 44, 47, 52, 100, 129,
Jeroboam II, King, 15, 17, 20, 25,
Jerome, Saint, 73, 129
Jesus, 9, 12, 56–57, 78, 89, 93, 107, 129, 130, 153, 157
Jethro, 95
Jezebel, Queen, 40, 111
Job, 12, 14, 21, 42, 73, 76, 79, 111, 132, 155
Joel, 16, 17, 52, 96, 98, 109–10
Jonah, biblical character
    as antihero, 9–10, 18, 23, 112, 113, 127
    in belly of fish, 55–57
    deliverance, 54–80
    described in Books of Kings, 15, 17–18, 20, 25, 35, 71
    disobedience, 31–53
    as Everyone, 9–10, 111, 135, 136, 152
    name, 36–37, 55
    as son of Amittai, 15, 18, 32, 35, 37, 71

Jonah, Book of,
  as allegory, 21–24, 79, 110
  Anti-Semitic interpretations, 52,
    93–94, 128–133
  canonization, 22
  casting lots in, 8, 48–49, 51, 148
  date, 24–26
  dove, 36–37, 55, 63
  Freudian interpretations, 119
  genre, 13–24
  as history, 15–16, 18–20
  humor in, 22–23, 61, 78–79, 114
  as *midrash*, 20–21, 109
  narrator's role, 35–36, 50–58, 68,
    72, 90, 95–96, 120, 124–25, 128,
    132
  as parable, 21–24
  parallel myths, 62–66
  as parody, 22–23, 78
  placement, 15, 17, 116
  as prophecy, 3, 12, 15, 17–18
  as satire, 12, 22–23, 71, 78–79,
    96
  structure, 26–30
  threshold imagery in, 58
"Jonah, sign of," 92–93
"Jonah and the Whale Complex"
  (Jung), 47–48
"Jonah complex." *See* "Jonah
  Syndrome"
"Jonah Syndrome" (Maslow), 38–39,
  48
Jones, Indiana, 10
Joppa, 25, 37–39, 61, 108
Joseph, 11, 41, 49, 55–56, 153, 154
Josephus, Flavius, 15–16, 41, 42–43,
  69, 71
Joshua, 60, 157
Jospin, Lionel, 143

journey literature, 11
Jung, Carl, 33, 47, 81

Kabbalah. *See* Zohar
Khmer Rouge, 140
King, Martin Luther, Jr., 107
Koran, 8, 12, 74, 79–80, 91, 93, 150
Kronos (Saturn), 63
Kushner, Harold, *When Bad Things
  Happen to Good People*, 140–41

Lamentations, 59, 71, 159
Levi, Primo, 141
Leviathan, 44, 58, 60, 84
Lewinsky, Monica, 2
Longfellow, Henry Wadsworth,
  Hiawatha, 65
Lorenzini, Carlo. *See* Collodi, Carlo
Lot, 45, 89
Lucas, George, 62, 64
Luther, Martin, 19, 129–30, 164

MacCool, Finn, 65
Maimonides, 12
Malachi, 16
Mandela, Nelson, 136–37, 143–46,
  162
Marduk, 45
Maslow, Abraham, 39, 48
Masoretic text, 9, 16
Media, 14, 25, 90
Mediterranean Sea, 43
Medusa, 63
Melville, Herman, *Moby Dick*, 39, 61,
  64, 69–70
Micah, 16, 17, 100, 147
Midrash, 13, 20–21, 23, 43, 51, 58,
  60, 76, 109
Minor Prophets, 14, 16
Mirkhond, 16, 55–56, 78

Mishnah, 104

Moab, 9, 79, 95, 131

"Monkey" Trial. *See* Scopes Trial

Moriah, Mount, 84

Moses, 20, 60, 111, 129

    communication with God, 40, 47,
        89, 147, 155, 158

    family history, 40, 95, 148, 153,
        154

    negotiations with Pharaoh, 22, 154

    wandering in desert, 11, 89, 158

Mosul. *See* Iraq

Nahum, 7, 17, 83, 90

Nathan, 118–19, 132, 158

Nazis. *See* Holocaust

Nebuchadnezzar, 25

Nehemiah, 31, 53

Nimrod, 84

Obadiah, 17

Oedipus, 42, 127

original sin, 146

Osiris, 65

Ovid, 62

Paul of Tarsus, 52, 130

Pawlikowski, John, 141

Perseus, 62–63

Pharaoh, 22, 31, 40, 41, 67, 127, 154

Philistia, 32, 54, 111, 157

Pol Pot, 140

Poseidon, 63

Prager, Dennis, 141

Pran, Dith, 140

Ptolemy II, 47

Rashi, 52, 91

Rawlinson, Henry, 84

Red Sea. *See* Reeds, Sea of

Reeds, Sea of, 60, 61, 67

Reformation, 19

Reparation and Rehabilitation
    Committee, 143

Robben Island, 144

Rosh Hashanah. See High Holy Days

Ruth, 9, 14, 53, 95, 131

Samson, 24, 111

Samuel, 32, 52, 100, 101, 106–7

Sarah, 38, 109, 112, 127

Saul, 24, 32, 100, 106

scapegoat, 148, 150

Scopes Trial, 19

Selihot, 1, 146–47, 150

Sennacherib, 82–83

Septuagint, 47, 57, 67, 89

Shakespeare, William, *Hamlet,* 41

Shakespeare, William, *King Lear,* 44

Shalmaneser, 82–83

Shamash, 45

sheol, 41, 47, 58, 72–74, 82, 117, 125

Shoah. See Holocaust

Siculus, Diodorus, 86

Simonides, 62

Sinai, Mount, 89

Sisulu, Walter, 144

Sobukwe, Robert, 144

Sodom and Gomorrah, 14, 40, 45, 82,
    89–91, 97, 131, 154

South Africa, ix, 1–2, 3, 4, 136,
    142–46

Speer, Albert, 141

SS. *See* Holocaust

Sukkot, 150

Syria, Damascus, 15–16, 17

Talmud, 32, 37–38, 46, 61, 64, 99,
    103, 112

Tammuz, 65

Tashlikh, 147
Telushkin, Joseph, 1, 150
Tent of Meeting, 148–49, 156
Tetragrammaton, 121
Thirteen Divine Attributes, 147
Thomas, Dylan, 58
Tigris River, 14, 84, 87
Tobias, 14
Tobit, 14
Tower of Babel, 14
townships, ix, 1
Truth and Reconciliation Commission, 142–43, 145
"Truth: The Road to Reconciliation," 2, 145
Turkey, Alexandretta, 18
Tutu, Desmond, 142
Twain, Mark, *The Adventures of Huckleberry Finn*, 11

Uzzah, 106–7, 114, 127

Verne, Jules, *Twenty Thousand Leagues under the Sea*, 64
Vishnu, 54

Wiesel, Elie, 43–44, 46, 52–53
Wiesenthal, Simon, 136–43, 145, 146
wisdom Literature, 13, 21, 24
witch of Endor, 32

Yom Kippur. *See* High Holy Days

Zechariah, 16, 24
"Zeigarnik Effect," 126
Zephaniah, 7, 16, 83
Zeus, 63
Zohar, 22, 47, 60

Breinigsville, PA USA
13 November 2009
227532BV00001B/65/A